AF870685

Wearable AI - The Future of Continuous Health Monitoring in the Metaverse

Editors:

Balasubramaniam S
Assistant Professor, School of Computer Science and Engineering
Kerala University of Digital Sciences, Innovation and Technology
Thiruvananthapuram, Kerala, India

Seifedine Kadry
Professor, Department of Computer Science and Mathematics
Lebanese American University, Beirut, Lebanon

CRC Press
Taylor & Francis Group
Boca Raton London New York

CRC Press is an imprint of the
Taylor & Francis Group, an **informa** business
A SCIENCE PUBLISHERS BOOK

First edition published 2027
by CRC Press
2385 NW Executive Center Drive, Suite 320, Boca Raton FL 33431

and by CRC Press
4 Park Square, Milton Park, Abingdon, Oxon, OX14 4RN

© 2027 Balasubramaniam S and Seifedine Kadry

CRC Press is an imprint of Taylor & Francis Group, LLC

Reasonable efforts have been made to publish reliable data and information, but the author and publisher cannot assume responsibility for the validity of all materials or the consequences of their use. The authors and publishers have attempted to trace the copyright holders of all material reproduced in this publication and apologize to copyright holders if permission to publish in this form has not been obtained. If any copyright material has not been acknowledged please write and let us know so we may rectify in any future reprint.

Except as permitted under U.S. Copyright Law, no part of this book may be reprinted, reproduced, transmitted, or utilized in any form by any electronic, mechanical, or other means, now known or hereafter invented, including photocopying, microfilming, and recording, or in any information storage or retrieval system, without written permission from the publishers.

For permission to photocopy or use material electronically from this work, access www.copyright.com or contact the Copyright Clearance Center, Inc. (CCC), 222 Rosewood Drive, Danvers, MA 01923, 978-750-8400. For works that are not available on CCC please contact mpkbookspermissions@tandf.co.uk

For Product Safety Concerns and Information please contact our EU representative GPSR@taylorandfrancis.com. Taylor & Francis Verlag GmbH, Kaufingerstraße 24, 80331 München, Germany.

Trademark notice: Product or corporate names may be trademarks or registered trademarks and are used only for identification and explanation without intent to infringe.

Library of Congress Cataloging-in-Publication Data (applied for)

ISBN: 978-1-041-30814-0 (hbk)
ISBN: 978-1-041-30815-7 (pbk)
ISBN: 978-1-003-77629-1 (ebk)

DOI: 10.1201/9781003776291

Typeset in Times New Roman
by Prime Publishing Services

Preface

Wearable AI - The Future of Continuous Health Monitoring in the Metaverse explores the dynamic intersection of artificial intelligence, wearable technologies, and immersive digital environments. As healthcare moves beyond clinics and hospitals into hybrid physical–virtual spaces, this volume examines how intelligent wearables and the metaverse are redefining the very nature of health, wellness, and human–technology interaction. This book brings together leading scholars, technologists, clinicians, and designers to investigate the scientific foundations, applications, and implications of continuous health monitoring. It delves into breakthroughs in biosensing, neural interfaces, digital twins, and AI-driven analytics that enable real-time physiological and behavioral insights. Through a series of interdisciplinary chapters, it showcases how wearable AI systems integrate seamlessly with metaverse platforms to deliver personalized, preventive, and participatory healthcare experiences.

Beyond technological innovation, the volume critically engages with the ethical, regulatory, and social dimensions of this transformation. It addresses pressing questions around data privacy, algorithmic transparency, equity, and the psychological impact of health virtualization. The discussions extend to global health policy, digital inclusion, and the future of medical governance in AI-enhanced environments. Combining visionary perspectives with practical case studies, *Wearable AI - The Future of Continuous Health Monitoring in the Metaverse* serves as a comprehensive reference for researchers, healthcare professionals, policymakers, and industry leaders. It envisions a future where continuous, intelligent health monitoring fosters not only longer lives but also more connected and empowered digital citizens.

Ultimately, this volume invites readers to imagine a world where the boundaries between body, data, and digital reality dissolve—creating a seamless ecosystem of care in which wearable AI and the metaverse converge to transform human health and experience.

Contents

List of Contributors

Abdelfateh Kerrouche
School of Engineering and the Built Environment, Edinburgh Napier University, Edinburgh, Scotland.

Alvin Ancy A.
Centre for Radar, Electronic and Communication Engineering, Rajalakshmi Institute of Technology, Chennai, Tamil Nadu, India.

Anitha Velu
Department of Electronics and Communication Engineering, Sri Sairam College of Engineering, Bengaluru, India.

Arun Kumar R.
Digital Forensics and Cybersecurity, University of South Wales, Treforest, United Kingdom.

Ashwini A.
Department of Electronics and Communication Engineering, Vel Tech Rangarajan Dr. Sagunthala R&D Institute of Science and Technology, Chennai, Tamil Nadu, India.

Azrour Mourade
Department of Computer Science, Faculty of Sciences and Technologies, Moulay Ismail University of Meknès, Morocco.

B. Aswini
Department of Biotechnology, Kalasalingam Academy of Research and Education, Virudhunagar, Tamil Nadu, India.

B. Hariharan
Department of Computational Intelligence, School of Computing, SRM Institute of Science and Technology, Chennai, Tamil Nadu, India.

B. Shanthini
Department of Computer Science and Engineering, St. Peter's Institute of Higher Education and Research, Chennai, Tamil Nadu, India.

B. Sreechandana
Department of Biotechnology, Kalasalingam Academy of Research and Education, Virudhunagar, Tamil Nadu, India.

Balasubramaniam S.
School of Computer Science and Engineering, Kerala University of Digital Sciences, Innovation and Technology (Formerly IIITM-K), Digital University Kerala, Thiruvananthapuram, Kerala, India.

Bhuvana B.P.
Department of Electronics and Communication Engineering, School of Electrical and Electronics, Sathyabama Institute of Science and Technology, Chennai, Tamil Nadu, India.

Bhuvana B.P.
Department of Electronics and Communication Engineering, School of Electrical and Electronics, Sathyabama Institute of Science and Technology, Chennai, Tamil Nadu, India.

C. Valarmathi
Department of Computer Science and Engineering, Sri Sairam College of Engineering, Bengaluru, India.

Ciro R. Rodriguez
Software Engineering Department, Universidad Nacional Mayor de San Marcos, Lima.

Danilo Pelusi
Department of Communication Sciences, University of Teramo, Balzarini, Italy.

Emmanvel Raj M. Chirchi
Department of Information Science & Engineering and Artificial Intelligence and Data Science, East-West Institute of Technology, Bengaluru, Karnataka, India.

F.G. Abaszadeh
National Aviation Academy, Baku, Azerbaijan.

G. Santhiya
Department of Information Technology, SRM Valliammai Engineering College, Kattangulathur, Tamil Nadu, India.

Geetha A.
Department of Electrical and Electronics Engineering, College of Engineering and Technology, SRM Institute of Science and Technology, Chengalpattu, Tamil Nadu, India.

Jagatheesan K.
Department of Electronics and Communication Engineering, M. Kumaraswamy College of Engineering (Autonomous), Karur, Tamil Nadu, India.

Jayaraj Ramasamy
Botha University, Gaborone, Botswana.

Jeysi B.
Department of Computer Science and Engineering, St. Peter's Institute of Higher Education and Research, Chennai, Tamil Nadu, India.

Joel Livin A.
Engineering Department, University of Technology and Applied Sciences, Sultanate of Oman, Ibra, North Al Sharqiah.

K. Suresh
Department of Computational Intelligence, School of Computing, SRM Institute of Science and Technology, Kattankulathur, Tamil Nadu, India.

Karthic Sundaram
Department of Computing Technologies, SRM Institute of Science and Technology, Chengalpattu, Tamil Nadu, India.

Lavanya M.
Department of Artificial Intelligence and Data Science (AI&DS), Adhiparasakthi College of Engineering, Ranipet, Tamil Nadu, India.

M. Santhanamari
Department of Biotechnology, Kalasalingam Academy of Research and Education, Virudhunagar, Tamil Nadu, India.

M. Sundarrajan
Department of Networking and Communications, SRM Institute of Science and Technology, Chengalpattu, Tamil Nadu, India.

Mani Deepak Choudhry
Department of Computing Technologies, SRM Institute of Science and Technology, Chengalpattu, Tamil Nadu, India.

Manoj Jayabalan
Bath School of Design, Bath Spa University, Bath, UK.

Mohakk Harshal Malvankar
Department of Computational Intelligence, School of Computing, SRM Institute of Science and Technology, Chennai, Tamil Nadu, India.

N. Sathish
Department of Electronics and Communication Engineering, Sri Venkateswara College of Engineering, Sriperumbudur, Tamil Nadu, India.

Nebojsa Bacanin
Faculty of Informatics and Computing, Singidunum University, Belgrade, Serbia.

P.G. Om Prakash
Department of Computational Intelligence, School of Computing, SRM Institute of Science and Technology, Chennai, Tamil Nadu, India.

P. Nagaraj
Department of Computer Science and Engineering, School of Computing, SRM Institute of Science and Technology, Tiruchirappalli, Tamil Nadu, India.

Raja Murugan
School of Civil and Mechanical Engineering, Curtin University, Perth, Australia.

Raja Rajakani
Plant Plastic Research Centre, Seoul National University, Seoul, South Korea

Rama Abirami K.
School of Engineering and Technology, PSB Academy, Singapore.

Rashad G. Abaszade
Electrical and Electronics Engineering, Turan International Research Institute, Baku, Azerbaijan.

S. Hemavathi
Department of Computing Technologies, School of Computing, SRM Institute of Science and Technology, Kattankulathur, Tamil Nadu, India.

S. Poonkodi
Department of Computing Technologies, School of Computing, SRM Institute of Science and Technology, Kattankulathur, Tamil Nadu, India.

S. Sheik Asraf
Department of Biotechnology, Kalasalingam Academy of Research and Education, Virudhunagar, Tamil Nadu, India.

T. Ravi
Department of Electronics and Communication Engineering, School of Electrical and Electronics, Sathyabama Institute of Science and Technology, Chennai, Tamil Nadu, India.

Uma M.
Department of Computational Intelligence, School of Computing, SRM Institute of Science and Technology, Chengalpattu, Tamil Nadu, India.

V. Kavitha
Department of Computing Technologies, School of Computing, SRM Institute of Science and Technology, Kattankulathur, Tamil Nadu, India.

Vanajaroselin Chirchi
Department of ISE, Dayananda Sagar Academy of Technology and Management (DSATM), Bengaluru, Karnataka, India.

Venkatesh Ramamurthy
NETS International, Dubai, United Arab Emirates.

Vijay Priya V.
Department of Computer Science and Engineering, SRM Valliammai Engineering College, Chengalpattu, Tamil Nadu, India.

Wilfred Blessing N.R.
College of Computing and Information Sciences, University of Technology and Applied Sciences-Ibri, Ibri, Oman.

Wilfred Blessing N.R.
College of Computing and Information Sciences, University of Technology and Applied Sciences-Ibri, Ibri, Oman.

Yokesh V.
Department of Electronics and Communication Engineering, School of Electrical and Electronics, Sathyabama Institute of Science and Technology, Chennai, Tamil Nadu, India.

Yokesh V.
Department of Electronics and Communication Engineering, School of Electrical and Electronics, Sathyabama Institute of Science and Technology, Chennai, Tamil Nadu, India.

Yuvaraja Teekaraman
Department of Electrical Engineering, Chair-Research and Ethics Committee, School of Engineering and Computing, American International University, Kuwait.

1 Introduction: The Convergence of AI Wearables and the Metaverse

V. Kavitha[1], S. Poonkodi[2*], K. Suresh[3], S. Hemavathi[4], Jayaraj Ramasamy[5] and Raja Rajakani[6]

The ongoing advancements in artificial intelligence (AI) and wearable sensors coupled with the metaverse touch every field of study, as they intertwine the physical, digital, and cognitive realms in an unprecedented way. In this work, we establish an initial AI, wearables, and metaverse interconnection point in the field. We focus on the possible collaborations, socio-ethical considerations, and challenges in the field of research. We present the arguments that AI-powered inference, which can run on wearable devices, is capable of real-time, situational awareness, and adaptive real-time granularity. Concurrently, metaverse applications deliver real-time profiles for social collaboration and teleportation, significantly extending the physical. We assist with adaptive health surveillance, augmented human work, and new modes of work and education that span the monolithic physical and virtual realms. We discuss the health and social applications of real-time, edge, and federated learning, and the privacy framework for digital systems. Finally, we determine the most critical social and technological needs in the field: real-time privacy systems, human-centred interoperability, and social/secondary real-time systems. This chapter also analyses the social threats of surveillance, the erosion of bias, and the loss of consent, and proposes future investigations aimed at addressing this surveillance and bias erosion through auditing models with transparency, preserving architectures with privacy, and guiding governance models with regulation. Identifying the potential of technology and proposing balanced innovations, this chapter aims to assist responsible researchers and professionals in the construction of integrated systems that provide high technical quality, ethical values, and social quality.

1. Introduction

An awesome paradigm shift is occurring in how digital systems communicate with humans and the physical world, mainly as a result of the convergence of artificial

[1-4] Department of Computing Technologies, School of Computing, SRM Institute of Science and Technology, Kattankulathur, Tamil Nadu, India.
[5] Botha University, Gaborone, Botswana.
[6] Plant Plastic Research Centre, Seoul National University, Seoul, South Korea.
* Corresponding author: Ps8078@srmist.edu.in

DOI: 10.1201/9781003776291-1

intelligence (AI), wearable technology, and the metaverse. Traditionally, these technologies were developed independently; today, however, they are increasingly being organized into ecosystems that are intelligent, immersive, and adaptive. When this integration is completed, we can achieve continuous sense-making, real-time awareness of what is happening around us, and a persistent virtual presence that effectively removes the old barriers among digital systems, how humans think, and the physical world we live in.

We can trace the speed of this convergence back to several key factors. AI algorithms have gotten much better, wearable sensors are now everywhere and cost way less than before, and the metaverse is becoming a world that just stays there all the time. These developments work together to help create new solutions for health, the education industry, and how people collaborate socially. But they also bring up some serious questions about keeping our data private, what is ethically right, and whether individuals still have control over their own choices. This section will set things up for the discussions that come later by examining how this convergence started in the first place, how it changed over time, and what it actually covers today.

1.1 Background and Motivation

Over the last decade, computing power, sensor techniques, and data analysis have really pushed forward this whole technological environment. AI has changed dramatically across pretty much everything. The field spans from basic rule-based systems all the way to advanced machine learning (ML) and deep learning models that can actually perceive, reason, and make decisions. Wearable tech has turned into sophisticated systems that monitor environmental, behavioural, and body related factors in real time. The metaverse concept has also come up as this unified, immersive digital space where identity, social interaction, and virtual economies can continue existing over time.

A key motivation behind the integration of advanced technological solutions (i.e., systems that are adaptable, personalized, and contextually relevant) is to meet contemporary societal needs (e.g., telemedicine, online education, augmented reality in the workplace, and monitoring of well-being). These needs necessitate systems that are capable of seamlessly operating in both the physical (or actual) and virtual (or digital) environments. We believe the use of advanced technologies, including AI-enabled wearable technologies and the metaverse, will allow us to provide more effective, human-centric services through the use of real-time feedback, immersive visualizations, and interactional collaboration.

The use of edge computing and distributed intelligence has provided a significant benefit to end users in terms of their ability to access and process critical or sensitive information from a location near them, thereby resulting in reduced latency and increased privacy. In addition, as more people use wearable devices and the growth of hyper-fast digital environments accelerates, there are several reasons to begin thinking about how we can create an integrated system that responsibly uses AI, wearables, and the metaverse.

1.2 Evolution of AI, Wearables, and the Metaverse

Advances in AI technology seem to be increasing at intervals over time. Initially, such a wave consisted of coding with AI techniques, followed by expert systems, and later it was replaced by ML. Deep learning models and generative adversarial models are dominating the current wave of AI. These innovative systems have created AI systems capable of processing and understanding complex, multifaceted data patterns and adapting their responses to real-time changes. Additionally, more systems have changed from relying on remote servers to local, small edge devices like wearables, which means that they can respond instantly to triggers without a cloud connection.

Wearable technology has also made huge strides. Old wearable devices are employed to track the basic metrics. Today's devices have multiple sensors and advanced processing capabilities. Smartwatches, fitness trackers, smart clothing, and medical wearables help users monitor their health and receive personalized feedback and services. These capabilities have positioned wearables, along with AI systems, to enable advanced embodied, context-aware systems.

The idea of the metaverse may now be associated with fully developed augmented reality (AR), virtual reality (VR), and mixed reality (MR) technologies, but in its early days, the metaverse was related to virtual worlds and game platforms. Most modern metaverse platforms try to incorporate persistence, interoperability, and real-time user social interaction, which makes it possible for users to keep their digital identities and have shared experiences with others. As wearable technology and AI advance, they will be incorporated into the metaverse, creating a system that is cyber-physical-social, and reflects and responds to the conditions and behaviours of users in the real world.

1.3 Scope and Contribution of the Chapter

This chapter examines the rapidly increasing convergence of AI, wearable devices, and the metaverse. More specifically, it addresses the conceptual core and the technology driving the human-centred design challenges, with the greatest focus on real-time intelligence, interoperability, and the three pillars of privacy architectures.

There are three key contributions made by this chapter. First, it conceptualizes the integrated AI–wearable–metaverse systems and how physical sensing, digital processing, and cognitive intelligence come together. Second, it emphasizes the value of edge intelligence, federated learning, and immersive environments in the advancement of adaptable and scalable applications, particularly those meant to function across disparate domains. Finally, it stresses the need for transparency, explicit consent, and responsible governance in the socio-ethical dilemmas arising from constant surveillance, digitally immersive environments, and the need for real presence.

This chapter aims to guide researchers, practitioners, and policymakers towards the development of systems that balance innovation with ethical values and social well-being by highlighting both the opportunities and challenges of technological integration.

2. Conceptual Framework for Technology Convergence

The integration of AI techniques, wearable technologies, and the metaverse can be explained using a layered conceptual framework that integrates the physical, digital, and cognitive domains. Instead of operating as isolated components, these domains continuously interact through data flows, intelligence inference, and human-centred feedback mechanisms. These models explain the sequential interaction between real-time, adaptive intelligence, and immersive perception that contributes to the advancement of cyber-physical-social systems.

2.1 Interoperation of Physical, Digital, and Cognitive Layers

The physical layer basically models what happens in the real world and involves the actual bodies of users, their bodily processes, how they move, and also the environment around them. Wearable sensors that are built into smart devices, clothes, and accessories actually measure different things about the human body, like heart rate, how the body moves, temperature, posture, and even environmental factors. This layer ends up providing the raw and immediate data that tells us about the current state of both the human body and the environment [1, 2].

The digital layer is the brain behind everything. The physical layer consists of local computing units, edge nodes, cloud computing, and data networks, which make it all work. The digital layer is responsible for making sure that the data can be accessed and synchronized in real time, as well as for processing and visualizing the data. At this level, dependability and privacy of data are ensured through reliable and secure communication and data flow [3, 4].

The cognitive layer augments the system's ability to reason with the help of AI models that are able to learn, comprehend, and make decisions. It helps in the understanding of different data streams, identifying and interpreting patterns, and making recommendations or predictions based on the information. The collaboration of these layers creates an ongoing feedback loop: data from the physical world is captured, processed in digital form, interpreted cognitively, and finally [5].

2.2 Role of AI in Context-Aware Intelligence

Artificial intelligence is the main catalyst for raising the level of contextual awareness in the deeply connected systems of the future. It is able to interpret ill-assorted, multi-modal data arising from several sources, e.g., wearables, to recognize an individual's context, such as their physical activities, health condition, feelings, and surroundings. Subsequently, the systems modify their functioning automatically to suit the needs of the particular user in the situation in time.

Another aspect of context awareness is edge AI, which takes it a step further by having the inference done right on the wearables or at a nearby edge server. This has the benefit of drastically cutting down the round-trip time of data for processing, thus enabling real-time decision-making and also lessening the amount of sensitive data that has to be sent to the central servers. Besides that, federated learning makes it feasible for isolated devices to jointly train a model while still not revealing any raw data, thus achieving privacy protection [6].

In the metaverse, the societal and collective layer of intelligence is integrated by AI along with the individual one. AI-powered avatars, virtual assistants, and constantly changing scenarios can understand the needs of a single individual as well as those of a group. Thus, they bring interaction on a more human level and make it possible to reach the goal of greater teamwork efficiency. In this sense, AI is the brain that connects physical sensing, digital processing, and immersive interaction to form a single system.

2.3 Wearables as Real-Time Sensing and Interaction Interfaces

Wearable devices are considered as the primary medium of communication between the human and the technologically converged ecosystem. Because these devices are almost always in contact with the human body, they can continuously and very discreetly collect data, which is why they are considered as the best option for long-term monitoring and immediate response. Current wearables are built with various sensors, a small computer unit, and the ability to connect to a network wirelessly; thus, they have been turned from simple data gatherers into smart, active devices.

Besides the sensing function, wearables also allow two-way communication through visual displays, audio cues, and haptic feedback. Wearables such as motion tracking devices, haptic gloves, and bio signal sensors play a crucial role in the interaction of the player with the metaverse-enabled applications. With these devices, players can navigate their virtual environments and alter them just like in reality. Such embodiment significantly increases the immersion and it is also very effective in rehabilitation, skill training, collaborative work, and experiential learning [7].

Wearables combining the features of sensing, computing, and interacting are like a conduit between the human body and digital intelligence; thus, they keep the virtual experiences from getting completely detached from real-world human emotions and needs.

2.4 Metaverse as a Persistent Immersive Environment

The metaverse in its pure form refers to a virtual shared world that is permanent and combines technologies such as AR, VR, and MR. Unlike traditional virtual worlds, the metaverse is characterized by continuity, the synchronization of events in real time, and social presence. Users retain their digital identities and avatars that record their activities, preferences, and moods across different sessions and platforms.

In combination with AI and wearables, the metaverse becomes a living cyber-physical-social world [8]. Data from wearables in real time can be used to create avatars, which in turn enable virtual representations of physical and cognitive states.

The metaverse has actually become much more than just another way to show information. It is turned into an interactive space where smart technology, physical experiences, and social connections all come together. These environments focus heavily on capabilities that go beyond what biology can do, and they really need ethical design that responds to users, smooth connections between different systems, and rules that build trust while including everyone [9] [10].

3. Enabling Technologies

The metaverse is changing the way we experience technology and have fun on computers. Instead of just using your computer to interact with other people through traditional online means (like email or instant messaging), you will now be able to use a virtual environment to collaborate, discover, and communicate in new and exciting ways within the same location that you would normally go to for these purposes. These shared spaces are powered by cutting-edge technologies, including VR and AR, allowing for dynamic and engaging environments that blur the lines between the physical and digital worlds. Figure 1.1 explains enabling technologies using metaverse.

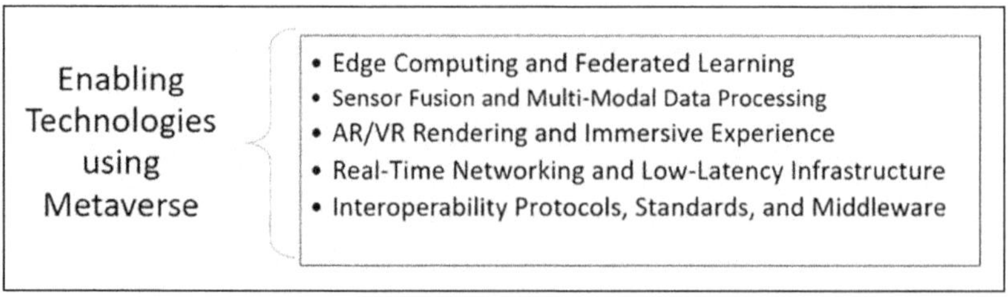

Fig. 1.1 Enabling technologies using metaverse.

3.1 Edge Computing and Federated Learning

A relevant application of edge computing is at the intersection of AI, wearables, and the metaverse, particularly smartwatches, headsets for AR and VR, and other wearable devices. The technology allows and processes data nearer to the source, in this case, the smartwatches, AR/VR headsets and other wearables, so rather than sending all of the data to centralized cloud servers, edge computing facilitates real-time analyses and decisions, thereby providing real-time critical monitoring, gesture tracking, and virtual engagement. Edge computing is particularly effective in the metaverse as it minimizes latency and maximizes engagement. Edge computing is particularly critical as it guarantees data privacy, reduced bandwidth consumption, and is cost-effective in the continuous streams of data generated by wearable devices.

In regard to the edge computing framework, federated learning facilitates the training of AI models on multiple wearables and edge devices without exposing any user data. The federated learning methodology is especially relevant to the metaverse since the wearable devices are responsible for the collection of sensitive personal data related to fundamental biological and behavioural data signals. Using federated learning, users can maintain privacy, security, and data collection while AI systems are optimized for continuous learning and enhancement across dispersed devices, resulting in a better metaverse experience that is personalized, secure, and intelligent.

3.2 Sensor Fusion and Multi-Modal Data Processing

These sensors produce an immense number of different types of data that are difficult to interpret and process. Multi-modal sensor fusion technology can combine different types of multi-modal data from multiple sensors to improve the quality and reliability of the combined data [11].

While sensor fusion was traditionally viewed as simply an amalgamation of data streams from multiple types of sensors, we instead view sensor fusion as the dynamic relationship between sensors performing under varying conditions in the real world. Just as humans rely on different types of senses (e.g., a person using light to see and their hands to feel for direction while walking in the dark) to form a more well-rounded perception of an object, autonomous systems can achieve robust capabilities by fusing different types of sensing modalities [12].

Multi-modal data processing refers to working together with multiple types of data (physiological signals, images, sounds, motion) using a combination of both AI and ML. With multi-modal processing, AI systems can assess and respond to various forms of input at the same time; thus, they can evaluate user intent, emotion, or environmental conditions at the intersection of AI, wearables, and the metaverse. For example, when using eye tracking, biometric data, and voice recognition technologies in combination, providing users with a more advanced way to interact within the metaverse is achievable using this approach, resulting in better responsiveness, greater realism, and a higher degree of personalization when working in a virtual environment.

3.3 AR/VR Rendering and Immersive Experience Design

The last few years have seen remarkable improvements in extended reality (XR) technologies such as VR, AR, and MR that have constructed new immersive experience possibilities that can entertain and engage users. These immersive experiences can also transform user experiences in everyday activities as they integrate with Internet of Things (IoT) and AI [13]. VR and AR technologies are increasingly being used in education. Students are able to interact with their environment in a more immersive way, increasing engagement and providing a greater understanding of concepts.

3.4 Real-Time Networking and Low-Latency Infrastructure

Edge computing solves this issue by providing real-time computational capacity with lower latencies. Nearby edge cloudlets process the data locally using IoE edge before sending it on to the central cloud. This decreases latencies and increases overall bandwidth through optimizing the use of available bandwidth. This is particularly useful for different types of metaverse applications including autonomous vehicles, low-latency healthcare services, digital twins or telepresence. However, despite the advancement of the IoE, it creates issues with regard to out-of-band privacy, security, and authentication [14].

Another means for meeting communications needs are advancements in the area of beyond 5G (i.e., 6G) technologies that will create high-reliability, low-latency (fast) connections to all metaverse devices. Intelligent virtual environments will be developed through AI while the ability to securely manage digital assets in the metaverse will require the use of both blockchain and non-fungible tokens (NFTs). The metaverse will incorporate a number of different technologies, including 3D modelling, AI/ML, blockchain, 6G, NFT, edge computing, and IoE [15].

The convergence of technologies such as AI, wearables, and the metaverse will depend on real-time networking and low-latency infrastructure to enable a seamless exchange between devices. To allow AI systems to quickly process all the data coming from wearable devices like smartwatch glasses, VR headsets, and biometrics, it must travel over low-latency networks that will use longer distance next-generation 5G-type technologies, edge computing, and high throughput cloud services. All these factors will help eliminate time delays and motion sickness when users interact with avatars in the metaverse by allowing for real-time instant gesture recognition that involves multiple users in the same virtual environment.

As individual users create and code their avatars, scenes, and interactions in real time via wearables, the volume of data packets being sent into the system will increase dramatically with each user in a multi-user environment. Low latency, as an example of such importance, will ensure that virtual meetings—as well as video games, healthcare simulations, and remote training events—are immersive, authentic, and immediate by maintaining a consistent level of immersion and realism for each user and provide a rapid response regardless of the number of users. Thus, real-time network and low-latency network are key partners to help the metaverse deliver a truly collaborative experience that replicates actual place of interaction one would have in person.

3.5 Interoperability Protocols, Standards, and Middleware

These areas of metaverse technology have many proprietary commercial solutions available off the shelf, as well as many open-source projects. While some components of the metaverse will share common building blocks, a good number will be independent of or orthogonally aligned with each other. Therefore, there are very few companies that possess the necessary resources to become well-versed in all building block technologies, as well as have the capabilities to integrate them adequately to handle the needs of commercial users. The current scenario is one where a few companies control the majority of the most valuable services within their respective vertically integrated silos while having significant influence over the core developers who are making these services available to the end user. This scenario has been demonstrated to negatively impact or pose a danger to society.

Interoperability protocols, standards, and middleware are important parts of enabling smooth cooperation between various types of software at the application layer of AI systems and through to smart wearable devices, the metaverse, etc. The interoperability protocols and standards create the common set of rules, data formats, and methods of communication among smart wearable devices, all different types of sensors, AR/VR headsets and AI services, that have been developed using different vendors' platforms, and provide an end-to-end solution for ensuring that data can be shared by different vendors in an efficient and reliable manner. The interoperability protocols and standards will continue to create a highly compatible, scalable, and always unified user experience across all types of virtual environments and all types of devices working together inside the metaverse in real time.

Middleware is the connection point across hardware, software, and applications for the control of data flow management, device coordination, and service orchestration of all types of data and devices. Middleware facilitates the integration of AI, wearables, and the metaverse by managing tasks such as data synchronisation, data security, data authentication, and data deployment for AI models. The benefit of the metaverse framework is that developers can easily create smart cross-platform applications without any of the device-specific limitations. Interoperability protocols and standards, along with middleware, provides the environment that enables the user to have a trustworthy, consistent, scalable environment for running truly immersive, AI-based experiences in both the physical and virtual worlds.

4. Application Domains and Use Cases

4.1 Personalized Healthcare and Rehabilitation

The metaverse is an ongoing (constant) worldwide interconnectedness and immersion through the use of a virtual and augmented digital ecosystem that utilizes multiple senses with users and AI utilizing many forms of smart technology and their interaction can be instantaneously created with other users and/or AI.

The metaverse is much larger in scope than a normal digital platform as it helps to blend physical and digital spaces by creating instant interactions between these two worlds. The metaverse also provides to users social, economic, and cultural opportunities as well as multiple opportunities for social interactions through a blend of digital and physical environments [16]. XR technologies such as VR, AR, and MR are what enable the metaverse to function. VR creates an environment that mimics the real-world environment yet creates a virtual environment. AR creates an environment that overlays digital items onto the physical environment. XR technology is looking to provide users with an experience (at once) that is real, interactive, and immersive.

In addition, aged individuals can now engage in social VR exergames within the metaverse for the purpose of rehabilitation. Participants enjoyed the social VR experience and felt that the collaborative nature of these experiences contributed greatly to their motivation level. Participants reported several health benefits associated with this type of VR experience and provided excellent usability ratings for virtual environments designed for rehabilitation. Due to the ability of the metaverse to allow patients to confront psychological problems (e.g., social anxieties or post-traumatic stress disorder [PTSD]), patients are able to gradually work through their psychological issues by being exposed to simulated social situations [17].

Combining AI, wearables, and the metaverse will provide an important application for personalized healthcare and rehabilitation in the home with the potential to close the medical support loop—this is an important step towards the advancement of medical/surgical tourism. Continuous streams of real-time data will be available on many critical indicators, such as heart rates, activity (during the day), hours of sleep each night, and muscle activity through a client's wearable technology, to refine their individualized health plans. AI algorithms will process this information to identify abnormalities, predict risk factors, and recommend personalized treatments/rehabilitation protocols.

To help with their recovery, patients may engage in virtual therapy sessions within an artificial environment, appearing as real. This environment would adapt to the changing condition of the patient over time, assisting them to recover. The merger boosts rehab by giving lively, urging, and safe virtual settings where users can do body therapy and mind drills under the watch of smart tech. Quick input from gear worn on the body lets AI tweak workout levels and methods to keep things working well and personalize recovery. Through personalized healthcare in the metaverse, patients are more engaged, their recovery is accelerated, and remote monitoring is enabled, thereby reducing the need for physical clinical visits.

4.2 Adaptive Fitness, Wellness, and Behavioural Monitoring

Adaptive fitness, wellness, and behavioural tracking is a major application of the integration of AI, wearables and the metaverse. Wearables endlessly collect the data of the physiological, motion, and behavioural activities of the individual, such as heart rate, sleep patterns, physical activity, posture, and stress levels. AI algorithms used to analyse data in real time provide users with personalized wellness, fitness recommendations, and behavioural analysis, all of which are delivered through interactive avatars and virtual environments.

The increasing interest of researchers and professionals in the effects of VR on our health—both physical and mental—has resulted in a wealth of studies demonstrating that participating in VR physical activity can produce a variety of physical improvements, such as improved cardiovascular fitness and strength improvements. Many people report having a significantly higher level of enjoyment when engaging in VR workout sessions than when they do similar activities using traditional forms of exercise, and as such, many of these individuals tend to remain committed to maintaining their regular exercise routine over the long haul due to the increased enjoyment associated with VR.

Thanks to this adaptive technology, virtual experiences can not only adapt based on how a person behaves while using them but also alter things like the intensity at which someone exercises, the amount of time they take to recover from those exercises, and even how much motivational support they receive in an organic way. Additionally, by analysing behavioural data, it is also possible to identify early indicators of poor lifestyle choices, mental fatigue, and other high-risk activities without overwhelming the user.

In gamified metaverse-like environments, behavioural tracking helps keep users engaged and accountable as they work to change their unhealthy habits, overcome mental exhaustion, and minimize the likelihood of engaging in high-risk behaviour. With access to a highly engaging virtual experience, as well as the use of wearable technology and AI in the metaverse, fitness and wellness solutions that are highly adaptive are available for people to achieve better health, improved well-being, and increased motivation both in the real world and virtually.

4.3 Distributed Telepresence and Remote Collaboration

The adaptive characteristic of this technology allows virtual experiences to adapt in a very natural manner to the users' actions, for instance, by varying the exercise intensity, rest time, and the provision of motivation. Additionally, although the gamified metaverse experiences keep the user involved, connected, and responsible for the improvements made, behavioural monitoring aids the system in identifying the user's hazards, unhealthy lifestyle, and mental overload. The amalgamation of AI technology, smart devices, and exciting VR in the metaverse provides the framework for adaptive fitness and wellness products that promote the adoption of a healthy lifestyle, the enhancement of well-being, and the encouragement of physical and virtual space users/persons. A multi-location telepresence essentially means people having a virtual presence together in a space of the metaverse while at different geographic locations of the world. Through the synergy of AI processing and appropriates such as AR glasses, VR headsets, haptic gloves, and biometric sensors, users can share real-time visual, auditory, and motion information. AI has a great potential to make the telepresence experience much better by giving avatars a human-like appearance, synchronizing the movements, reducing the delay time, and identifying the user's facial expressions and body language. This is the highest form of presence and continuity between the two realms (physical and virtual), and thereby remote communication will be easier and more natural with immersion. In the metaverse, remote collaboration uses distributed telepresence to connect people, allowing them to collaborate in real time regardless of where they are in the world. With AI tools analysing multi-modal data from wearables, intelligent features such as live language translation, hand gesture detection, sentiment analysis, and adaptive virtual working environment become available. Besides that, users can synergize on virtual whiteboards, 3D models, simulations, and shared digital resources as if they were physically collocated in a room. Wearables, AI, and metaverse platforms are the three main drivers of increased productivity, engagement, and communication. As a result, work, education, and social interaction are being transformed at a distance.

4.4 Intelligent AR/VR Assistants and Smart Learning Environments

Intelligent AR/VR assistants use a combination of AI, wearable devices, and immersive technologies to offer up-to-the-minute information and highly individualized help in the metaverse. They take data from wearables like eye-tracking sensors, motion sensors, and biometric monitors to find out user context, behaviour, and performance. Such AR/VR assistants, by combining natural language processing, computer vision, and adaptive AI models, can give step-by-step guidance, virtual coaching, as well as provide valuable tips and ideas from the surrounding environment. Hands-free help, life-like simulations, as well as increased work efficiency in the fields of training, healthcare, maintenance, and teamwork will become possible through the use of these technologies in the metaverse.

Smart learning environments are a perfect example of the AI, wearables, and metaverse coming together to provide immersive, adaptive, and student-centred educational settings. Wearables gather time-sensitive information regarding the student's focus, mental activity, and physical reactions. AI evaluates this information to customize the learning materials and speed of the instruction. Students can learn through various senses in VR/AR classrooms and simulations, paying closer attention than they would if they were taught in a more conventional manner.

4.5 Human–Machine Teaming in Industrial and Defence Settings

Human–machine teaming shows how AI, wearables, and the metaverse can come together in industry and defence. This allows humans and intelligent machines to work together, improving decision-making and enhancing performance and safety. AI systems use data from AR headsets, exoskeletons, and smart helmets to support workers and soldiers. These systems are represented as digital twins in the metaverse to simulate human and machine interaction. This technology is useful for training, planning missions, and rehearsing as operation prior develop each of the objectives of the metaverse. To further support these objectives, the metaverse proposes the accelerated development of a variety of foundational technologies, including but not limited to XR (VR/AR/MR), AI, computer graphics, blockchain, robotics, 3D printing, edge computing, 5G (and even 6G), all creating a large-scale and immersive digital world where users can connect, work, play, and perform other activities with their respective avatars. In addition to the guidance of AI, which helps humans concentrate on the more strategic and creative parts of their tasks, it also offers alerts, insights, and guidance in an adaptive manner.

In high-risk, complex environments, and in defence and industrial operations, human–machine teaming augments situational awareness, improves operational precision, and reduces overall cognitive load. Human–machine teaming incorporates the metaverse for training simulations with drones and other systems. With the combination of wearable technology, immersive virtual environments, and AI analytics, human–machine teaming offers more effective collaboration and autonomy between humans and machines, and it results in faster operational responses and enhanced safety.

5. System-Level Requirements and Design Considerations

5.1 The Architectural Triad: Latency, Reliability, and Scalability

Nowadays, the performance of modern data storage/databases and embedded systems is not calculated based only on the speed of execution. Alternatively, it can be determined by using complex communication among the three non-productive panorama: reliability, latency, and scalability. The system architecture combines the core of these three elements, improvement from one domain to another frequently involves a concurrence in another, requiring originators to voyage a "Pareto Frontier".

- **Latency: Temporal Bounds and System Integrity**

Latency is defined as the intermission between a stimulus and its observable response. In high-grade environments, such as independent vehicular control or high-frequency trading, it is also measured by functional correctness; system failure can be measured when it exceeds the corresponding temporal threshold.

Latency represents an aggregate delay spectrum, encompassing complexity in algorithm, obstacles in memory hierarchy, operating system context switching, and input/output hardware-level. Consequently, design efforts are categorized "Tail Latency", especially the ultimate delays evaluated from more incorporates (e.g., P99). In feedback-controlled systems, unexpected delays in these perceptible can induce phase lag, destabilizing mechanical characteristics and increasing failure in the physical system.

- **Reliability: Continuity under Fault Conditions**

Reliability is the possibility that a system will act upon its considered amount of function without failure over corresponding mentioned time. As system elaborateness increases, the imaginable surface area for expands the system failure that leads to fault tolerance a basic requirement which are mandatory.

Reliability is highly achieved in distributed systems environment, particularly the duplicates are received through redundancy and concurrency. Raft and Paxos are the protocols Paxos are introduced to monitor a single beginning of truth contempt node failures. However, these communication protocols are introduced to rectify "coordination overhead", authenticating a direct exchange where reliability implements are used to increase latency. Simultaneous engineering highlights proactive residency using digital twins and holter monitoring to counterfeit failure modes and recombine resources prior to courages.

- **Scalability: Architecting for Elastic Demand**

Scalability indicates to the structural measures of a device to handle expanding workloads by expanding resources without transforming the inner space architecture. A hyper-critical perfection exists between estimating methodologies: upright scaling (upgrading existing hardware) is defined by physical limitation because horizontal scaling (distributing load across multiple nodes) allows near-infinite development.

Horizontal scaling clearly explains the strong foundation for cloud-native and microscopical architectures. Efficient scaling methods need to follow the "decoupling principle", and make use of the techniques such as knowledge sharding and nonsynchronous message queues. To improve separately to look forward to local rushes from concluding the broader framework closer techniques are used for different system segments.

The integration of these necessaries produces essential infrastructure conflicts:

- **Latency vs Reliability:** Synchronous counterpart ensures data rightness but acknowledgments are required from the receiver side to improve the time of response.
- **Scalability vs Reliability:** Horizontal scaling improves the statistical feasibility of failure in hardware, necessitating complex recovery logic.
- **Latency vs Scalability:** Global distribution improves scalability but increases the geographic distance, thus increasing the latency by using the speed of light.

5.2 Privacy-Preserving Analytics and Secure Architectures

Privacy-preserving analytics (PPA) can be implemented using the new and modern computing technology and devices that are always connected with it. This gives protection to the system design, particularly for compliance with the new regulations as such as the General Data Protection Regulation (GDPR).

The PPA technologies allow the estimate consequent from the rebuilt datasets while protecting confidentiality, for the given time being they also charge translation overheads:

- *Homomorphic Encryption (HE)*: It also permits mathematical demands on ciphertext. While managing maximum confidentiality, it controls significant calculation overhead, always challenging hardware accelerators to protect responsiveness.
- *Differential Privacy (DP)*: It injects evaluated statistical noise to secure individual data points. The important design objections are the privacy–utility trade-off, where supplemental noise creates analytics inaccurate.
- *Federated Learning (FL)*: It concentrates workout to the wirework edge, producing weight improvements only. This used to improve scalability but it also posed reliability challenges and required update accumulation from the nodes which are not stable.
- *Secure Multi-Party Computation (SMC)*: It prepares collaborative computation without expressive private inputs. The necessary communication protocols are terrible and can multiply network latency.

A private architecture ensures data at rest, in charge, and its application. Identity management, providing attribute-based access control (ABAC) and several-factor confirmation is demanding. In microservices, separated identity providers are applicable to secure scalability. However, key governance using in cryptographic method explains failure in single point; if the benefits inhibit, its agreement providing latency and reliability system-wide. The "scalability–complexity paradox" explains that as a system scales horizontally, its attack portion expands, using new intelligent security techniques like Service Meshes. Mitigation measurements encompass offloading services in cryptographic to security modules and also applying "zero trust" infrastructures.

5.3 Interoperability and Human-Centred Design

■ Interoperability

Interoperability organizes systems across the following layers:

- *Technical Interoperability*: This layer guarantees physical integration across systems (e.g., IoMT sensors).
- *Syntactic Interoperability*: Classifying data formats (e.g., REST, MQTT) to allow data parsing at every event of internal rules.
- *Semantic Interoperability*: Managing data significance across platforms, enabling convenient clinical evaluations.

Architects need to protect restrictions from the proprietary by using principles that are open to all. To reduce the latency introduced and by virtualization, system design asynchronous communication and secure hierarchical fault tolerance.

■ Human-Centred Design (HCD)

The HCD is the explanative layer between precious data and human decision-making. Even when network communication has minimal latency, efficiency is reduced if the interface is untrained.

- *Active Feedback*: Systems device should always give immediate feedback to improve "perceived latency".
- *Predictability*: Designs should include high recovery capabilities and also give correct error messaging.
- *Psychological Time*: UX designers shape user perception by using techniques like Skeleton Screens to secure architecture before data can be loaded.
- *Transparency*: If a node finds failure, then the interface should provide the user of remodelling efforts preferably freezing, thereby protecting trust.

6. Socio-Ethical and Policy Challenges

6.1 Surveillance Risks and Data Governance

Modern digital technology produces integration and enables information management, but it also introduces substantial supervision risks and administration challenges.

- **Mass Surveillance and Detection**

Surveillance has moved from final targeted interception to large-scale data retention by regulatory and private entities. This produces a "chilling effect", where individuals modify their behaviour to protect themselves from negative algorithmic evaluations, combining data tracking with self-control of human agency. In regions with regulatory gaps, as such as parts of Africa, the expansion of spyware and CCTV introduces risks of civil rights abuses. Technological detection capabilities often outpace ethical governance. For example, during the COVID-19 pandemic, tracking architectures were established for public health usages despite their intruding nature, raising questions about data control during at the time of emergencies.

- **Ethical Data Governance**

Effective governance provides policies for pure ethical decision-making, distinguishing between data governance (setting policies) and IT governance (technical implementation). Infrastructures such as GOSLING help standardize problem assessment in clinical related research, providing the important quantitative measures for routine use, particularly for collected data.

6.2 Bias Amplification in AI-Driven Analytics

Data processing through AI introduces the threat of bias amplification. When biased practices are integrated into automated systems, they are operationalized, thus reinforcing environmental inequalities.

- **Sources of Algorithmic Bias**

Bias often originates from training data produced via surveillance, which may reproduce existing historical inequalities. Integrated with the, developer design methods and feature selection can inadvertently create specific demographics. This modifies AI from an objective tool into a technique for discrimination.

- **The Accountability Deficit**
The ambiguity of deep learning methods—often described as "black boxes"—produces a "transparency paradox". If the derivation of an outcome cannot be explained, holding an organization accountable for unequal outcomes, such as unfair resource accommodation, becomes difficult.

6.3 Legal and Regulatory Frameworks

Robust legal and regulatory frameworks have been provided to protect against socio-ethical challenges. One of the most paramount policy objections revolves around the complete lack of global synchronization within data security. Although the GDPR provides a large-scale measure to set certain universal standards, international harmonization exists solely based on non-binding guidance, making communication at an international level difficult.

There are currently no adequate techniques available for AI systems requesting large amounts of data; thus, "consent or anonymize" are not valid means for successful request completion with these types of systems. New technological platforms developing "dynamic consent", which enables continual communication types between data subjects through their use of the platform, are emerging and will also provide users the ability to ensure transparency when repurposing data.

6.4 Ethical Frameworks and Responsible Deployment

Beyond legal compliance, associations must adopt cautious ethical frameworks. Digital rights and digital justice link digital index or digital privilege with social benefits and seek to have a governance structure that allows for measurable treatment through technology and not just through technocracy. This will create an environment in which marginalized people are given a technological solution to their marginalization, such as smart community care.

The responsible use of technology for the benefit of people requires translating ethical theories into action by having necessary technical guardrails and explainable AI (XAI). This form of communication is valuable in the application of technologies like sewage surveillance, where public health monitoring should be considered along with "group privacy" rights.

7. Future Research Directions

7.1 Transparent and Auditable AI Models

Trust, accountability, and ethical compliance are genuinely needed for integrating AI-driven wearables and metaverse for which transparent and auditable AI models are significant. Wearable tech devices incessantly gather incredibly private personal information including health related metrics, exercise patterns, and what we do within metaverse (immersive environments), and this feeds directly into the AI systems. XAI models provide explanations for predictions and actions (e.g., health recommendations or avatar behaviour). Auditable AI models make it possible to supervise, validate, and examine AI processes for fairness, accuracy, and adherence to data privacy regulations. Transparency and auditability ensure that AI-driven metaverse experiences are trustworthy, ethical, and user-focused.

7.2 Privacy-by-Design and Security-by-Design Approaches

Privacy-by-design is a pre-emptive strategy of integrating privacy measures into the design of AI, wearable devices, and metaverse platforms. Given that (most) wearables operate on a constant feed of very sensitive private data, including biometric information and health records, as well potentially more general behavioural data, quantified self-principles benefit from privacy-by-design measures in order to minimize the amount of data collected; to enable user consented processing as far as possible; to facilitate anonymous processing; and to utilize local (non-cloud based) modes for managing users' personal information. In the metaverse, this process protects the identities of users and their interactions (and digital belongings), so entities can trust these as they relate to both compliance with data protection laws and interaction for personalized experiences.

Security-by-design involves building strong security up front into our AI modelling, wearable hardware and metaverse infrastructure—as opposed to adding it in at the end. This comprises secure authentication, encryption, access controls, security device firmware, and ongoing threat monitoring. In the intersection of AI, wearables, and the metaverse, security-by-design secures systems against cyberattacks and data breaches as well as against identity theft—it assures integrity, availability, and confidentiality in virtual environments. In combination, these various techniques yield a safe, reliable, and robust environment for next generation.

7.3 Sustainable and Inclusive Technology Ecosystems

An inclusive and sustainable technology ecosystem is essential to support the convergence of AI, wearable devices, and the metaverse, enabling long-term environmental stewardship and providing digital experiences for everyone. Sustainable technology can be evaluated to establish research areas and goals for energy-efficient AI systems, low-power wearable devices, and edge computing technologies that minimize carbon emissions and reduce resources consumed. The metaverse will be able to develop in a sustainable manner without causing adverse effects to our environment through the use of sustainable technologies and software.

It is this ecosystem inclusivity that makes it possible for the metaverse technologies to be used more broadly, including people of all abilities, ages, and socio-economic statuses. This is where AI-driven personalized experiences, adaptive interfaces, and wearable assistive technologies allow everyone to be part of the action through voice control, gestural interaction, vibrational response (think: haptic feedback), and on-the-fly language translation. By emphasising ethical AI, affordability, accessibility, and universal design principles, the sustainable and inclusive technology ecosystems ensure that fair and human-centric as well as globally accessible metaverse environments are offered.

7.4 Long-Term Vision for AI–Wearable–Metaverse Ecosystems

The ultimate goal for AI–wearable–metaverse ecosystems is a fully integrated digital and physical world in which smart machines constantly interact with human beings in natural and meaningful ways. In such a vision, AI models embedded in wearable devices will be personal digital companions that learn the user's behaviour, health data, emotions, and context to help users out virtually and physically. The metaverse will be a persistent shared space that supports work, learning, and healthcare as well as entertainment and socializing, with wearables serving as the primary interface between humans and digital worlds.

All this will be possible thanks to technologies like edge computing, federated learning, sensor fusion, and immersive AR/VR that learn from you with increasing relevance while preserving your privacy. Studies have proven that economic, social, and governance (ESG) performance positively influences firm value through transparent disclosure. ESG performance in the metaverse is therefore essential for improving both the company's economic viability as well as its societal contribution.

Sustainability and scalability are two of the most critical considerations for the metaverse as it develops into an integrated digital ecosystem. This section builds upon the previous sections by discussing the structural architecture of the metaverse's multilayered network. This multilayer network is how users, their avatars, and platforms are connected to the real world, the internet, and virtual environments, and allows all users to interact seamlessly with each other. By using this type of analysis on the metaverse's position in relation to the greater economy and ecology, this lens also illustrates how multilayered networks can promote and provide ES/GS compliance and sustainability over time. Narrows consist of nodes that exist as virtual representations of an individual (in this case, individuals in the metaverse) connected through edges, which connect those nodes together [19, 20].

Countless applications exist using AI in the metaverse, such as creating personalized content for each end user; enhancing virtual environment realism and immersion; and creating intelligent assistive technologies that will enable users to explore and navigate their environments in the metaverse. Beyond these examples, AI could enable a more inclusive metaverse experience for those who are physically or cognitively impaired and enhance security and privacy via improvements made to current systems [21].

8. Conclusion

To summarize, examining the role of emerging metaverse technologies as they relate to the healthcare sector positions this research at the frontiers of healthcare, technology, and innovation. Focusing on the analysis of patent data and employing state-of-the-art analytical techniques, the research has identified the principal domains of potential application and possible trajectory of the metaverse in the healthcare delivery ecosystem [22]. The research illustrates the magnitude of metaverse technologies in the reconfiguration of healthcare delivery, with diverse applications in fitness, entertainment, surgery, medical education, training, and the pharmaceutical supply chain. While the initial capital outlay to develop the requisite infrastructure to support the integration of the metaverse in healthcare delivery may be significant, the potential returns are likely to surpass the initial investment significantly. The research strikes a balance between the unprecedented potential in the transformational reconfiguration of the delivery of healthcare services and the need to optimize the research focus to relatively emergent levels in the increasingly digital environment. The pace at which the metaverse is integrated into the healthcare delivery system is likely to be determined by the nature and extent of partnerships established among the technology companies, the regulators, and the healthcare system. The design of the accessible and the usable systems that embody the principles of anti-privacy, with the adaptive and implementable frameworks of AI, is likely to be more successful and more readily accepted by the health system. Furthermore, VR with haptic feedback systems that monitor a user's real-time physiology has the potential to transform therapy in ways beyond what decades of innovation and advanced technology can do to revolutionize healthcare post-surgery, thus providing means for doctors to virtually follow the recovery of their patients. There is a need for healthcare to become one whole unit when using AI, XR, and blockchain technology with quantum computing, in order to maximize the potential of the healthcare system through developments in the metaverse.

The researchers should investigate using quantum computing in conjunction with AI to improve the metaverse potential for healthcare technologies. ML based on quantum computing has the ability to greatly improve the rapidness and correctness of providing complex diagnosis of medical data gathered in a number of various ways; e.g., genomic and personalized medicine. The utilization of quantum encryption as a protocol could potentially redesign the infrastructure used to secure information within the metaverse and reduce the potential for cybersecurity concerns. In addition, using federated learning as a reinforcement tool would enable hospitals and researchers to collectively develop large, patient-centric AI systems while keeping patient data secure but without having to provide any direct access to that data. Exploring these technologies will play a key role in advancing the future of healthcare that utilizes the metaverse in the most novel ways.

References

[1] Rajkumar, R., Lee, I., Sha, L. and Stankovic, J. (2010). Cyber-physical systems: The next computing revolution. *Proceedings of the 47th ACM/IEEE Design Automation Conference (DAC)*, Anaheim, CA, USA, pp. 731–736.

[2] Sargolzaei, A.B., Yen, K.K. and Abdelghani, M.N. (2019). Wearable sensors and IoT-based systems for healthcare monitoring. *IEEE Internet of Things Journal*, 6(2), 2278–2289.

[3] Satyanarayana, M. (2017). The emergence of edge computing. *Computer*, 50(1), 30–39.

[4] Zhou, P., Hu, Y., Liang, Z. and Zhang, W. (2019). Edge intelligence: Paving the last mile of artificial intelligence with edge computing. *Proceedings of the IEEE*, 107(8), 1738–1762.

[5] Kim, J.K., Park, S. and Kim, H. (2020). Context-aware systems: A survey on sensors, computing platforms, and applications. *IEEE Access*, 8, 193970–193988.

[6] Lee, J., Bagheri, B. and Kao, H.A. (2015). A cyber-physical systems architecture for Industry 4.0-based manufacturing systems. *Manufacturing Letters*, 3, 18–23.

[7] B. McMahan, B., Moore, E., Ramage, D., Hampson, S., Blaise Aguera y Arcas, et al. (2017). Communication-efficient learning of deep networks from decentralized data. *Proceedings of the 20th International Conference on Artificial Intelligence and Statistics (AISTATS)*, pp. 1273–1282. arXiv:1602.05629.

[8] Xu, D., Guo, F. and Chen, Z. (2021). Human–machine interaction in wearable computing systems: A survey. *IEEE Transactions on Human–Machine Systems*, 51(3), 214–227.

[9] Thrun, S. (2004). Toward robotic assistants. *Communications of the ACM*, 47(6), 25–31.

[10] Jain, A.K., Ross, A. and Prabhakar, S. (2004). An introduction to biometric recognition. *IEEE Transactions on Circuits and Systems for Video Technology*, 14(1), 4–20.

[11] Tang, Q., Liang, J. and Zhu, F. (2023). A comparative review on multi-modal sensors fusion based on deep learning. *Signal Processing*, 213, 109165.

[12] Bibri, S.E. (2023). The Metaverse as a Virtual Model of Platform Urbanism: Its Converging AIoT, XReality, Neurotech, and Nanobiotech and Their Applications, Challenges, and Risks. Smart Cities, 6(3), 1345–1384. https://doi.org/10.3390/smartcities6030065.

[13] Bibri, S.E. (2023). The metaverse as a virtual model of platform urbanism: Its converging AIoT, XReality, neurotech, and nano biotech and their applications, Challenges, and Risks. *Smart Cities*, 6, 1345–1384.

[14] Zhou, P., Braud, T., Zavodovski A. et al. (2020). Edge-facilitated augmented vision in vehicle-to-everything networks. *IEEE Transactions on Vehicular Technology*, 69(10), 12187–12201.

[15] Rafique, W. and Qadir, J. (2024). Internet of everything meets the metaverse: Bridging physical and virtual worlds with blockchain. *Computer Science Review*, 54, 100678.

[16] Morone, G., Ciancarelli, I., Calabro, R.S. et al. (2025). Meta rehab verse: The great opportunity to put the person's functioning and participation at the center of healthcare. *Neurorehabilitation and Neural Repair* , 39(3), 241–255.

[17] Calabrò, R.S. and Morone, G. (2025). Advancing rehabilitation medicine with the metaverse: Opportunities and challenges. *Brain Sciences*, 15(3), 321.

[18] Choi, S., Jung, T. and Bae, S. (2023). The rolling hills: ESG metaverse platform. In Tom Dieck, M. C., Jung, T., and Kim, Y.S. (eds), XR and Metaverse. XR 2023, pp. 238–244. Cham: Springer.

[19] Moro-Visconti, R., Rambaud, S.C., Pascual, J.L. et al. (2025). Sustainable metaverse ecosystems: From ESG compliance to multilayer network scalability. *Financial Innovation*, 11, 117.

[20] Dhanaraj, R.K. (2024). A comprehensive exploration of artificial intelligence methods for COVID-19 diagnosis. *EAI Endorsed Transactions on Pervasive Health & Technology*, 10(1).

[21] Soliman, M.M., Ahmed, E., Darwish, A. et al. (2024). Artificial intelligence powered metaverse: Analysis, challenges and future perspectives. *Artificial Intelligence Review*, 57, 36.

[22] Balasubramaniam, S., Vijesh Joe, C., Prasanth, A. and Satheesh Kumar, K. (2025). Computer vision systems in livestock farming, poultry farming, and fish farming: Applications, use cases, and research directions. In Dhanaraj, R. K., Balusamy, B., Samuel, P. et al. (eds), *Computer Vision in Smart Agriculture and Crop Management*, pp. 221–258. Wiley.

2 The Evolution of Wearable Technologies: From Fitness Tracker to Intelligent Companions

Yokesh V.[1*], N. Sathish[2], Bhuvana B.P.[3], Abdelfateh Kerrouche[4] and Danilo Pelusi[5]

The development of wearable technologies has turned personal devices into the intelligent companions to individuals that can easily adjust to everyday life and do not seem like a mere activity tracker. Early fitness trackers were mainly known to count the number of steps, check the heart rate, and promote better health habits. With the development of sensors, wireless connectivity, artificial intelligence (AI) and miniaturized electronics, the functionality of wearables has grown significantly beyond mere health data in the long term. The wearable devices in the modern world are able to read patterns in behaviour, make customized suggestions, offer real-time decision support, and even anticipate possible health risks. The connection to smartphones, cloud environments, and the Internet-of-Things systems has allowed them to be constantly monitored, to enhance their interaction with the users, and provide them with adaptive functionality based on their needs. As wearables move to the next stage of their development, they are transforming into proactive, context-aware assistants which can improve productivity, well-being, safety, and the quality of life, in general. In this chapter, the authors examine this extraordinary journey with the most important technological discoveries and design changes that led to the creation of wearables as smart digital assistants.

1. Introduction to Wearable Technologies

Wearable technologies can be defined as electronic and computational systems that are effectively incorporated into clothes or accessories, or worn directly on the human body to allow around-the-clock sensing, processing, and communication of data concerning physiological, behavioural, and environmental parameters.

[1,3] Department of Electronics and Communication Engineering, School of Electrical and Electronics, Sathyabama Institute of Science and Technology, Chennai, Tamil Nadu, India.
[2] Department of Electronics and Communication Engineering, Sri Venkateswara College of Engineering, Sriperumbudur, Tamil Nadu, India.
[4] School of Engineering and the Built Environment, Edinburgh Napier University, Edinburgh, Scotland.
[5] Department of Communication Sciences, University of Teramo, Balzarini, Italy.
* Corresponding author: yokesh.inba@gmail.com

DOI: 10.1201/9781003776291-2

Technically, wearables are distributed embedded systems, which consist of sensing hardware, low-power electronics, wireless communication, and intelligent data analytics in small-scale ergonomic form factors [1].

On the hardware side, wearable devices have a plethora of micro- and nano-scale sensors, such as inertial (accelerators, gyroscopes, magnetometers), biomedical (ECG, PPG, EMG, EDA, temperature), and environmental (pressure, gas, light) ones [2]. These sensors are connected by low-noise analogue front-end (AFE) and signal conditioning stages and high-resolution analogue-to-digital converters (ADCs) to provide reliable data acquisition of a sensor by motion and environmental perturbations. Ultra-low-power microcontrollers or system-on-chip (SoC) platforms process the sensed data, and contain computation, memory, power management, and communication modules on a single package.

The wearable systems are based on wireless communication protocols like the Bluetooth Low Energy (BLE), Zigbee, Wi-Fi, and new cellular standards (LTE-M, NB-IoT) to send data to smartphones, gateways, or cloud hubs [3]. They are connected, which allows real-time monitoring, long-term data storage, and massive analytics. Improved wearables have started to integrate edge intelligence with machine learning (ML) and signal processing algorithms running directly on-board to do activity recognition, anomaly detection, and context inference with low latency and low energy usage.

The central purpose of wearable technology is to enhance the human abilities by allowing uninterrupted non-obstructing communication between humans and computer systems.

Wearable devices can aid remote patient monitoring, early disease identification, rehabilitation, and custom medicine in healthcare since they can record longitudinal physiological data outside of the clinical setting [4]. They also measure physical activity, the quality of sleep, and metabolic measures in the context of fitness and wellness to facilitate evidence-based lifestyle solutions. In non-health usage, wearables are used in the military to monitor soldiers, in sports to streamline performance, in occupational health and safety to detect hazards, and in human–computer interaction to provide intuitive user-friendly context-aware interfaces.

The development of wearable technologies as autonomous and intelligent companions with adaptive decision-making through the integration of artificial intelligence (AI), Internet of Things (IoT) architectures, flexible electronics, and smart textiles is underway. With these advances, wearables are already a core element of new cyber-physical systems, and make personalized, pervasive, and human-centric computing possible [5].

The available wearable technologies today could be built on the principles of low-power construction, wireless connectivity, and on-board intelligence to make them comfortable, dependable, and possess long battery life, as shown in Figure 2.1. The wearable technologies are rapidly evolving as there are applications of AI, IoT, and new materials, such as flexible electronics and smart fabrics.

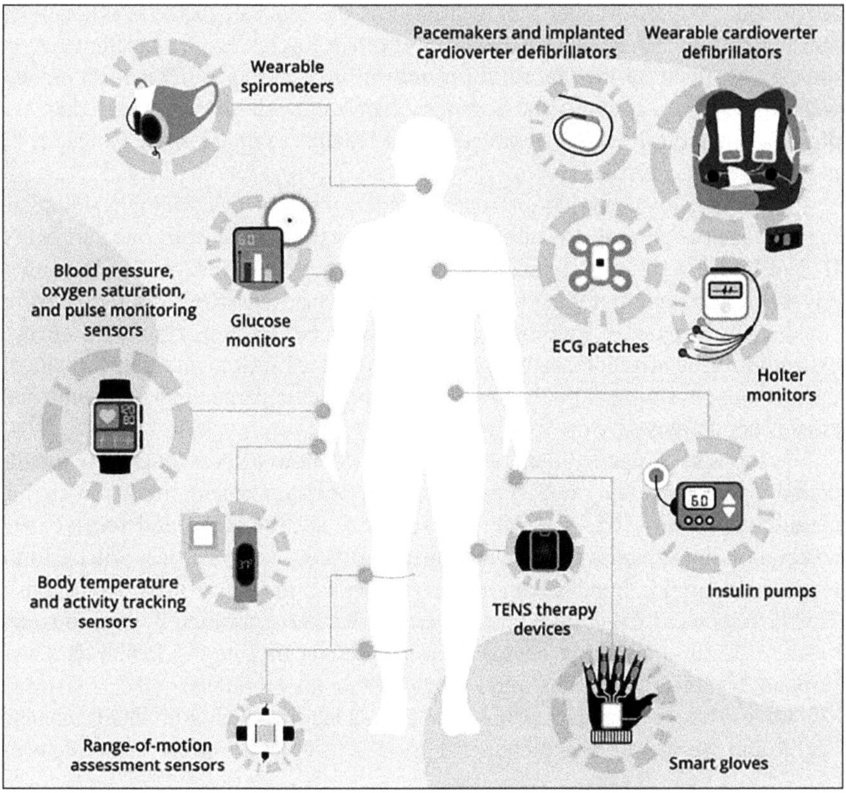

Fig. 2.1 Examples of wearable devices we work with.

They are, in turn, humanizing technology and making it more approachable, thus enabling personalized services, smarter healthcare, and ubiquitous computing.

2. From Pedometers to Fitness Trackers

The technological advancement of the wearable systems that is driven by the advancement of the sensing technology, embedded processors with the ability to communicate wirelessly is evident in the development of pedometers into modern fitness trackers. Basic early pedometers were typically of a simple electronic nature or mechanical spring-lever, and involved a simple electronic contact switch or a single axis accelerator-based design [6]. They operated on the principle of identifying vertical movement of the body to accumulate a count of steps that was not very precise, and they could not analyse a signal or offer any context.

With the beginning of the maturity of technology of the microelectromechanical systems (MEMS), the idea of pedometers was digitalized into sensor platforms. The emerging generation of fitness trackers is accommodative of multi-axis accelerators and gyroscopes that measure motions and categorize activities with much precision. Sensors fusion algorithm refers to classes of algorithm fusing the data obtained by the inertial measurement unit (IMU) to distinguish among walking, running, cycling, and sedentary behaviour. These raw sensor data are digitally filtered followed by extraction into features to improve the resilience of noise and motion artifacts [7].

In addition to motion sensors, current fitness trackers include biophysiological sensors, such as photoplethysmography (PPG) heart rate and heart rate variability (HRV), pulse oximetry (SpO2), and skin temperature sensors [8]. The other advanced sensors include galvanic skin response (GSR/EDA) to measure stress, GPS module to determine location and speed. To approximate the energy expenditure, the metabolic equivalents (METs), which seek to integrate the data of the motion, physiological indicators, and user-specific parameters, mathematical models are employed.

Systems wise, these systems employ ultra-low power SoCs which have inbuilt digital signal processing (DSP) cores and power management circuits to enable continuous monitoring. The data are sent through the BLE, and received by companion smartphones or gateways where the cloud-based services will perform long-term analytics, trend detection, and personalization based on ML algorithms. This development has transformed wearable devices from merely step counters to smart health-monitoring devices that can deliver meaningful health data and respond dynamically to users' physiological state in real time.

Fitness trackers have revolutionized the manner in which individuals manage health and wellness, as depicted in Figure 2.2. They are more convenient to

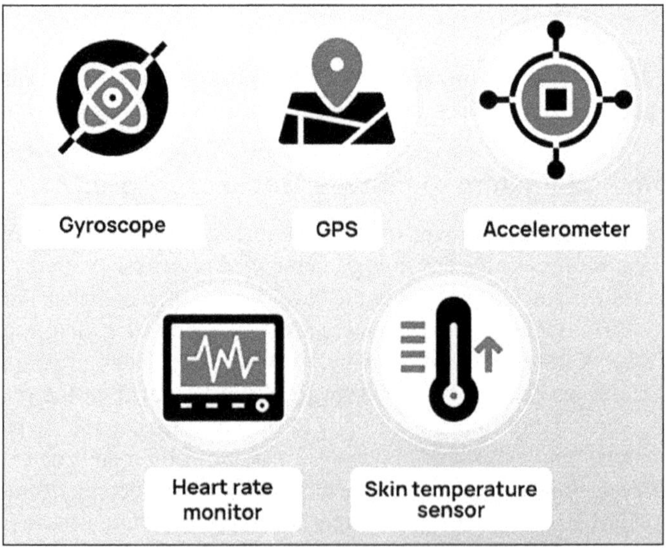

Fig. 2.2 Key sensors integrated in fitness trackers.

help users to lead healthy lifestyles since they are likely to provide real-time feedback, goal setting, and performance tracking. Besides, AI and data analytics can be integrated to provide the fitness tracker with the ability to provide personal suggestions and forecasts. This will be a major step towards wearable technologies enabling holistic ease of health monitoring with the transformation of pedometers into smart fitness watches.

3. Advances in Sensors and Miniaturized Electronics

A constant transformation has been witnessed in the wearable technologies which was boosted by the continuous advancement of sensor design, micro/nano-fabrication, and ultra-miniaturized electronic systems. Contemporary wearables are not merely innovative sensing systems anymore, they have become compact, smart, cyber-physiological, and contextual, continuous real-time monitoring devices subject to extreme size, power, and comfort requirements.

3.1 MEMS and Nano-Fabricated Sensors

The modern wearable systems are greatly based on MEMS and nano-fabrication technology in order to deliver high-performance sensing in millimetre-scale dimensions [9]. Inertial sensors such as accelerometers, gyroscopes, and magnetometers are developed by MEMS-based applications through silicon micromachining process which facilitates the capability of high sensitivity, low noise, and low power usage. These detectors are the main components of IMUs and they have found extensive use in motion tracking, posture estimation, gait analysis, and activity recognition. Sensor fusion algorithms also improve the accuracy with an integration of multi-axis inertial data to reduce drift and noise; hence, they are applicable in the long-term continuous monitoring.

At the nano scale, nanowires, carbon nanotubes, graphene, and piezoelectric nanomaterials have been developed, which have made it possible to record the mechanical, electrical, and chemical stimuli with ultra-sensitivity. These materials are greatly used in enhancing signal-to-noise ratio (SNR) and at the same time consuming very low energy.

3.2 Biomedical and Biosensing Technologies

Wearable biomedical sensing has also advanced through incorporation of electrical, optical, and chemical sensors, as shown in Figure 2.3. PPG optical biosensors utilize light absorption and scattering within living tissues in order to non-invasively determine heart rate, blood oxygen saturation (SpO2), and vascular dynamics [10]. It enhances the accuracy of PPG which is advanced to multi-wavelength under motion and different skin conditions.

Wearables have electrocardiogram (ECG) sensors that rely on dry, capacitive, or textile-based electrodes, eliminating the need to use gels or adhesives to perform

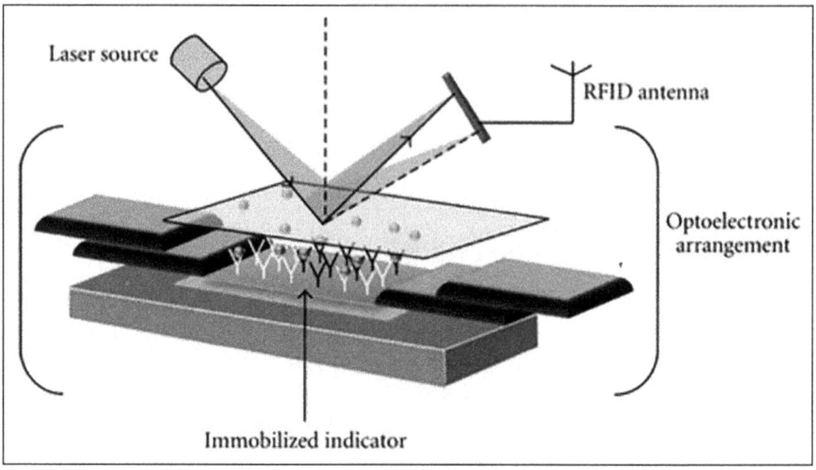

Fig. 2.3 Architecture of an optical biosensor.

long-term cardiac monitoring [11]. Such systems are helpful in promoting high-grade heart metrics like HRV, arrhythmia, and cardiac stress measurements. Also, the electromyography (EMG) and electrodermal activity (EDA) sensors are becoming more popular in measuring muscle activity, fatigue, and stress levels.

The latest developments in electrochemical and sweat-based biosensors have facilitated real-time detection of biochemical indicators of glucose, lactate, sodium, potassium, and cortisol. The enzymatic reactions, ion-selective electrodes, or redox-based detection mechanisms are used in these sensors, making it possible to continuously measure metabolic parameters and stress without blood sampling.

3.3 Miniaturized Electronics and System Integration

Wearable sensors produce an enormous amount of data that can only be processed, stored, and transmitted using miniaturization of electronics. Current wearables use SoC and system-in-package (SiP) platforms comprising of AFE circuits, digital signal processors, microcontrollers, embedded memory, power management unit, and wireless transceiver in one small package [12, 13], as shown in Figure 2.4. Low-noise AFEs are essential to enhance the amplification of weak biosignals and to reduce the interference and motion artifacts.

Power-efficient design methods and techniques, including duty cycling, dynamic voltage and frequency scaling (DVFS), event-based processing, and edge-based signal analytics have played an important role in minimizing energy usage. Such techniques can provide constant tracking and also extend battery life, which is a vital limitation in wearable technology.

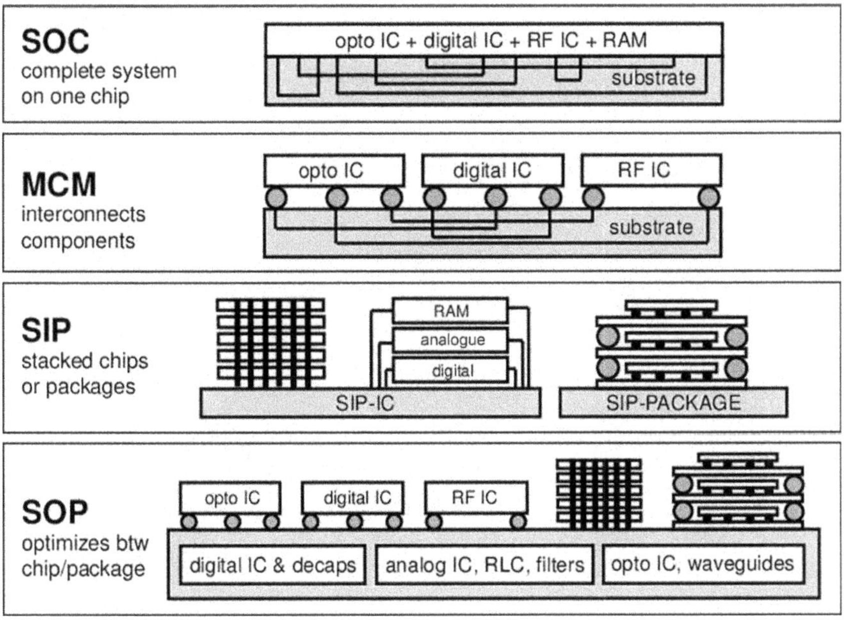

Fig. 2.4 Architecture of system-on-chip (SoC) and system-in-package (SiP).

3.4 Flexible, Stretchable, and Conformal Electronics

The advent of flexible and stretchable electronics has changed the form factor and usability of wearables, as shown in Figure 2.5. Electronic components can be made to conform to the human body using polymer substrates, conductive elastomers, and thin-film transistors (TFTs), and do not deform under mechanical stress. This facilitates the production of intelligent clothes, epidermal electronics, and implantable or skin-mounted systems that offer better comfort and signal stability in day-to-day processes.

Such conformal systems reduce motion-induced artifacts, enhance long-term wearability, and support unobtrusive sensing in real-world environments [14].

3.5 Impact on Next-Generation Wearable Applications

Combining advanced sensors with miniaturized electronics to form a synergistic system leads to wearable systems that are more accurate, have a lower latency, and can be more reliable. These abilities constitute the technological foundation of the next generation application in individualized healthcare, remote care, rehabilitation engineering, human machine interface, and intelligent cyber-physical systems. Coupled with the further evolution of fabrication technologies, materials, and low-power electronics, these wearable systems will be more of active companions, and not merely monitoring devices [15].

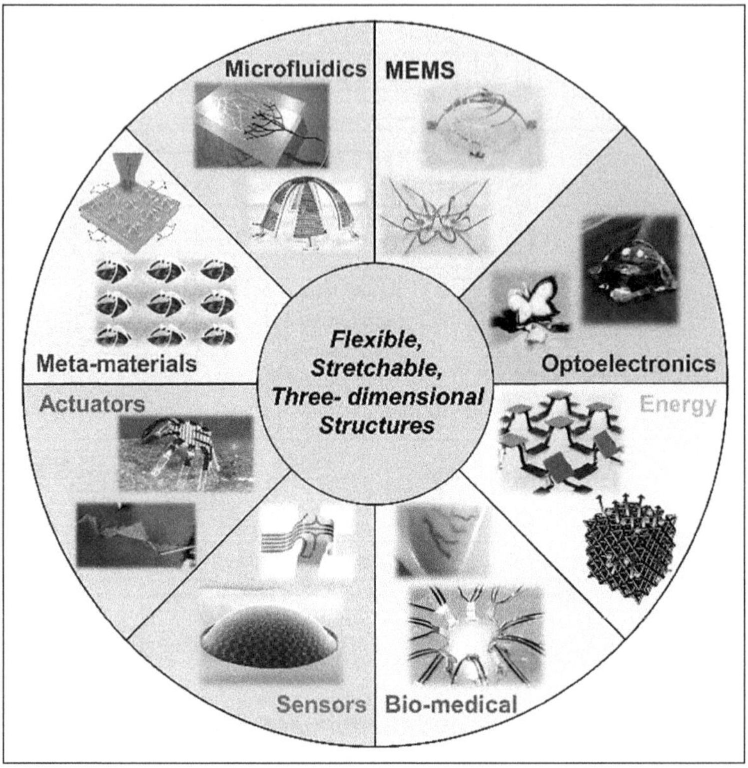

Fig. 2.5 Applications of flexible and stretchable three-dimensional structures for soft electronics.

4. Integration of Wireless Communication and Cloud Connectivity

Wearable technologies can only be successfully implemented through seamless application of wireless communication systems and cloud-based computing systems. The modern wearables are operational in the IoT and Wireless Body Area Network (WBAN) systems as distributed networked sensing nodes that are used to gather physiological, behavioural, and environmental data and transmit them to external devices, gateways, or cloud platforms. Such connectivity may be exploited to offer real-time monitoring, remote accessibility, large-scale analytics as well as intelligent decision support [16, 17].

4.1 Wireless Communication Technologies in Wearables

Wearables use low-power, short- and long-range wireless protocols at the device level which are chosen based on application-specific constraints of data rate, latency, transmission range, reliability, and energy efficiency.

- BLE is the most prevalent technology to use in short-range communication between wearables and smartphones or edge gateways. BLE has been designed to accommodate low-latency data transfer, adaptive duty cycling, and efficient power usage; therefore, it is convenient to use in continuous physiological monitoring.
- Zigbee and IEEE 802.15.4-based protocols are the most prevalent in multi-node WBANs and IoT ecosystems since they have mesh networking properties and can be powered by very low power.
- Near Field Communication (NFC) is mainly used to perform secure authentication, device pairing, and intermittent data transfer with minimal power consumption.
- Wi-Fi (IEEE 802.11) is used when used cases demand high data throughput, e.g., streaming biosignals or firmware updates in high resolution but at a cost of using more energy.

Cellular IoT technologies including LTE-M and NB-IoT are also being used more extensively in the healthcare, industrial, and remote monitoring applications with a need to maintain wide-area and infrastructure-independent connectivity. The standards provide long-distance coverage, low power usage, and consistent connectivity allowing to connect directly to the clouds without the support of the intermediate gateways.

4.2 Wearable–Edge–Cloud Architecture

Multi-tier architecture wearable systems are generally based on the wearable, an intermediate edge node (e.g., smartphone or a gateway), and cloud infrastructure.

- On-device processing does initial signal conditioning, feature extraction, and event detection with ultra-low-power microcontrollers or SoCs.
- Edge computing lowers the latency and bandwidth consumption of the network by doing localized analytics, buffering, and connectivity management.
- Cloud services offer a scalable storage, high-performance computing, and advanced analytics, which can be used to support long-term data aggregation and cross-user analysis.

This hierarchical architecture allows the effective use of resources as well as supports the real-time and non-real-time applications.

4.3 Cloud-based Analytics and Intelligence

Cloud connectivity allows using sophisticated data analytics, ML, and AI algorithms to work with the data generated by wearables [18]. Statistical models and deep learning structures are used to process high-dimensional, multi-modal time-series data to extract trends and identify anomalies and predict health risks. Cloud platforms support:

- longitudinal health modelling and digital phenotyping
- predictive disease initiation and disease progression analytics

- individualized feedback and recommendations systems
- populational health knowledge and clinical decision support.

A combination with cloud-based dashboards and the use of mobile applications would enable clinicians, caregivers, and end users to view real-time and historical data remotely, which would be useful in telemedicine and remote patient monitoring.

4.4 Security, Privacy, and Interoperability

The continuous stream of vulnerable physiological and behavioural data presents a significant challenge of high security and privacy. Wearables ought to have powerful encryption algorithms [e.g., Advanced Encryption Standard (AES), Transport Layer Security (TLS)], powerful authentication, and key management protocols to manage data relay and storage. Privacy-saving techniques which are relied on to reduce the exposure of raw data are data anonymization and federated learning.

Heterogeneous devices and platforms should also be compatible with wearables, which is also a key problem of interoperability, and healthcare information systems. In line with the standardized communication protocol, data structure and healthcare interoperability models offer the seamless flow of data and system scalability.

5. AI and ML in Wearables

Artificial intelligence and ML have become the key technologies that may transform wearable technology into more than a data-gathering tool and convert it into a smart, customizable, and self-adjusting unit. Due to modern wearables, inertial, physiological, and environmental time-series data of wearables are produced in multi-modal, high-frequency large volumes [19]. It can be efficiently processed with the assistance of AI and ML algorithms; discriminative features are identified, user context is predicted, health conditions are predicted, and real-time decision-making is assisted under the strict resources constraints.

5.1 Data Characteristics and Preprocessing in Wearables

The acquired data of wearables is non-stationary and noisy, and user-dependent, which requires robust preprocessing pipelines. The most popular steps in signal conditioning include motion artifact removal, baseline drift correction, signal normalization, and temporal window segmentation. The feature extraction methods are: time-domain, frequency-domain, time-frequency, statistical moments, spectral entropy, wavelet coefficients, and HRV. Fusion in heterogeneous sensors enhances better context and strength.

5.2 Classical ML Techniques

Wearable systems still use the traditional ML algorithms due to their interpretability, low-power performance, and computational efficiency. Traditional machine learning algorithms has been applied to support vector machines (SVMs), decision trees, random forests, and k-nearest neighbours (k-NN) as some of the commonly used methods in activities recognition, posture classification, fall detection, and anomaly detection [20]. These models are driven by inherent properties of design, and in the majority of designs they employ dimensionality reduction algorithms such as principal component analysis (PCA) to maximize consumption in cases where memory and energy are scarce.

5.3 Deep Learning for Biosignal Analysis

The latest advances in the sphere of deep learning have contributed to the improvement of the wearable intelligence regarding its accuracy and strength. Convolutional neural networks (CNNs) are effective in the discovery of both spatial and temporal patterns in raw or minimally processed biosignals; recurrent neural networks (RNNs) and long short-term memory (LSTM) networks are effective in the prediction of long-range temporal relationships. The hybrid CNN and LSTM structures are usually used in processing the ECG, PPG, EEG, and EMG signal, which makes it possible to detect arrhythmias, sleep, stress, fatigue, and neurological abnormalities with high precision. New attention mechanisms and transformer-based models have been developed that have improved time representation.

5.4 Edge AI and Resource-Aware Intelligence

To curb latency, and bandwidth and privacy congestion, edge AI architectures are increasingly being transferred to wearable devices to execute AI inference. Inference with compressed models with neural processing units (NPUs) and ultra-low power microcontrollers are implemented on the devices. Quantization, knowledge distillation and event-driven inference, and model pruning are methods that reduce the computations and energy cost. Edge computing brings the possibility of real-time notification and remote work, without necessarily having to always be connected to the cloud.

5.5 Federated Learning and Privacy-Preserving AI

Federated learning structures allow wearable devices to collaboratively learn shared models but retain the raw data in the devices. The models are aggregated in the cloud servers rather than the sensitive information. This will assist in augmenting personalization, preserve the privacy of the users, and comply with the guidelines of the data protection. Secure aggregation in conjunction with the various methods of privacy augmentation in federated learning assists in implementing intelligence-soul aware learning that is scalable over large populations [21].

5.6 Hybrid Edge–Cloud Intelligence

Most improved wearable frameworks adopt a hybrid intelligent paradigm in which lightweight inference is fulfilled at the edge and also more intricate training and population-level analysis is finished on the cloud. It allows the feature of constant enhancement of models, both adaptive personalization and longitudinal modelling of health, and is an aspect of this architecture. Cloud-based AI is also applicable in the digital phenotyping, risk prediction, and clinical decision support system [22, 23].

6. Expansion into Healthcare and Medical Monitoring

The growth of wearables into the sphere of healthcare and medical surveillance is the convergence of biomedical sensing, embedded system design, wireless communication, and intelligent data analytics to provide real-world, continuous, and non-invasive health assessment. Unlike consumer-grade fitness wearables, medical wearables are developed to stringent clinical requirements, i.e., precision, reliability, security, durability, and regulatory specifications. These systems can be described as longitudinal physiological monitoring platforms, which optionally quantify the high-resolution biosignals used in long periods of time to provide assistance in preventive, predictive, and personalized healthcare [24].

6.1 Signal Acquisition and Embedded Electronics

The low-noise AFE circuits, the programmable gain amplifiers, and the high-resolution ADCs are used to get high-fidelity signal acquisition. In their wearable medical applications, adaptive filtering, motion artifact reduction algorithms, and real-time signal quality measurements have been used to ensure that measurements are accurate in ambulatory settings. Under strict power and latency limits, feature extraction and event detection are done by embedded processors and digital signal processing (DSP) units.

6.2 Feature Extraction and Physiological Modelling

Diagnostic and prognostic analytics are based on extracted physiological features. The common parameters are HRV to assess the autonomic nervous system, pulse transit time (PTT) to estimate blood pressure, respiratory patterns to determine pulmonary health, and sleep micro-architecture to determine sleep disorders. The next-generation techniques turn raw biosignals into data that can be used by clinicians to interpret them, and with the help of further refined techniques, this data could be used to predict the presence of an anomaly and disease development [25].

6.3 Edge–Cloud Architecture and Intelligent Analytics

Medical wearables are generally used in a secure edge cloud system, as shown in Figure 2.6. On-device (edge) processing allows detecting events in real time, setting alerts based on thresholds, and notifying of an emergency with a minimum of latency. Computationally heavy analytics, such as ML and deep learning models of arrhythmia classification, apnea detection, seizure prediction, gait assessment,

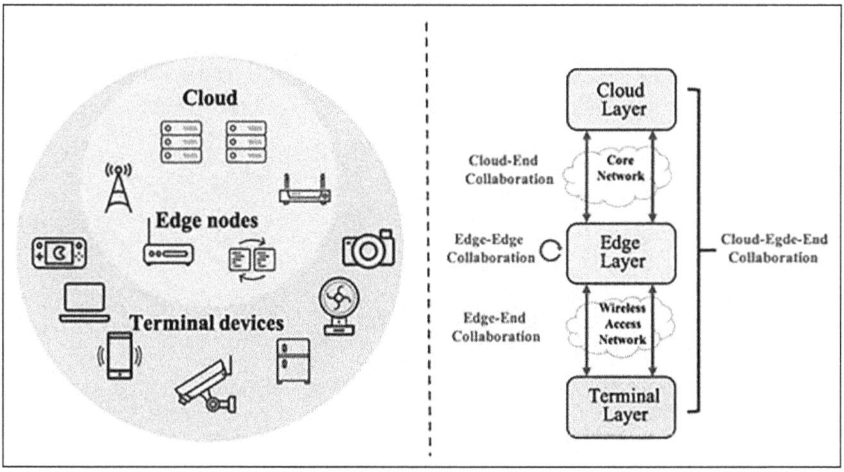

Fig. 2.6 Layers of edge computing architecture.

and chronic disease progression modelling, can be run on cloud-based platforms. Digital phenotyping and population-level health insights can be made possible through the use of longitudinal data aggregation.

6.4 Remote Patient Monitoring and Clinical Applications

There is a growing implementation of wearable medical devices in remote patient monitoring (RPM) systems to enable clinicians to monitor patients beyond the hospital environment. The most important areas of use are chronic diseases (cardiovascular diseases, diabetes, respiratory disorders), post-operative recovery, geriatric, and rehabilitation engineering. The constant data monitoring enhances patient interaction, minimizes hospital readmissions, and facilitates clinical intervention.

6.5 Regulatory Compliance and Clinical Validation

Medical wearables should also be in accordance with international standards and regulatory measures, such as international electrical equipment safety standard, IEC 60601, quality management system, ISO 13485, and regulations on healthcare data protection. Clinical validation should be conducted by controlled trials and real-life studies to prove accuracy, repeatability, and clinical utility. Integration into the clinical workflows is also supported by interoperability with electronic health record (EHR) systems, as shown in Figure 2.7 [23].

7. Challenges and Ethical Considerations

Table 2.1 presents a layer-by-layer breakdown of the challenges of wearable technologies, including technical, data-driven, security, and ethical. It illustrates

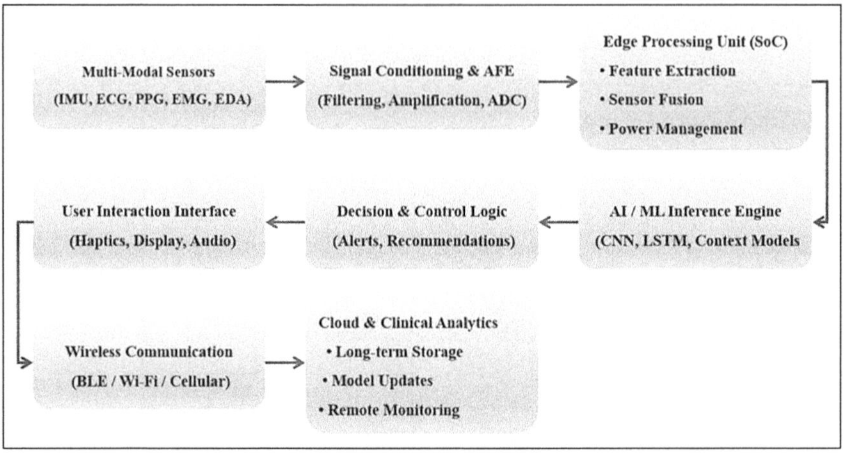

Fig. 2.7 Layered abstraction (hardware → intelligence → interaction).

the role played by each system layer constraint, such as sensors and embedded computing, to AI, communication, and regulation, in influencing the performance, the reliability, and the acceptance of wearable systems. The systematic perspective can be used to determine specific research and design solutions for the next generation of smart wearables.

Table 2.1 Layer-wise analysis of challenges in wearable technologies.

System Layer	*Key Challenges*	*Technical Description*
Sensor Layer	Sensor accuracy & drift	Motion artifacts, skin impedance variation, sweat, and placement errors degrade biosignal quality (ECG, PPG, EMG)
	Miniaturization limits	Smaller sensors reduce signal-to-noise ratio (SNR) and thermal stability
	Calibration & aging	Long-term wear causes sensor degradation and baseline drift
Signal Conditioning & AFE	Noise suppression	Power-line interference, motion noise, and baseline wander affect analogue signals
	Low-power design	Trade-off between resolution (ADC bits) and energy consumption
Edge/Embedded Processing	Energy constraints	Limited battery capacity restricts continuous sensing and AI inference
	Real-time computation	Strict latency constraints with limited CPU, memory, and clock speed
	Thermal management	Continuous processing increases device temperature, affecting comfort and reliability

Contd...

Table 2.1 *Contd...*

System Layer	*Key Challenges*	*Technical Description*
AI/ML Layer	Data quality & labelling	Noisy, sparse, and poorly labelled biosignals reduce model robustness
	Model generalization	Inter-subject variability leads to reduced accuracy across populations
	Edge AI limitations	Model size, memory footprint, and inference latency constraints
	Explainability	Black-box models hinder clinical trust and regulatory acceptance
Wireless Communication	Connectivity reliability	Packet loss, interference, and mobility issues affect data continuity
	Bandwidth limitations	High-resolution biosignals strain low-power protocols like BLE
	Security threats	Vulnerability to eavesdropping, spoofing, and man-in-the-middle attacks
Cloud & Backend Systems	Scalability	Handling continuous, multi-user data streams at scale
	Latency & availability	Dependence on network and cloud uptime for real-time applications
	Data storage & management	Long-term storage of high-frequency physiological data
Security & Privacy Layer	Data privacy	Continuous collection of sensitive physiological and behavioural data
	Data ownership	Ambiguity over control, access, and secondary use of data
	Consent management	Dynamic consent for long-term and secondary data usage
User Interaction Layer	User comfort	Wearability, skin irritation, and ergonomic constraints
	Cognitive overload	Excessive alerts and feedback reduce usability and trust
	User compliance	Long-term adherence affected by comfort and perceived value
Regulatory & Ethical Layer	Clinical validation	Requirement for accuracy, repeatability, and safety evidence
	Regulatory compliance	Adherence to IEC 60601, ISO 13485, HIPAA/GDPR equivalents
	Algorithmic bias	Unequal performance across age, gender, or ethnicity
	Ethical autonomy	Over-reliance on automated decisions affecting human judgment

These wearable technology issues and ethical issues described in Table 2.1 show that wearable technologies are not single-use devices but multidisciplinary layers of challenges and ethical concerns. The limitations of sensing, processing, and communication are technical issues related to data privacy, security, and ethics, and are especially crucial in medical applications. To achieve user-centric, explainable AI, privacy-by-design, and regulatory compliance, it is important to address these challenges in the process of designing robust systems, creating trustful and scalable wearable technologies.

8. Future Directions and Emerging Trends

The emerging trends in wearable technologies are being established by parallel progress in materials science, at-the-device computing structure, and smart data processing models, and pushing wearables towards completely autonomous, adaptive cyber-physical systems. One of the directions is the creation of flexible, stretchable, and textile-integrated electronics which has been made possible with the help of thin-film transistors, conductive polymers, graphene-based interconnects, and elastomeric substrates. These technologies enable sensors and circuits to fit the human body, enhancing signal fidelity, comfort, and wearability. The future of nanomaterial and bio-compatible interfaces advances is assisting in continuing biochemical sensing by sweat, interstitial fluid, or skin-contact electrodes to support monitoring of non-invasive glucose, electrolytes, hydration, hormones, and stress biomarkers.

Migration of cloud-centric processing to edge intelligence and distributed AI architecture is another important trend that is critical. Wearable devices are also getting the ability to run compressed deep learning models through ultra-low-power NPUs and AI accelerators that run the model locally. In order to have real-time analytics in a very narrow power and memory energy consumption, techniques like quantization, pruning, knowledge distillation, and event-driven inference can be used. Federated and perpetual learning models facilitate a personalized model adaptation in populations that lack the delivery of raw data, privacy handling, bandwidth, and control.

Connected health ecosystems also include wearables, and they can be used with infrastructures that rely on the IoT and WBAN. It is possible to do longitudinal health modelling, early risk stratification, and proactive intervention by being connected with digital twins of patients, remote patient monitoring systems, and predictive analytics systems. Multi-source data fusion of wearables, electronic health records, and environmental sensor data are used to enable the population-level insights and precision medicine.

Simultaneously, autonomy in energy is emerging as one of the key research domains. Thermoelectric generators (body heat), piezoelectric and triboelectric (motion) and flexible photovoltaics are among the energy harvesting schemes which are being combined into better power management circuits in order to reduce use of conventional batteries. Lastly, interoperability, secure system architecture, and ethical-oriented AI systems will need to emerge in order to achieve scalable execution, clinical trust, and equitable utilization. All these tendencies make wearable technologies a foundation of intelligent healthcare of the future, human–machine symbiosis, and everywhere-intelligent systems.

References

[1] Minaoglou, P., Efkolidis, N., Manavis, A. and Kyratsis, P. (2024). A review on wearable product design and applications. *Machines*, 12(1), 62.

[2] Azeem, M., Shahid, M., Masin, I. and Petru, M. (2025). Design and development of textile-based wearable sensors for real-time biomedical monitoring: A review. *The Journal of The Textile Institute*, 116(1), 80–95.

[3] Bhatti, D.S., Saleem, S., Imran, A. et al. (2022). A survey on wireless wearable body area networks: A perspective of technology and economy. *Sensors*, 22(20), 7722.

[4] Williams, G.J., Al-Baraikan, A., Rademakers, F.E. et al. (2023). Wearable technology and the cardiovascular system: The future of patient assessment. *The Lancet Digital Health*, 5(7), e467–e476.

[5] Huang, G., Chen, X. and Liao, C. (2025). AI-driven wearable bioelectronics in digital healthcare. *Biosensors*, 15(7), 410.

[6] Hazell, T., Ellery, C., Cohen, T. et al. (2016). Assessment of pedometer accuracy in capturing habitual types of physical activities in overweight and obese children. *Pediatric Research*, 80, 686–692.

[7] Bancroft, J.B. and Lachapelle, G. (2011). Data fusion algorithms for multiple inertial measurement units. *Sensors*, 11(7), 6771–6798.

[8] Xu, J., Zhang, Y., Xie, M. et al. (2024). Real-time intelligent on-device monitoring of heart rate variability with PPG sensors. *Journal of Systems Architecture*, 154, 103240.

[9] Wang, Q., Ruan, T., Xu, Q. et al. (2021). Wearable multifunctional piezoelectric MEMS device for motion monitoring, health warning, and earphone. *Nano Energy*, 89, 106324.

[10] Duarah, R., Torné-Morató, H., Zhang, G. et al. (2026). Next-generation wearable optical sensors for personalized health and point-of-care diagnostics—A systematic review. *Advanced Healthcare Materials*, e04419.

[11] Khan, B., Khalid, R.T., Masrur, M.H. et al. (2025). Next-generation wearable ECG systems: Soft materials, AI integration, and personalized healthcare applications. *Chemical Engineering Journal*, 525, 170117.

[12] Wu, K.-C., Tamborini, D., Renna, M. et al. (2022). Open-source FlexNIRS: A low-cost, wireless and wearable cerebral health tracker. *NeuroImage*, 256, 119216.

[13] Dei, M., Aymerich, J., Piotto, M. et al. (2019). CMOS interfaces for internet-of-wearables electrochemical sensors: Trends and challenges. *Electronics*, 8(2), 150.

[14] van den Brand, J., de Kok, M., Koetse, M. et al. (2015). Flexible and stretchable electronics for wearable health devices. *Solid-State Electronics*, 113, 116–120.

[15] Li, J., Zhao, Y., Fan, Y. et al. (2025). Flexible wearable electronics for enhanced human–computer interaction and virtual reality applications. *Nano Energy*, 138, 110821.

[16] Yuce, M. R. (2010). Implementation of wireless body area networks for healthcare systems. *Sensors and Actuators A: Physical*, 162(1), 116–129.

[17] Zhumayeva, M., Dautov, K., Hashmi, M. and Nauryzbayev, G. (2023). Wireless energy and information transfer in WBAN: A comprehensive state-of-the-art review. *Alexandria Engineering Journal*, 85, 261–285.

[18] Ghadi, Y.Y., Shah, S.F. A., Waheed, W. et al. (2025). Integration of wearable technology and artificial intelligence in digital health for remote patient care. *Journal of Cloud Computing*, 14(1), 39.

[19] Seng, K.P., Ang, L.-M., Peter, E. and Mmonyi, A. (2023). Machine learning and AI technologies for smart wearables. *Electronics*, 12(7), 1509.

[20] Khan, M.A., Mazhar, T., Mateen Yaqoob, M. et al. (2024). Optimal feature selection for heart disease prediction using modified artificial bee colony (M-ABC) and K-nearest neighbors (KNN). *Scientific Reports*, 14(1), 26241.

[21] Mohammadi, S., Balador, A., Sinaei, S. and Flammini, F. (2024). Balancing privacy and performance in federated learning: A systematic literature review on methods and metrics. *Journal of Parallel and Distributed Computing*, 192, 104918.

[22] Kurul, F., Aydoğan, D., Janat, S. et al. (2026). Wearable sensors for health monitoring: Current applications, trends, and future directions. *Biosensors and Bioelectronics: X*, 28, 100727.

[23] Balasubramaniam, S., and R. Bharathi. (2012). Performance analysis of parallel FIR digital filter using VHDL. *International Journal of Computer Applications*, 39(9), 1–6.

[24] Ravizza, A., De Maria, C., Di Pietro, L. et al. (2019). Comprehensive review on current and future regulatory requirements on wearable sensors in preclinical and clinical testing. *Frontiers in Bioengineering and Biotechnology*, 7, 495557.

[25] Subhadra Sarngadharan, A., Narasimhamurthy, R., Sankaramoorthy, B. et al. (2022). Hybrid optimization model for design and optimization of microstrip patch antenna. *Transactions on Emerging Telecommunications Technologies*, 33(12), e4640.

3 Wearable AI Architecture for Continuous Health Monitoring

Yokesh V.[1], Bhuvana B.P.[2*], T. Ravi[3] and Venkatesh Ramamurthy[4]

Wearable artificial intelligence (AI) has emerged as a transformative technology for continuous health monitoring, enabling real-time physiological sensing, intelligent data interpretation, and proactive healthcare delivery. This chapter presents a comprehensive overview of wearable AI architecture, focusing on the integration of biosensors, edge intelligence, communication frameworks, and cloud-assisted analytics for uninterrupted health surveillance. The architecture emphasizes low-power operation, real-time decision-making, and adaptive learning to support long-term monitoring of vital signs such as heart rate, activity patterns, sleep quality, and metabolic indicators. Key design considerations, including data security, privacy preservation, interoperability, and scalability, are discussed in the context of personalized and preventive healthcare. The chapter further explores the role of edge AI and federated learning in reducing latency and preserving user data confidentiality. By highlighting current applications, challenges, and future directions, this chapter provides valuable insights for researchers, engineers, and healthcare professionals aiming to develop intelligent, reliable, and user-centric wearable health monitoring systems.

1. Introduction to Wearable AI in Healthcare

The global healthcare is in the midst of a paradigm shift, which is being facilitated by digital technologies, data analytics, and intelligent systems. The creation of wearable artificial intelligence (AI) to monitor health continuously is one of the most important transformations in the given change. AI-based wearables enable continuous monitoring of physiological and behavioural variables which transform healthcare from an episodic, hospital-centric healthcare model to proactive, personalized, and preventive healthcare. The change of paradigm is especially concerning in terms of the increasing prevalence rate of chronic diseases, the aging of the population, and the need to provide remote and home-based healthcare services due to the increasing demand. Conventional disease monitoring methods are very dependent on periodic clinical readings which in most cases

[1-3] Department of Electronics and Communication Engineering, School of Electrical and Electronics, Sathyabama Institute of Science and Technology, Chennai, Tamil Nadu, India.
[4] NETS International, Dubai, United Arab Emirates.
* Corresponding author: bhuvanabp1509@gmail.com

DOI: 10.1201/9781003776291-3

are incapable of identifying possible physiological alterations or an indication of disease development [1]. Such disorders like cardiovascular disorders, diabetes, respiratory diseases, and partition sleeping problems need consistent and constant monitoring since slight changes in vital signs can be precursors to an emergency situation. Wearable devices may overcome this drawback by allowing data to continuously be collected in the real world to give a more detailed and more representative picture of the health of an individual. Nevertheless, the volume, variability, and complexity of the information collected by wearable sensors are large and therefore require intelligent processing mechanisms, where AI is the key component.

Wearable AI combines biosensing technology with machine learning and deep learning technologies to derive meaningful insights based on continuous streams of data. AI-enabled wearables are able to recognize trends, identify abnormalities, forecast health threats, and provide real-time actionable feedback. Such functions make it less dependent on close clinical monitoring and enable early intervention, which is the key to preventive care. More so, personalization, enabled by AI, enables wearable devices to be better adapted to the physiological baseline of an individual, enhancing the monitoring accuracy and clinical relevance. Technologically, wearable AI systems are a complicated combination of embedded systems, communication technologies, and smart algorithms. Wearable devices have stringent limitations with regards to power consumption, processing power, memory, and physical footprint unlike traditional computing platforms. Simultaneously, they will be required to provide credible sensing, real-time decision-making, and safe data management, as well as long-term usability. These conflicting needs put a lot of weight on the system architecture as the main factor of the performance and the scalability [2].

Wearable AI systems have an architectural design that goes beyond the device itself and incorporates various layers in a network, such as biosensors, embedded intelligence, communication systems, edge and cloud computing systems, and healthcare interfaces. This distributed architecture allows to effectively distribute the workload with time-sensitive tasks being run locally and computationally intensive analytics off-loaded to external resources. This kind of design minimizes latency, increases energy savings, and improves the data privacy, which is especially important in healthcare applications [3]. The other significant aspect of wearable AI in healthcare is its presence in the larger Internet of Medical Things (IoMT) ecosystem. Wearables are commonly used as a node in a wireless body area network that allows them to be connected to smartphones, gateways, and cloud platforms that facilitate remote patient monitoring and telemedicine. This interconnectedness can also allow clinicians to access real-time and historical health data to support data-driven clinical decision-making outside of the traditional clinical environment.

However, the implementation of wearable AI in healthcare has a number of technical and ethical issues despite the promise it has brought. The data security and privacy preservation, interoperability, and transparency of the algorithms have to be solved to guarantee the trust of users and the adherence to the regulations. In addition, the reliability and clinical validity of AI-based health insights are a highly important issue, especially in safety-related applications. In this chapter, the authors are concerned with architectural principles of wearable AI–based continuous health monitoring. Instead of focusing on the results of the applications, it focuses on how the elements of sensing, intelligence, communication, and security are effectively coordinated into a unified system of functionality that can be launched and operated in real-world settings [4]. Through the discussion of system architecture, biosensors, edge intelligence, cloud integration, and ethics, the chapter offers an overall outlook to researchers, engineers, and health practitioners interested in the design and implementation of intelligent wearable health monitoring systems.

2. System Architecture for Continuous Health Monitoring

The wearable AI–based continuous health monitoring system architecture contributes significantly to facilitating the aspects of reliable sensing, real-time intelligence, scalable data management, and secure healthcare integration. In contrast to traditional healthcare information systems where systems are used sporadically and under regulated clinical settings, wearable AI systems need to be continuously used in unregulated, real-world situations. This need presents major architectural concerns of power efficiency, latency, data reliability, interoperability, and privacy. As a result, an adequately developed, stratified, and distributed architecture is required to facilitate extended, continuous health surveillance [5]. Recent wearable AI systems are typically implemented as a distributed intelligence paradigm, with sensing, computers, and decision-making activities being strategically distributed across multiple layers. This model does not rely heavily on centralized cloud resources and at the same time facilitates that time-sensitive operations are done near the source of data. These types of architectures are best adapted to healthcare applications, where data loss or delays can be very severe.

2.1 Layered Architectural Model

Figure 3.1 demonstrates the example of a layered architecture that is typically used in wearable AI–based continuous health monitoring systems. The architecture is structured into three major layers which include terminal layer, edge layer, and cloud layer which are connected with trustworthy communication networks and cooperative processing mechanisms. These abstraction layers give an organized structure on how the complexity of the continuous health monitoring can be handled yet maintaining scalability and flexibility. The wearable and end-user devices that have direct contact with the human body and environment make up the terminal layer. They comprise smartwatches, fitness wearable gadgets, medical-grade wearable sensors, and other body-worn devices that can constantly record

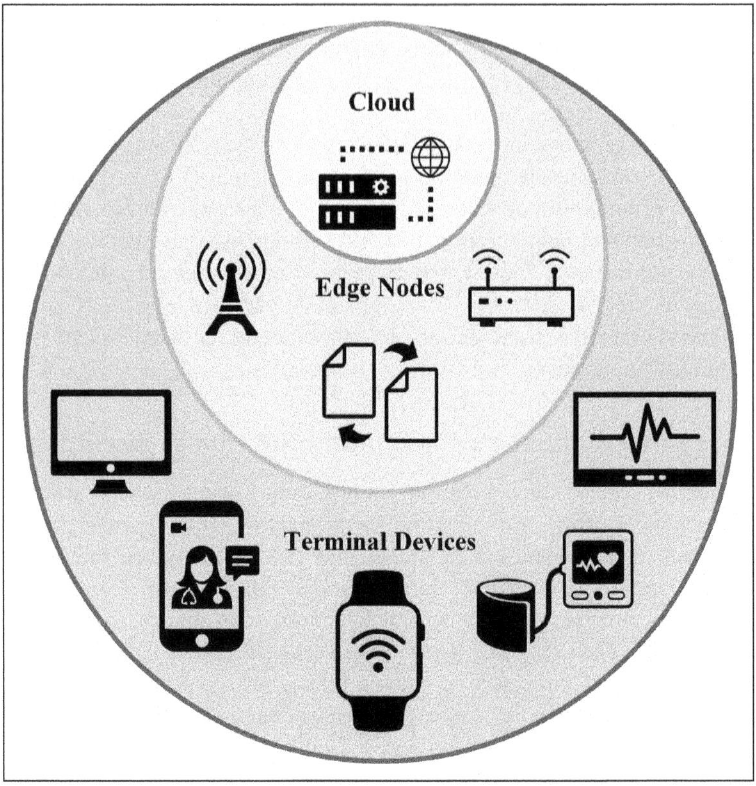

Fig. 3.1 General architecture of wearable AI.

the physiological data. The main role of this layer is to measure vital parameters like heart rate, movement, temperature, and activity patterns. There are stringent energy, processing power, and memory capacity limitations in the operation of the terminal devices. Consequently, the architectural designs focus on lightweight processing, effective data buffering, and minimal communication overhead on this layer.

The edge layer is used as a conduit between end devices and distributed cloud computing infrastructure. Examples of typical edge nodes are smartphones, personal gateways, local servers, or dedicated edge computing units that are near the source of the data. The addition of this layer will overcome the major drawbacks of cloud-centric architectures, specifically the latency, bandwidth usage, and the privacy issues. Wearable AI systems can react to critical health events quickly by processing and analysing preliminary data on the edge and minimizing unnecessary data transmission. Cloud layer is a centralized computing platform that can be used to support large-scale data storage, sophisticated analytics, and long-term health assessment. Cloud systems can offer the calculational capabilities needed to train advanced AI models, analyse population health on a scale, and work with electronic health record systems. Scalability and global accessibility are the features that the cloud layer provides, and it is an indispensable part of large-scale healthcare rollouts.

2.2 Collaborative Processing across Layers

The architecture in Figure 3.2 is unique, in the sense that it focuses on distributed processing among cloud, edge, and terminal layers. These layers communicate continuously and work collaboratively to execute distributed processing tasks, rather than functioning as isolated components with fixed responsibilities. This cooperation allows the best allocation of work according to the latency sensitivity, computational needs, and energy limits. Edge end collaboration enables terminal devices to delegate computational-intensive tasks to edge nodes that are in their immediate vicinity and maintain control of critically important aspects sensing and generating instantaneous alerts. Indicatively, wearable devices can be used to do simple signal preprocessing and event detection on-node, whereas edge nodes can extract features or perform short-term trend analysis [6]. This partnership saves time on responding and also improves reliability, particularly in cases where cloud connectivity is unreliable. As shown in the architecture, edge collaboration allows collaborative processing between two or more edge nodes. Edge nodes in a large-scale healthcare setting, e.g., a hospital or a smart community, can distribute processing loads, collect data on multiple users, and offer redundancy in the event of node failure. This dispersed system improves the fault tolerance and scalability of the system.

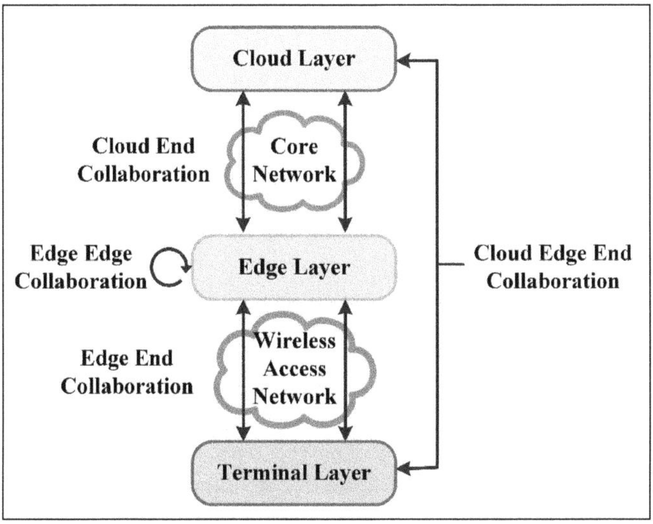

Fig. 3.2 Cloud edge terminal architecture for health monitoring.

Cloud-edge collaboration facilitates adaptive intelligence, whereby the cloud can be used to train and update AI models on large datasets and then deploy optimized models to edge or terminal devices. The personalized healthcare has a special role in this feedback loop, with the model required to adjust to the unique physiological traits whilst enjoying the advantages of learning at the scale of the entire population.

2.3 Architectural Support for Real-Time Monitoring

Constant surveillance of health involves the architecture to provide real-time or near real-time processing of physiological data. This requirement is made through the layered design, which makes certain that the tasks that are latency sensitive are run near the data source. An example is that abnormal heart rate detection or fall detection should be processed in one of the terminal or edge layers in order to provide instantaneous alerts. Any delay of such decisions to cloud may add unacceptable latency and threat to patient safety. Meanwhile, the architecture enables long-term monitoring and predictive analytics to aggregate history on the cloud layer. The two features provide the system with a unique ability to respond immediately and conduct long-term planning in healthcare, which makes it appropriate in preventive and tailored healthcare models.

2.4 Energy Efficiency and Resource Management

Wearable AI functionality is highly energy-demanding due to the fact that the constant operation exerts considerable battery resource pressure on the wearable AI systems. The architecture will deal with this issue by assigning smart tasks and adopting adaptive functionality. The terminal devices can save energy by transferring the heavy processing to either the edge or cloud layer and still save on energy, yet the continuity in monitoring is not compromised. Moreover, the event-based communication techniques minimize the unwarranted data transmission to prolong the devices even further. Resource management devices in the architecture dynamically vary processing and communication as determined by contextual factors like user activity, network conditions, and battery status. Such flexibility is necessary in longer-term application in healthcare-related practice.

2.5 Interoperability and Scalability

Interoperability with the current healthcare infrastructures is also achieved through the layered architecture. The system may be interconnected with various devices, communication procedures, and clinical platforms by introducing sensing, processing, and data management capabilities. Modular principles of design and standardized interfaces can be deployed with scalability in any healthcare environment, whether individual-home-based monitoring or high population programmes. The level of scalability is also improved by the fact that the cloud layer can manage growing amounts of data and execute complex analytics without compromising the work of terminal devices. Such flexibility of architecture will guarantee that the wearable AI systems will be updated as the technology evolves and healthcare requirements grow.

2.6 Reliability and Fault Tolerance

Healthcare applications require high reliability because failures of the system may be disastrous. The architecture is distributed which increases the fault tolerance, since it does not have single points of failures. In case of temporary unavailability due to cloud connectivity, edge and terminal layers may keep on working independently. On the same note, edge layer redundancy is provided to guarantee that there is service continuation even where failures of nodes occur.

3. Biosensors and Data Acquisition Layer

The biosensors and data acquisition layer is the underlying element of the wearable AI architecture that provides unceasing health checks since the quality, dependability, and utility of clever health analytics will be directly associated with the quality of the physiological data obtained at this phase. This layer forms the base interface between digital healthcare ecosystem and human body, which allows the continuous sensing, signal digitization, and early data processing in natural settings. Biosensors in wearable health monitoring systems have to be non-obtrusive, use limited power, and have to be stable over long periods, as they are required to record a wide range of physiological and behavioural parameters. Health monitoring platforms that are wearable generally based on a heterogeneous array of biosensors that can be used to observe human physiology in a multimodal manner. Some of the common sensing modalities are electrocardiogram (ECG) sensors that detect cardiac activity, photoplethysmography (PPG) sensors that sense heart rate and percentage of oxygen saturation in blood, blood pressure sensors, body temperature sensors, electromyography (EMG) sensors that sense muscle activity, and inertial sensors like accelerometers and gyroscopes that sense motion and posture. Combination of these sensors will allow monitoring of all health indicators of cardiovascular, metabolic, and physical activity associated with health, which is important for continuous and preventive healthcare.

Contrary to clinical grade tools that are confined in controlled settings, wearable biosensors are used to work in dynamic settings that are frequently not predictable. Body motion, sensor motion, sweating, changes in ambient temperatures, and electromagnetic interference are some of the factors that add noise and artifacts to the signals obtained. Particularly, motion artifacts have a major effect on cardiovascular responses, including ECG and PPG, in the everyday life scenario. As a result, the data acquisition layer would need to be designed to facilitate strong signal capture, noise elimination at an early phase, and quality evaluation to deliver high-quality data to the downstream AI models.

Sampling, digitization, synchronization, and buffering of signals of various biosensors are done by the data acquisition subsystem. The choice of sampling frequency is a design choice that is important and can determine signal resolution, computational cost, and energy consumption. Higher sampling rates provide better signal fidelity at the cost of more power consumption and data storage, and may not be feasible in the long term to have wearables operating on this kind of sample rate [7]. Adaptive sampling mechanisms are embraced to overcome this trade-off, and the sampling rate can be dynamically changed based on the perceived activity level, physiological condition, or context information gathered by other sensors.

The importance of sensor fusion can be determined in the context of improving wearable data acquisition robustness and reliability. Wearable systems can also integrate information across several sensing modalities, which can help in compensation of sensors with drawbacks and performance on the overall accuracy of measurements. As an example, cardiovascular signals can be corrected and accurately detected using motion information provided by inertial sensors. This multi-modal fusion allows the sensibility of the context and allows more precise interpretation of physiological conditions. In the majority of wearable health monitoring, biosensors are arranged in a Wireless Body Area Network (WBAN) that supports structure and energy-efficient communication between on-body sensors and a central coordinating device. A common WBAN comprises a series of sensor nodes on various body areas and each node will be monitoring a certain physiological parameter. These sensor nodes are connected wirelessly to a local coordinator which is frequently incorporated into a wearable hub or a personal digital assistant like a smartphone.

Figure 3.3 represents an exemplary WBAN-based biosensor data collection and transfer system of continuous healthcare. In such a design, physiological sensors which are attached on the body create an intra-WBAN network that is short-range, low-power, and allows communication with the sensor nodes and the central coordinator. The coordinator consolidates sensor information and synchronizes, schedules, and preliminary validates the information, and then forwards the data outside the WBAN. Beyond-WBAN in communication is a linkage of the wearable system with external infrastructure such as gateway, base stations, and the Internet, and can allow access to health data by clinical databases and medical professionals remotely. The intra-WBAN layer of communication is meant to reduce energy, and at the same time guarantee the dependability of information transfer between sensor nodes [8]. Low-power wireless protocols are generally used so that they can operate continuously and not often change their batteries or recharge. Coordinator is very important in achieving network traffic management, reducing redundancy, and ensuring efficient delivery of time-sensitive physiological data.

Beyond WBAN communication allows wearable systems to work within a broader IoMT system. Information sent outside the body network is relayed to remote servers or cloud computing through base stations and Internet access. This architecture will facilitate the remote monitoring of patients, storing of long-term

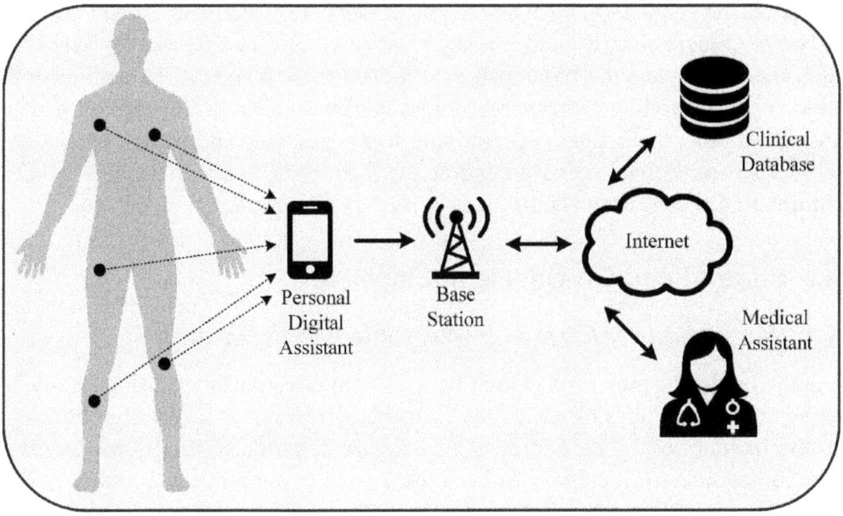

Fig. 3.3 WBAN-based biosensor data acquisition and transmission framework.

data, and connections with clinical decision-support systems. It is also capable of providing health workers and researchers with real-time and past health data to be evaluated, diagnosed, and treated. Power efficiency is an overwhelming constraint all through the biosensor and data acquisition layer. Constant sensing and wireless communication may exhaust battery resources very fast unless well controlled. The wearable AI architectures to deal with this difficulty are energy-conscious sensing plans, such as duty cycling, event-based gain, and selective data delivery. Sensors can stay in low-power sleep and only when a relevant change or predetermined event in the physiological state is detected, it obtains power and starts acting. This strategy dramatically increases service life as well as sustains the monitors.

The aspects required in successful biosensing are personalization and calibration. The physiological indicators have significant inter-individual variation which depends on age, body structure, lifestyle, and medical history. There might be inaccurate interpretations and false alarms with static thresholds and generic models. With time, we can constantly update such baselines through continuous data sampling, and enhance sensitivity and specificity to health monitoring. Another important role that the data acquisition layer plays is early-stage signal conditioning [9]. The raw biosensor stream is usually filled with noise and artifacts that compromises the performance of AI models otherwise unstated. Signal conditioning methods like filtering, normalization, segmentation, and artifact suppression are used at the sensor level or close to the sensor level in order to enhance the quality of the data and to minimize the complexity of the computation. Early implementation of these operations helps to avoid the spread of corrupted data over the system and increases the credibility of edge and cloud-based intelligence.

The data acquisition layer and the biosensors are also not an exception when it comes to data security and privacy protection. Health data is very sensitive and, therefore, reducing redundant data transmission is one of the architectural objectives. Wearable systems can communicate small representations of data instead of raw sensor data by performing local validation and feature extraction. This also minimizes communication overhead and helps to keep sensitive information secret, which contributes to privacy conscious system design.

4. Edge AI and On-Device Intelligence

4.1 Motivation for Edge AI in Wearable Health Monitoring

Continuous health monitoring wearable AI systems are used to create high amounts of heterogeneous physiological data by using biosensors as a part of or attached to the human body. These streams of data are continuous, time-sensitive, and sometimes safety-critical, as has been mentioned in the preceding sections. The process of handling this kind of data in centralized cloud-based systems only creates major problems in terms of latency, bandwidth usage, reliability, and privacy. These constraints have led to the emergence of edge AI as a platform architecture element in the contemporary health monitoring wearable systems [10]. One of the most important issues in healthcare applications is latency. Some physiological anomalies, e.g., cardiac arrhythmia, acute decrease of oxygen saturation, or collapses, need urgent identification and intervention. The use of cloud-centric processing also creates inevitable delays caused by transmission of data, network overload, and server processing, which can prove to be intolerable in the time-sensitive environment. Edge AI allows addressing this problem by making inferences in real time or near real time nearer to the source of data, and hence enables faster decision-making and prompt alerts.

Data privacy is another reason why edge AI is very motivated. Smart gadgets are the constant gathering of intimate personal health data, and sending raw physiological data to remote servers poses a greater risk of information disclosure and unauthorized access. The edge AI architecture enables localization of preprocessing of data, feature extraction, and inference at the immediate edge nodes and, therefore, at proximity nodes, prompting the reduction of the raw data transfer to the outside wearable ecosystem. This technique helps in privacy conscious system design and helps in adhering to healthcare data protection rules. The decisive role in motivating edge intelligence is energy efficiency also. Wearable technologies are inevitably restricted by the limited battery capacity and there is a need to enable them to operate over a long period of time and not have to be replenished frequently. The act of transmitting raw sensor data wirelessly to the cloud continuously is both energy-consuming and cannot be used over a long period of time. Edge AI minimizes the communication overhead, as it allows local inference and selective data transmission, and thus increases the lifetime of the device and enhances the user experience.

4.2 Edge AI Architecture and On-Device Intelligence

The edge AI of wearable health monitoring systems is executed by a hierarchical and distributed architecture of intelligence, in which computational tasks are distributed strategically among wearable devices, edge or fog nodes, and cloud computing. This architecture allows efficient distribution of work load according to urgency of the tasks to be done, the complexity of the computation as well as the availability of the resources. Figure 3.4 depicts an edge AI–based wearable health monitoring system architecture, points out the relationship among wearable sensors, smartphones or personal gateways, fog or edge node, and the cloud infrastructure. Under this architecture, the wearable sensors constantly gather physiological information and send it to the edge devices which are close, like smartphones or local gateways. These edge elements do low-latency processing and real-time inference, which allow detecting an abnormal health event quickly and producing emergency alerts.

The illustration shows a clear difference between the low-latency edge processing and the high-latency cloud processing with the complementary nature of the layers. Activities that are time-sensitive, such as anomaly detection and emergency alerts creation, are processed at the edge, which also guarantees immediate reaction even when Internet connectivity is unreliable or lacking. Conversely, the cloud layer is useful in computationally intensive tasks like long-term data analytics, model training, and medical records management. At the bottom of the edge hierarchy, on-device intelligence is of significant importance. Wearable devices and smartphones run small machine learning models that can identify activities, anomalies that are detected by thresholds, and initial health analysis [11]. This means that the models are low-power and low-memory consumption due to hardware restrictions. Model compression, quantization, pruning as well as lightweight neural network architectures are the techniques that are often used to allow efficient on-device inference.

More advanced analytics and intermediate processing are supported using edge or fog nodes that have more computational power than wearable devices. These nodes combine the readings of various wearables, analyse trends in the short run, and organize the sending of alerts among users. Fog or edge nodes increase the scalability and reliability of the system especially in hospital, smart home, or community healthcare settings. The hierarchical structure presented in Figure 3.4 allows collaborative intelligence across layers. Information is constantly exchanged among wearable devices, edge nodes, and a cloud platform, and this enables the system to be dynamically adjusted to changing circumstances. As an example, the cloud-trained models can be deployed to the edge devices periodically, and the edge performance feedback can be utilized to improve the models centrally [12]. This two-way communication helps active learning and system development without revealing raw data of users.

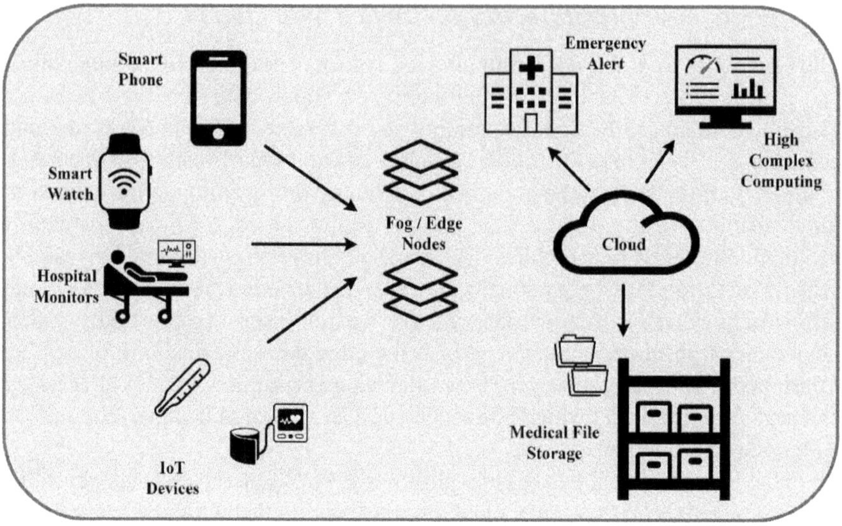

Fig. 3.4 AI-enabled wearable health monitoring architecture.

4.3 Benefits and Challenges of Edge Intelligence

Edge AI implementation in wearable health monitoring systems has a number of important advantages. Real-time responsiveness can be cited among the most significant benefits. Edge intelligence guarantees the prompt detection of health events and is necessary to support fast action, which is a crucial aspect of patient safety and effective healthcare provision. Personalized health monitoring can also be achieved with the help of edge AI. Patterns of physiology differ in individuals as they are different in terms of age, lifestyles, and medical backgrounds. Edge intelligence helps wearable systems to acquire user-specific baselines and learn inference models over time. Such personalization makes the system more sensitive to abnormal conditions and the number of false alarms decreases, which increases the reliability of the system and user confidence. This is the case especially in wearable devices that were designed to take care of the elderly and those that were to be used in managing chronic diseases. Regarding reliability, edge intelligence improves the robustness of a system as it allows operating autonomously when the network is disrupted. Edge-enabled wearable systems can also keep on monitoring without the need to be connected to the clouds, identify critical events, and make alerts, even when the device is not connected to the clouds [13]. Although these are the benefits, edge AI is also associated with a number of challenges. The wearable and edge levels have resource constraints that restrict the ability to train more complex models and their complexity.

The implementation of updates in models between heterogeneous devices and the fact that they can be deployed in a wide range of environments is an open research problem. Also, there should be adequate distribution of intelligence across the cloud and edge layers that must be carefully designed to prevent redundancy and inefficiency. These issues are normally resolved by hybriding edge and cloud architecture wherein inference is done locally with training and large-scale optimization done centrally. These hybrid solutions merge the power of edge intelligence and cloud analytics to get a workable scale of responsiveness, scalability, and the depth of analytical power.

5. Communication and Cloud Integration

Wearable AI architecture is a vital part of communication and cloud integration that will constantly monitor health. Although it is possible with biosensors and edge intelligence to gather local data and make real-time inferences, scalable data aggregation, long-term analysis, clinical access, and system-wide intelligence require the reliable mechanisms of communication and cloud platforms. This part explains the communications of wearable devices in network layers and the integration of clouds in the provision of advanced healthcare services in the IoMT ecosystem.

5.1 Communication Framework in Wearable Health Monitoring

Health monitoring systems that are wearable are served in a multi-tier communication environment involving the linkage of body-worn devices to healthcare providers using intermediate gateways and cloud systems. The wearable devices at the bottom level constantly record the physiological information on heart rate, blood pressure, ECG signals, and body temperature. Such devices usually use short-range wireless communication to send the data to the closest aggregation points. The communication structure needs to have met a few major needs such as low power consumption, reliability, scalability, and capability to support continuous data transmission. Given the power-limited nature of wearable devices, communication protocols are tailored towards reducing the transmission overheads whilst the critical health information being delivered in time. The selection of communication technologies is based on the requirements of the data rate, latency tolerance, and the deployment environment.

Wearable devices in IoMT-based architectures are connected with intermediate nodes (smartphones, IoT (Internet of Things) gateways, or base stations). These middle ground nodes are connectors between body-worn sensors and upper-level network infrastructure. They consolidate information across several devices, do pre-validation, and send information to edge or cloud platforms to further process it.

5.2 Role of Edge Computing in Communication

Edge computing is crucial towards improving the efficiency and responsiveness of communications in wearable health sensors. As computation and data handling are brought nearer to the data source, edge computing eliminates the amount of

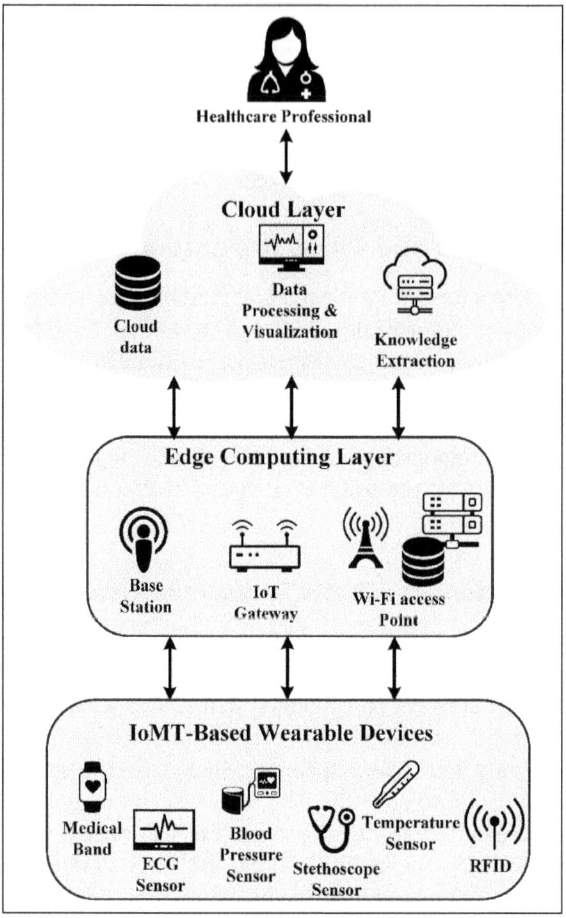

Fig. 3.5 Communication and cloud integration architecture for IoMT-based wearable health monitoring systems.

data sent to the cloud and decreases end-to-end latency. It is especially critical to continuous monitoring applications, which may require transmitting large amounts of data regularly, and therefore pressurize network resources and consume more energy.

The edge nodes, e.g., Wi-Fi access points and IoT gateways, serve as intermediaries between the wearable devices and cloud platforms. Such nodes include data aggregation, buffering, preprocessing as well as local analytics. Transmission of data to the cloud is only with clinically relevant information by filtering and compressing data at the edge, reducing bandwidth consumption and enhancing scalability [14]. Figure 3.5 shows a stratified communication and cloud integration design of wearable health monitoring systems. On the device layer, wearable IoMT devices receive physiological information and send it to the edge computing layer via base stations, IoT gateways, and wireless access points. The edge layer allows efficient routing of data and processing locally and then passes information onto the cloud. The two-way communication in Figure 3.5 shows the flow of data in both directions; devices to the cloud and cloud services to the healthcare professionals and edge devices. Adaptive monitoring, dissemination of alerts, and clinical critique require this bi-directional communication.

5.3 Cloud Integration for Health Data Management

Health data management and analytics are offered on a large scale through cloud platform providers. After information has been delivered by the edge nodes to the cloud, it is aggregated, stored, and processed using sophisticated analytics and AI-based methods. Cloud integration makes available the long-term storage of health records, trend analysis, and population-level insights, which cannot be calculated by wearable and edge devices. As indicated in Figure 3.5, the cloud layer helps in supporting key functions like data aggregation, processing, visualization, and extraction of knowledge. An analysis of aggregated data on many users can be made to determine patterns, associations, and risk factors to reinforce predictive and preventive models of healthcare. The visualization tools facilitate intuitively representing the health data, which plays an important role in enabling clinicians to keep track of the health of patients and thereby make informed decisions. The cloud systems are also interoperable with the current healthcare information systems, such as electronic health records and telemedicine platforms. This connection enables medical professionals to obtain wearable-based data in conjunction with clinical data, which gives them a broader picture of patient health.

5.4 Communication Latency and Reliability Considerations

The important performance measures associated with wearable health monitoring communication systems are latency and reliability. Some of the health events are urgent and any delay in sending data may undermine patient safety. The layered architecture depicted in Figure 3.5 would solve this challenge as it allocates communication and processing tasks to device, edge, and cloud layers. Alerts and notifications that are time-sensitive can be created at the edge or cloud layer and relayed back to healthcare workers with a minimal delay [15]. In the meantime, the data that are not time-sensitive, like long-term trends or historical records, can be delivered asynchronously to minimize network congestion. Reliability can be applied by creating redundant communication routes, and buffering at edge nodes. With temporal disruptions in the network, the edge devices are capable of local storage and provision of data when network connectivity is restored and then as the network goes on, the monitoring continuity is not lost.

5.5 Security and Controlled Data Access

The security issue is also induced by communication and cloud integration because the health data is sensitive. Despite the elaborate security measures, which are explained in the following section, it is worth mentioning that secure communication protocols, encrypted transmission of data, and controlled mechanisms of access are part and parcel of wearable systems connected to the cloud. Figure 3.5 architecture underpins the regulated access of data because it uses trusted edge and cloud platforms to route information. Secure interfaces allow healthcare professionals to access processed and authorized data, which leads to the confidentiality and integrity of patient information.

6. Data Security, Privacy, and Ethical Considerations

The implementation of wearable AI systems as the means of the constant health monitoring raises considerable concerns regarding the aspect of data security and privacy protection as well as ethical responsibility. With such systems continuously gathering, processing, and sending sensitive physiological information, the privacy, integrity, and proper utilization of health information is one of the most significant architectural and social issues. Wearable AI systems function in real-time settings, which are more susceptible to security and privacy risks compared to traditional healthcare systems, where data is usually gathered periodically in controlled clinical settings. The architectural design of wearable AI systems should thus not be handled as an afterthought; hence, security and privacy should be incorporated into the design. All of the layers of architectures mentioned in the previous sections, including wearable devices, edge nodes, and cloud platforms, demand coordinated security systems on all levels to safeguard sensitive health information in its lifecycle.

6.1 Data Security in Wearable AI Architectures

Wearable health monitoring systems' range of data security will include protection against unauthorized access, data tampering, and malicious attacks at device, communication, and cloud layers. The wearable devices are especially prone as they have small computational capabilities, and their bodies are physically exposed. Because of this, to protect data at the collection point, lightweight yet strong security mechanisms should be utilized. The secure transmission of data is one of the basic needs of wearable AI systems. The physiological information sent from wearable devices to edge gateways and cloud platforms should be secured through encryption algorithms to avoid eavesdropping and interception. End-to-end encryption helps in making sure that the data is not disclosed in the process of transmission even when it passes through a public or shared network. Authentication also plays a significant role to authenticate devices and users involved in communication process [16]. At cloud and edge levels, data aggregation health security and access control mechanisms are necessary to secure the health data. Any unauthorized access to centralized health databases may have devastating results such as loss of privacy and abuse of sensitive data. Secure authentication methods as well as role-based access control measures avert the misuse of patient information by unauthorized healthcare providers and systems.

6.2 Privacy Preservation in Continuous Health Monitoring

A key issue in wearable AI health monitoring is privacy preservation because data is gathered on a continuous and pervasive basis. Wearable devices record intimate information about the physiological condition of a person, his/her daily routines, and behavioural tendencies, and this raises the issue of surveillance and deprivation of personal autonomy. User privacy must be ensured by giving much attention to the nature of data collected, processed, and accessed. Reducing the transmission of raw physiological data is one of the effective methods of preservation of privacy. As has been explained in previous paragraphs, edge AI can facilitate local data processing and inference, which means that wearable devices can only send high-level features, notifications, or anonymized summaries to third-party services. This minimizes the vulnerability of the raw data that is sensitive and the chances of intrusion to privacy.

Further protection of privacy is provided with the help of data anonymization and pseudonymization which erase or mask personally identifiable information prior to data storage or sharing. The techniques prove to be especially significant when it comes to the population-level analytics and research use, where aggregated data is processed across multiple users. Transparency and user consent are other critical features of wearable AI that are privacy-conscious. People have to know what type of data is gathered, how it is utilized, and who is the recipient. Clear data use policies and privacy options enable people to make wise judgment concerning their use in ongoing health monitoring schemes.

6.3 Ethical Implications of Wearable AI in Healthcare

In addition to technical aspects of security and privacy, the wearable AI systems present more ethical issues of fairness, accountability, and trust. Health monitoring systems driven by AI are becoming an aspect of clinical decision-making, life advice, and emergency response, so any form of ethical insight must be the primary concern of space utilization and system deployment. Algorithms bias is one of the major ethical issues. However, AI models that are trained using non-representative datasets might develop biased behaviour and thus provide incorrect or unfair services to specific groups of the population. Examples of ways in which biases may lead to poor performance in healthcare are misdiagnosis, unequal treatment, or less effective monitoring because of underrepresentation. To handle this problem, it is necessary to pay close attention to the selection of the dataset, its constant assessment, and represent various populations in the process of constructing the model.

The most essential ethical considerations also include explainability and transparency of AI models. Users and healthcare professionals should be in a position to comprehend the way that the decision-making of the AI is undertaken, especially in situations that are critical in safety. Black-box models that are not explanatory and provide predictions may lead to lack of trust which in turn makes their use in clinical practice difficult. The use of explainable AI methods can be used to make AI outputs interpretable and clinically meaningful. The other significant ethical dimension is accountability. In case the AI systems provide recommendations or raise an alarm, it is to be understood who will take the actions. There must be clear accountability models to establish the roles and duties of the device manufacturers, software developers, healthcare providers, and users.

6.4 Regulatory and Compliance Considerations

Health monitoring UI (User Interface) systems should be in conformity with regulatory frameworks on medical equipment and health data security. Data security, data privacy, and reliability of the systems are usually required by regulation. It is necessary not only to comply with these regulations in order to be approved by the law, but also to evoke trust among users and healthcare professionals. The architectural designs should consequently aid in compliance through the practice of safe data handling, auditing, and controlled access. Security updates and vulnerability tests should be done regularly so that threats that arise can be dealt with and that the systems are kept intact in the long run.

6.5 Trust and User Acceptance

The popularity of wearable AI systems in the healthcare sector relies on trust as a preconditioning element. The users need to be assured that their information is safely processed, that their privacy is not violated, and that the insights collected by AI are accurate and helpful. The combination of the ethical design principles, open communication, and strong security ensures the creation and preservation of user trust. Perceptions of autonomy and control also impact the user acceptance [17]. AI wearable devices must empower users instead of monitoring them, and it must be controlled by the users themselves to decide on the monitoring type they want to use. Creating systems that observe autonomy among users increases adoption and engagement in the long term.

7. Applications and Use-Case Scenarios

Continuous health monitoring with wearable AI architectures provides a wide range of applications in healthcare through multimodal biosensing, edge intelligence, robust communication, and cloud-assisted analytics. Wearable AI systems can provide context-aware and personalized health measurement continuously through wearable technology, unlike traditional medical systems that are used to provide episodic measurements. The architectural structure, which is presented in previous paragraphs, enables such systems to work independently, adjust to specific users, as well as scale to different healthcare environments. The section expounds on the major areas of application and typical use-case scenarios where wearable AI systems have been shown to have a major contribution.

7.1 Cardiovascular Health Monitoring

Cardiovascular diseases still pose as one of the major causes of death globally, and thus there is a need to maintain a continuous and proactive monitoring plan. Wearable AI devices can be connected to ECG, PPG, and heart rate sensors, which allow to continuously monitor the cardiac activity throughout the everyday, as depicted in Figure 3.6. Wearable devices offer longitudinal data in comparison to traditional clinical monitoring which only provides limited snapshots, which is a reflection of the real world physiological behaviour. With the help of AI, one can identify arrhythmias, abnormal variation of heart rate, and violations of individual baselines early through the analysis of constant cardiac data. Edge intelligence enables real-time response to occurrence of critical events, including abnormal heart rhythm, in order to provide real-time warning to the user or caregiver. Cloud analytics also contributes to long-term trend analysis, risk stratification, and clinician review, which makes preventive cardiology easier [18].

7.2 Chronic Disease Management

Such chronic conditions as diabetes, hypertension, and respiratory disorders need continuous monitoring and not a periodic clinical evaluation. AI wearable platform

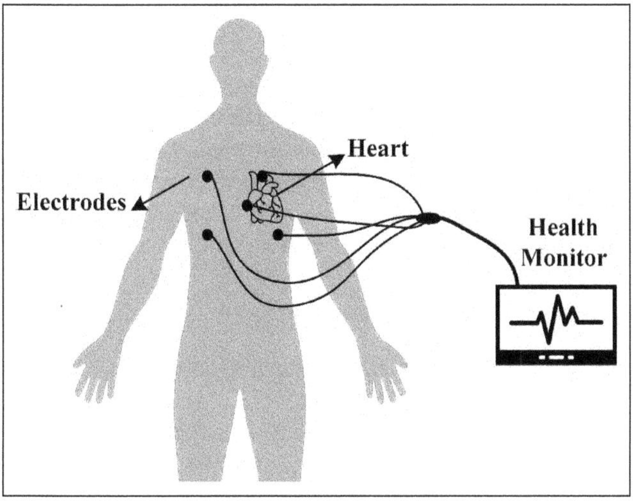

Fig. 3.6 Cardiovascular health monitoring.

allows tracking of physiological indicators and lifestyle trends continuously, giving information about the disease progress and the efficacy of the treatment. To treat diabetes, wearable sensors can be used to track the activity level, sleep cycles, and physiological reactions so that AI models could be used to conclude about metabolism dynamics and the onset of dysregulation. Continuous blood pressure estimation, monitoring of activities and stress in hypertension treatment provide individual feedback and early intervention [19]. Longitudinal analysis and clinician control are enabled by cloud platforms, whereas edge intelligence is needed to provide timely notifications. This ongoing and tailored methodology decreases the number of visits to the hospital, increases adherence to treatment, and enhances patient empowerment.

7.3 Elderly Care and Assisted Living

The issue of aging population presents special healthcare problems such as risk of falls, mobility reduction, and acute health decline. Wearable AI systems are important in the area of elderly care as they allow continuous, unobtrusive monitoring at home and assisted-living care. Fall, prolonged inactivity, or abnormal movement patterns can be detected in real time with wearable machines that have motion sensors and physiological monitors [20]. Edge AI allows to generate alerts in real time, which guarantees fast reaction of caregivers or emergency services. Cloud integration aids in tracking of mobility tendencies and health conditions over time, enabling prompt detection of the functional deterioration.

7.4 Remote Patient Monitoring and Telemedicine

Wearable AI architectures make it possible to monitor patients remotely, which can be used in post-surgery treatment, long-term illnesses follow-ups, and remote healthcare delivery (in rural settings). Wearable gadgets constantly gather physiological information and relay it using edge gateways to cloud services, which clinicians may view as real-time dashboards and historical data. The AI-based analytics can help clinicians with highlighting abnormal trends, prioritization of critical cases, and minimizing information overload [21]. This use case helps the telemedicine models through the fact that patients outside of hospitals can be monitored by the healthcare professional and that this facilitates access to care, as well as decreases the burden on the healthcare system.

7.5 Mental Health and Stress Monitoring

One of the new ways in which wearable AI systems can be used is in mental health monitoring. There are physiological indicators of stress, fatigue, and emotional well-being which are indirectly shown by physiological markers like heart rate variability, sleep patterns, activity levels, and changes in circadian rhythm. Cloud analytics help to analyse long-term trends and provide personal recommendations, whereas edge intelligence ensures privacy-saving inference. The presented area of application indicates the potential of wearable AI to facilitate comprehensive healthcare including physical and mental health. Daily events like work, physical activities, and sleep are some of the potential stressors that affect the physiological and behavioural responses [22].

In wearable sensors, there is constant acquisition of stress-related signals (activity patterns, physiological variations). Such information is sent to personal gadgets to monitor stress markers in real time. The analysis with the assistance of AI makes it possible to detect stress tendencies and the deviation of individual baselines. The system is interactive in the assessment of stressors as it correlates daily tasks with the observed stress levels. An intelligent personal assistant offers customized feedbacks and suggestions on the basis of deduced stress levels. Stored processed information is placed in a longitudinal mental health assessment personalized archive. Such a feedback loop can be adapted and help to detect mental health risks at an early stage. This framework assists in the personalized, preventive, and contextual mental health management. This is depicted in Figure 3.7.

7.6 Rehabilitation and Physical Activity Monitoring

The applications of wearable AI systems in rehabilitation and physical activity monitoring are also significant, as they can be used to continuously monitor patient movements and functional recovery by utilizing various sensors, including accelerometers, gyroscopes, electromyography (EMG), and inertial measurement units (IMUs). The devices provide real-time data of gait, posture, joint motion, balance, exercise intensity, and exercise performance, which helps AI algorithms evaluate the progress of rehabilitation and identify abnormal movement patterns. Edge computing ensures immediate analysis and personalized feedback during exercise sessions, and cloud platforms store exercise recovery data over time, support the predictive model, and produce detailed exercise reports for healthcare professionals. This smart system helps rehabilitative treatment to be performed remotely, promotes compliance with prescribed exercise regimens, allows for the detection of deviations in recovery during early rehabilitation stages and empowers the clinician to tailor rehabilitation plans according to objective measures of performance. Wearable AI, therefore, is improving the outcomes of rehabilitation, encouraging patients to recover at home on their own, and elevating the quality of patient-centred care [23].

7.7 Occupational Health and Safety Monitoring

Wearable AI systems aid health and safety in the workplace and industry setting by monitoring physiological stress and fatigue, environmental exposure, and so on [24]. On-the-job monitoring helps to identify in time cases of heat stress, exhaustion, or unsafe conditions and helps to prevent accidents in the workplace and enhance the safety of workers. Edge-generated real-time alerts can be used

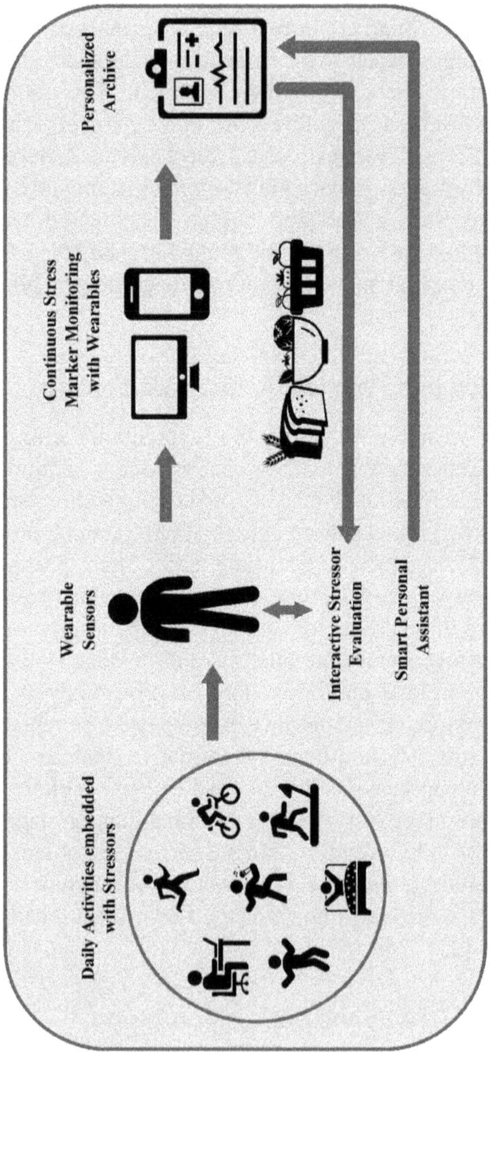

Fig. 3.7 Wearable AI–based stress and mental health monitoring using physiological and behavioural indicators.

to take immediate preventive measures, whereas cloud analytics can be used to provide compliance reporting and risk assessment over the long term.

8. Challenges and Future Research Directions

Although there has been a tremendous advance in wearable AI systems in the area of continuous health monitoring, there are still a few technical, operational, and social issues that constrain large-scale implementation and scalability. These challenges need to be tackled to transform the wearable AI systems that currently exist as experimental and consumer-grade technologies into systems that are clinically reliable and universally accepted as healthcare technologies. This section defines the critical issues and mentions the prospective avenues for future studies. Energy efficiency and battery life are among the main issues of wearable AI systems. Constant sensing, communication, and inference of AI impose high burdens on limited power resources. Even though edge AI and event-driven processing can be used to lower the amount of energy consumed, additional advances are required in the field of ultra-low-power hardware, energy-conscious algorithms, and adaptive duty-cycling techniques. Future studies should address co-design strategies that can be used to optimize hardware, firmware, and AI to exist in the long run.

The quality and strength of the data is still a significant issue when it comes to real-world wearable applications. Uncontrolled environments can usually cause physiological signals to be influenced by noise, motion artifacts, sensor movement, and environmental change. These aspects may undermine the performance of AI models and result in false alarms or false detections. The future research should focus on strong signal processing, adaptive filtering, and AI models that are immune to imperfect and incomplete data. Self-calibration sensors and context-based data verification algorithms are some of the promising research directions. Generalization and personalization of models is also another critical challenge. Personalized health monitoring by AI models based on population-level data might lack accuracy in terms of the effectiveness of individual physiological features. Although edge intelligence allows one to learn the baselines on a personal scale, the challenge of balancing between personalization and generalization has yet to be resolved. Future research ought to investigate the hybrid method of learning that integrates the population knowledge and individual adaptation strategies such as federated and continual learning techniques that do not compromise privacy.

Large-scale healthcare deployments also have scalability and interoperability issues. Wearable AI systems should be seamlessly able to connect with heterogeneous devices, communication protocols, and healthcare information systems. Interoperability may be impaired by the absence of standardization, which will reduce widespread adoption. The next step in research is standardized data formats, interoperable architectures, and open platforms that will enable integration among different healthcare ecosystems. The threats of security and privacy keep on changing in line with technological changes. AI-based wearables can be attacked by attackers through their devices, networks, and through cloud-based assets.

The security mechanisms implemented in the past might not be enough as the attackers become more advanced. Future studies are needed to investigate more sophisticated security systems, including hardware-based trust anchors, machine learning privacy preserving systems, and adaptive threat detection systems adapted to wearable and edge-based settings [25].

Another important area that needs to be investigated in the future is the ethical and societal considerations. The concerns of algorithmic bias, fairness, transparency, and accountability are still not addressed in most of the AI-based healthcare systems. The impact of wearable AI systems on any health-related decision is getting larger, and thus ethical design and responsible implementation become crucial requirements. Explainable AI methods, bias reduction methods, and governance policies that specify accountability among stakeholders should be the subject of research activity [26]. Clinically speaking, validation and regulatory approval are still big challenges. Numerous wearable AI devices have not been through clinical rigor, and thus they are not easily accepted in the formal healthcare system. Future research should focus on evidence-based assessment, longitudinal research, and collaboration with healthcare providers to prove clinical efficacy and safety. The wearable AI development ought to be oriented in alignment with the regulatory standards to facilitate the shift of wellness to medical-grade applications [27].

A number of new research directions are quite promising in the future. The development of flexible and biocompatible sensors will be more comfortable and can be worn over the long term. Federated learning and distributed intelligence will facilitate cooperative model training without centralized data gathering to improve privacy and scale. A combination of wearable AI and digital twins and cyber-physical healthcare systems can potentially facilitate predictive and simulation-driven healthcare planning. Moreover, the intersection of wearable AI with the next-generation communication technology like 5G and others will further increase responsiveness and connectivity.

References

[1] Patel, S., Park, H., Bonato, P. et al. (2012). A review of wearable sensors and systems with application in rehabilitation. *Journal of Neuroengineering and Rehabilitation*, 9(1), 21.

[2] Ray, P. P. (2018). A survey on Internet of Things architectures. *Journal of King Saud University-Computer and Information Sciences*, 30(3), 291–319.

[3] Hiremath, S., Yang, G. and Mankodiya, K. (2014). Wearable Internet of Things: Concept, architectural components and promises for person-centered healthcare. In *2014 4th International Conference on Wireless Mobile Communication and Healthcare—Transforming Healthcare through Innovations in Mobile and Wireless Technologies (MOBIHEALTH)*, pp. 304–307.

[4] Dias, D. and Paulo Silva Cunha, J. (2018). Wearable health devices—Vital sign monitoring, systems and technologies. *Sensors*, 18(8), 2414.

[5] Movassaghi, S., Abolhasan, M., Lipman, J. et al. (2014). Wireless body area networks: A survey. *IEEE Communications Surveys & Tutorials*, 16(3), 1658–1686.

[6] Islam, S.M.R., Kwak, D., Kabir, M.D.H. et al. (2015). The internet of things for health care: A comprehensive survey. *IEEE Access*, 3, 678–708.

[7] Kim, J., Campbell, A.S., de Ávila, B.E.-F. and Wang, J. (2019). Wearable biosensors for healthcare monitoring. *Nature Biotechnology*, 37(4), 389–406.

[8] Yetisen, A.K., Martinez-Hurtado, J.L., Ünal, B. et al. (2018). Wearables in medicine. *Advanced Materials*, 30(33), 1706910.

[9] Heikenfeld, J., Jajack, A., Rogers, J., Gutruf, P., et al. (2018). Wearable sensors: Modalities, challenges, and prospects. *Lab Chip*, 18(2), 217–248.

[10] Shi, W., Cao, J., Zhang, Q. et al. (2016). Edge computing: Vision and challenges. *IEEE Internet Things Journal*, 3(5), 637–646.

[11] Banbury, C.R., Reddi, V.J., Lam, M., Fu W., et al. (2021). Benchmarking TinyML systems: Challenges and direction. arXiv preprint arXiv:2003.04821.

[12] Abdulmalek, S., Nasir, A., Jabbar, W. A., Almuhaya, M. et al. (2022). IoT-based healthcare-monitoring system towards improving quality of life: A review. In *Healthcare* 10(10), 1993..

[13] Chen, M. and Ran, X. (2019). Deep learning with edge computing: A review. *Proceedings of the IEEE*, 107(8), 1655–1674.

[14] Zhang, Y., Qiu, M., Tsai, C.-W. et al. (2017). Health-CPS: Healthcare cyber-physical system assisted by cloud and big data. *IEEE Systems Journal*, 11(1), 88–95.

[15] Abdulmalek, S., Nasir, A., Jabbar, W. A., Almuhaya, M. A., Bairagi, A. K., Khan, M. A. M., & Kee, S. H. (2022, October). IoT-based healthcare-monitoring system towards improving quality of life: A review. In Healthcare (Vol. 10, No. 10, p. 1993). MDPI.

[16] Alsubaei, F., Abuhussein, A. and Shiva, S. (2019). Security and privacy in the Internet of Medical Things: Taxonomy and challenges. *IEEE Access*, 7, 87067–87084.

[17] Obaid, Omar Ibrahim, and Saba Abdul-Baqi Salman. (2022). Security and privacy in IoT-based healthcare systems: a review. *Mesopotamian Journal of Computer Science*. 29-39.

[18] Hannun, A.Y., Rajpurkar, P., Haghpanahi, M., et al. (2019). Cardiologist-level arrhythmia detection with convolutional neural networks. Nature Medicine, 25(1), 65–69.

[19] Kamei, T., Kanamori, T., Yamamoto, Y. and Edirippulige, S. (2022). The use of wearable devices in chronic disease management to enhance adherence and improve telehealth outcomes: a systematic review and meta-analysis. *Journal of telemedicine and telecare*, 28(5), 342–359.

[20] Noury, N., Fleury, A., Rumeau, P., Bourke, A. et al. (2020). Fall detection—Principles and methods. *Annual Review of Biomedical Engineering*, 22, 353–379.

[21] Tan, S.Y., Sumner, J., Wang, Y. and Wenjun Yip, A. (2024). A systematic review of the impacts of remote patient monitoring (RPM) interventions on safety, adherence, quality-of-life and cost-related outcomes. *NPJ Digital Medicine*, 7(1), 192.

[22] Kang, M. and Chai, K. (2022). Wearable sensing systems for monitoring mental health. Sensors, 22(3), 994.

[23] Li, S., Chen, S., Yu, X., Shang, H., Tu, T. and Quan, M. (2026). AI-enabled wearables for motor function assessment and rehabilitation in parkinson disease: scoping review. *Journal of Medical Internet Research*, 28, e85596.

[24] Danilenka, A., Sowiński, P., Rachwał, K., Bogacka, K., Dąbrowska, A., Kobus, M. and Paprzycki, M. (2023). Real-time AI-driven fall detection method for occupational health and safety. *Electronics*, 12(20), 4257.

[25] Balasubramaniam, S., Prasanth, A., Kumar, K. S. and Kadry, S. (2024). Artificial intelligence-based hyper automation for smart factory process automation. In Dhanaraj, R. K., Nalini, M., Daniel, A. et al. (eds) *Hyperautomation for Next-generation Industries*, pp. 55–89. Wiley.

[26] Rieke, N., Hancox, J., Li, W., et al. (2020). The future of digital health with federated learning. *NPJ Digital Medicine*, 3(1), 1–7.

[27] Nelson, S. G., Arishma, M., Rajan, A. S. and Satheesh, K. K. (2023). Machine learning based disease and pest detection in agricultural crops. *EAI Endorsed Transactions on Internet of Things*, 10.

4 Cognitive and Neural Interfaces in Bridging Brain, Body, and Virtual Worlds

Ashwini A.[1*], Alvin Ancy A.[2], Joel Livin A.[3] and Balasubramaniam S.[4]

The neural interface, coupled with wearable artificial intelligence (AI) and cognitive computing, is reshaping the way human beings interact with digital ecosystems, especially in immersive metaverse worlds. This chapter explains that cognitive and neural interfaces may be an epochal nexus among the human brain, physiological systems, and the virtual world. Wearable AI may be employed to decipher neural and biosignals continuously with the assistance of brain–computer interfaces, neuro-wearables, and sensor-laden body interfaces. These technologies are opening the way to adaptive, personalized, and context-sensitive health monitoring, which crosses the physical boundaries of previous years. The conversion of raw biosignals into actionable data in the metaverse, relying on AI-based analytics and the models of the digital twin, is instrumental in predicting diagnostics and providing biofeedback-based therapies. Specific attention is given to closed-loop systems in which neuroplasticity, rehabilitation outcomes, and human–machine symbiosis are fostered by the dynamic adjustment of virtual environments using neural feedback. Finally, the chapter deals with future problems and trends, such as ethics, data privacy, neural security, interoperability, and long-term user safety. This chapter discusses the possibility of a future wherein smart neural interfaces can readily augment human capabilities without triggering a breach of trust, transparency, and social welfare.

1. Fundamentals of Cognitive and Neural Interfaces

Cognitive and neural interfaces are multidisciplinary and a meeting point of neuroscience, engineering, and cognitive science, seeking to determine a direct line of communication between the nervous system and external devices. In its most

[1] Department of Electronics and Communication Engineering, Vel Tech Rangarajan Dr. Sagunthala R&D Institute of Science and Technology, Chennai, Tamil Nadu, India.

[2] Centre for Radar, Electronic and Communication Engineering, Rajalakshmi Institute of Technology, Chennai, Tamil Nadu, India.

[3] Engineering Department, University of Technology and Applied Sciences, Sultanate of Oman, Ibra, North Al Sharqiah.

[4] School of Computer Science and Engineering, Kerala University of Digital Sciences, Innovation and Technology (Formerly IIITM-K), Digital University Kerala, Thiruvananthapuram, Kerala, India.

* Corresponding author: a.aswiniur@gmail.com

DOI: 10.1201/9781003776291-4

simple form, this field attempts to decode neural signals which are representative of a cognitive intention and convert them into actionable commands that drive a machine, virtual world, or a prosthetic. Neural signals are the result of complex electrochemical events in both the peripheral nervous system and the brain, and they can be adequately measured under the condition of understanding the physiological processes that lead to their origin and the artifacts that may corrupt the neural signals. Electroencephalography (EEG), intracortical microelectrodes, electrocorticography (ECoG), and new optical techniques have their own set of trade-offs in terms of spatial resolution, invasiveness, and signal fidelity [1]. The modality of sensing used has a direct effect on interface performance, ethical issues, and clinical applicability.

One of the principles of neural interfacing is the ability to process and decode signals. Raw neural recordings are always noisy and high-dimensional, which require state-of-the-art algorithms to isolate the required features associated with cognitive states or motor intentions. Classical methods use filtering, spectral analysis, and statistical classifiers, whereas modern paradigms continue to employ more and more machine learning and deep neural networks to detect complex temporal and spatial patterns. These decoding structures should trade accuracy with computational efficiency to enable real-time interaction and closed-loop systems where immediate feedback is very important [2]. Further progress in adaptive and personalized decoding strategies is used to complement the robustness by allowing inter- and intra-individual differences in the neural responses, as shown in Figure 4.1.

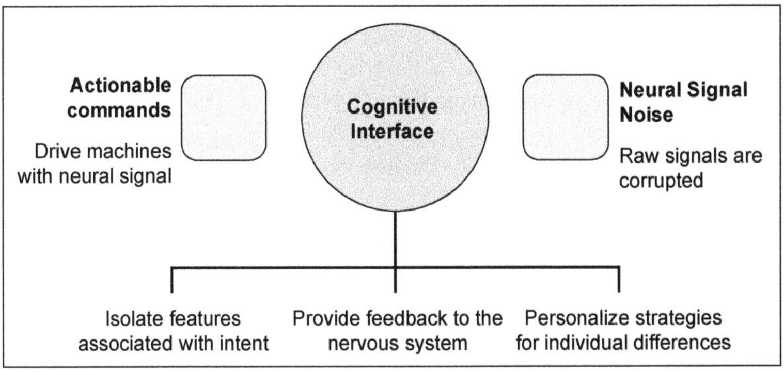

Fig. 4.1 Interfacing Brain and Machine.

In addition to signal recipients and signal decoding, cognitive and neural interfaces are based on two-way communication channels that, in addition to reading neural activity, provide feedback to the nervous system. This closed-loop design allows dynamic adaptation, where the user can tighten control through real-time sensory feedback, be it of visual, auditory, or somatosensory. These feedback mechanisms are crucial to applications both in the neurorehabilitation domain, where the goal is to enhance or realize a lost function, and in the immersive virtual reality field, which can increase or decrease cognitive state feedback with high fidelity [3]. Basic research still investigates the best way to encode artificial sensory stimuli so that they can be intuitively understood, with little cognitive load and maximum embodiment. With the development of the field, the moral issues of autonomy, privacy, and fair access to neural interface technologies have been the focus of responsible innovation.

2. Brain–Computer Interfaces for Wearable AI

Wearable artificial intelligence (AI) brain–computer interfaces (BCIs) mean devices which identify and process brain neural signals in real time and utilize the data to control intelligent wearable or on-body devices [4]. Wearable BCIs, unlike traditional ones, are made to look like common objects and can be used in day-to-day activities, embedded into headsets, caps, or even earbuds, and are meant to mimic natural interactions with AI devices. These interfaces provide a bridge between cognition and machine intelligence and find applications in augmentative communication, adaptive assistance, and human–machine collaboration.

2.1 Signal Acquisition and Wearable Modalities

Non-invasive technologies, such as EEG in comfortable headgear or dry sensors in wearable devices, are the most commonly used technologies in wearable systems. These sensors record electrical activity in the brain which is caused by the cerebral cortex involved in cognitive functions such as attention, error processing, and motor imagery [3]. Wearable modalities are challenging because it is necessary to have quality signals and at the same time be comfortable, mobile, and consume little power. Recent developments in flexible electronics, miniaturized electrodes, and dry contact sensors are quickly making the feasibility of the long-term use of BCI outside the laboratory setting a reality.

2.2 Real-Time Decoding and AI Integration

After the acquisition of neural signals, real-time decoding is used to convert raw data into meaningful features on which an AI system can take actions. It includes preprocessing to eliminate noise (e.g., muscle artifacts), feature extraction (e.g. frequency bands such as alpha, and beta), and machine learning models that are trained to identify patterns that correlate with particular cognitive states. Wearable BCIs currently utilize portable AI-based algorithms either on edge computing devices or on smartphones paired with these devices. These models are able to determine when the user is concentrated, exhausted, or wants to do a task and are able to initiate the right action, such as adjusting the assistive feedback, placing an order with a virtual assistant, or adjusting the behaviour of a wearable device [5]. The harmonious integration of neural decoding with AI allows responsive systems that respond to the internal conditions of the user instead of being dependent on external stimuli, such as buttons or gestures.

3. Neuro-Wearables and Multimodal Biosignal Acquisition

Neuro-wearables are new intelligent, body-embedded devices that constantly measure neural and physiological signals in natural settings. With the integration of wearables, sensor miniaturization, and AI, these systems can be used to gain brain and body signals in real time and capture cognitive, emotional, and physiological states [6]. Multi-modal biosignal acquisition enhances neuro-wearable devices by integrating neural signals with other physiological variables to produce a holistic human state, which is essential to adaptive human–AI and human–virtual world interactions. Neuro-wearables are divided into biosignals obtained, the site of sensing, and the context of use. These types have a specific role in capturing the neural and physiological information that is required in intelligent adaptive systems.

3.1 EEG-based Neuro-Wearables

Neuro-wearables based on EEG are the most popular neural signal non-invasive devices. These machines record a portion of the electrical activity of neurons in the cortex with electrodes on the scalp. EEG neuro-wearables are generally used as headbands, smart caps, or ear-EEG devices, and are widely used in BCIs, cognitive state monitoring, and neurofeedback systems. They have high time resolution and can therefore detect mental states including attention, fatigue, and motor intention in real time, hence suitable for wearable AI and virtual environments.

3.2 fNIRS-based Neuro-Wearables

Neural activity–related changes in cerebral blood oxygenation are measured by wearable devices (functional near-infrared spectroscopy [fNIRS]) devices. In comparison with EEG, fNIRS measures hemodynamic performance, and it offers information about the enduring cognitive workload and executive functioning. Such systems are commonly part of lightweight headgear, and they have found application in environments where EEG quality is impaired by electrical noise [7]. fNIRS wearable is finding use in cognitive workload measurement, neuroergonomics, and adaptive human–machine interfaces.

3.3 Multi-modal Neuro-Wearables

Multi-modal neuro-wearables are neural sensors that integrate physiological signal with neural sensors, such as electrocardiography (ECG), galvanic skin response (GSR), respiration, and skin temperature. This combination provides deeper insights into cognitive, emotional, and autonomic states. To illustrate, EEG is used to reveal the intent of the neuron, whereas ECG and GSR are used to show signs of stress and arousal. Multi-modal systems enhance robustness and minimize ambiguity during neural interpretation and ensure high-performance during real-world use in cases like mental health monitoring and adaptive virtual reality systems.

3.4 Muscle–Brain Integrated Wearables

The EEG–EMG wearable devices provide not only neural activity but also the muscle activity patterns. EEG indicates motor intention, whereas electromyography (EMG) measures muscle responses, which can be used more accurately in the interpretation of movement-related tasks. These systems have found specific use in neurorehabilitation, prosthetic control, and exoskeleton-assisted mobility, in which intention and execution can be enhanced by giving them both [4]. EMG integration is also useful for proving neural commands in motion-intensive or noisy environments.

3.5 Peripheral Neuro-Wearables

Instead of measuring actual brain activity, peripheral neuro-wearables are sensitive to biosignals related to the autonomic nervous system. These include ECG, photoplethysmography (PPG), GSR, and respiration sensors on smartwatches, chest straps, or smart clothes. These wearables are vital indirect indicators of cognitive load, stress, and emotional regulation, although they do not measure neural activity directly. Multi-modal inference and contextual awareness areas are improved with the use of peripheral wearables in conjunction with central neural signals.

3.6 Hybrid Neuro-Wearables for Immersive and Virtual Environments

Hybrid neuro-wearables are created with the purpose of immersive use like augmented reality (AR), virtual reality (VR), and metaverse technologies. These systems are based on a combination of EEG or fNIRS, motion sensors, eye tracking, and haptic feedback modules. Multi-modal information allows virtual environments to be adapted in real time according to user cognition, attention, and emotional interest.

3.7 Implant-Assisted Neuro-Wearables (Transitional Systems)

Although neuro-wearable ecosystems are mostly non-invasive, other ecosystems include neuro-minimally invasive or neuro-assisted devices, e.g., subdermal sensors transmitting wirelessly to wearable devices. These systems have greater signal fidelity than user mobility. Their main area of use is in clinical and assistive applications, such as long-term neurological monitoring and advanced prosthetic control, which is a compromise between fully invasive and wearable neural interfaces.

4. Integration of Brain, Body, and Virtual Platform

The union among the brain, body, and virtual worlds is a paradigm shift in the interaction between humans and machines, whereby neural intent, physiological reactions, and immersive digital worlds are interwoven in a seamless manner. Through this integration, it can be bidirectional, with cognitive states and bodily actions acting upon virtual systems, and virtual stimuli dynamically acting on neural and physiological responses [8]. The basis of next-generation applications in healthcare, rehabilitation, education, and immersive computing is such closed-loop ecosystems, which can facilitate more natural, adaptive, and embodied interactions between human beings and intelligent virtual agents.

The heart of this integration is the brain–body interface, which coordinates neural impulses to body biosignals to capture both intention and action. Neural data recorded by BCIs: EEG or fNIRS: Neural data represent cognitive functions such as attention, decision-making, and motor planning. EEG or fNIRS recordings can give real-time feedback on cognitive activities and can be used to track specific body actions and autonomic functions; EMG to monitor heartbeat; EEG to monitor muscles; (posture). Sensor fusion methods match heterogeneous data streams in terms of time and space, enabling AI systems to understand the human state more accurately. This integrated representation closes the divide between mental intent and physical action to respond, and allows to be responsive and intuitive to virtual worlds.

Virtual platforms (AR, VR, and metaverse environments) are overlays on which integrated brain–body data can be converted into an immersive experience [9]. Virtual systems created with AI can change the content, difficulty level, and sensory feedback in response to real-time neural and physiological inputs. For example, a virtual rehabilitation system can change the difficulty of tasks according to cognitive load and muscle fatigue, or an immersive training system can vary the visual and haptic feedback according to the level of attention. This flexibility improves interest, authenticity, and educational achievements, as well as minimizes intellectual load.

A hallmark of brain–body–virtual integration is the closed-loop feedback system, which continuously gets the system behaviour refined by providing real-time feedback to the user. Neural plasticity and embodiment are supported through sensory feedback, that is, visual, auditory, or haptic, and are used to match virtual actions with bodily sensations. This kind of closed-loop system has found especially useful applications in neurorehabilitation, where coordinated neural feedback can be used to speed up motor recovery, and in mental health, where adaptive virtual environments can be used to regulate emotions and manage stress.

Brain, body, and virtual platform integration is not easy, even though it has potential, due to issues of synchronization latency, signal variation, and ethical issues regarding the privacy of neural data and user autonomy [10]. To be responsible for deployment, it is necessary to assure a secure, transparent, and user-friendly system design. With the ongoing convergence of advances in AI, neuro-wearables, and immersive technologies, integrated brain–body–virtual ecosystems will become the defining new way humans become integrated with digital worlds—no longer as a tool of interaction but as an embodied and smartly integrated experience.

5. AI-Driven Interpretation of Neural and Physiological Data

The successful processing of neural and physiological data is key to facilitation of intelligent adaptive brain–body–virtual systems. Neural (EEG, fNIRS) and physiological (ECG, EMG, GSR, respiration) biosignals are complex, high-dimensional, and noisy in nature [11]. AI is the computer-based basis needed to convert these unrefined biosignals into appropriately meaningful representations of cognitive, emotional, and physical conditions. By learning latent patterns and temporal dependencies in multi-modal streams of data, AI-based frameworks can easily comprehend human intent and condition in real time in ways that traditional rule-based approaches cannot.

Another important ingredient of AI-based interpretation is signal preprocessing and feature learning. State-of-the-art algorithms are used to remove artifacts, normalize and time-align heterogenous modalities to have consistent input to learning models. Whereas classical methods use handcrafted characteristics like power spectral densities or heart rate variability indices, contemporary deep learning networks acquire discriminative characteristics using raw or low-level signals. Convolutional neural networks (CNNs) represent neural data along the spatial and frequency domains, whereas recurrent neural networks (RNNs) and transformer-based models represent the temporal dynamics of cognitive transitions and physiological responses, respectively. Such data-driven feature learning contributes greatly to robustness and cross-user cross-environment generalization.

The AI-based interpretation is multi-modal data fusion. Neural and physiological indicators offer complementary views of the human condition, and AI models combine modalities based on early, intermediate, or late fusion approaches. Graph-based learning models and attention mechanisms are becoming more popular to calculate modality relevance dynamically, and enable systems to adapt to changes in signal quality and context changes [12]. The accuracy of the classification of these fusions in activities such as estimation of cognitive workload, stress detection, and motor intention recognition is improved, which allows for more dependable human–AI interaction in real-life conditions.

Adaptive and personalized intelligence is also under the support of AI-driven interpretation based on continuous learning. The neural and physiological patterns of human beings have a high degree of inter- and intra-individual variability;

hence, the AI models have to evolve during their activities to stay relevant, as shown in Figure 4.2. Online learning, transfer learning, and federated learning strategies enable the systems to facilitate personalization of meanings without compromising privacy of data [5]. The AI models are used to ensure that the predictions are updated continuously in response to the feedback provided by the users and outcomes of the system, and they improve the responsiveness and user embodiment of the virtual and assistive environments in a closed-loop application.

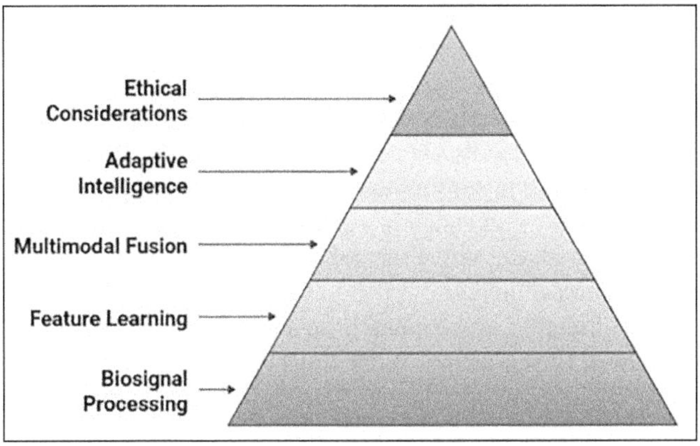

Fig. 4.2 AI-Driven Biosignal Interpretation.

Even though it has the potential to transform medicine, AI-driven biosignal interpretation is associated with issues of explainability, data bias, and ethical accountability. The lack of transparency of deep learning models may restrict the belief in safety-related applications, including healthcare and neurorehabilitation. As a result, explainable AI methods are becoming more and more widespread in order to shed light on decision-making processes and make them transparent. With the convergence of AI, neuroscience, and wearable technologies, neural and physiological data interpretation, aided by AI, will continue to be one of the pillars that will define the connection among the brain, body, and virtual world via intelligent, ethical, and human-centred systems.

6. Metaverse-based Neurorehabilitation and Mental Healthcare

The metaverse presents a novel paradigm of neurorehabilitation and mental health care, through its interaction and immersive therapeutic environments, and personalized and interactive nature. Metaverse platforms can form continuous care environments that go beyond the conventional clinical facilities by incorporating VR, AR, digital twins, and persistent virtual worlds.

Metaverse-based environments in neurorehabilitation can offer controlled but engaging virtual environments that can be used to promote motor recovery, cognitive retraining, and enhancement of neuroplasticity [13]. Task-oriented virtual worlds can communicate with stroke survivors, traumatic brain injury victims, and neurodegenerative patients, and react dynamically to their intended activities and movements. EEG, fNIRS, and neural signals indicate the presence of motor planning and cognitive activity, whereas physiological biosignals are used to determine the fatigue and stress levels. AI-based feedback also changes task difficulty, intensity, and sensations in real time to encourage repetitive practice, inspiration, and functional recovery via a closed-loop brain–body–virtual interaction.

Mental healthcare in the virtual world is also of great benefit since a virtual world can be used to provide an immersive treatment process for various disorders like anxiety, depression, post-traumatic stress disorder, and attention disorders. Virtual environments can be created to imitate stressors or peaceful conditions in real life, and neuro-wearables keep checking the cognitive load, emotional arousal, and autonomic activity. AI computer programs then read these signals to customize therapeutic exposure, relaxation programs, or cognitive behavioural programs. This dynamic immersion increases treatment effectiveness by matching therapeutic stimuli with the active mental state of the patient, while being a safe and manageable clinical model.

One of the strengths of care based on metaverse is its ability to perform remote, continuous, and collaborative therapy [14]. Therapeutic environments can be provided for patients in their homes; thus, they have fewer barriers associated with mobility, geography, and access to clinical resources. Digital biomarkers based on neural and physiological data provide clinicians with the opportunity to monitor progress and make decisions about treatment and longitudinal evaluation. Furthermore, group therapy, training social skills, and peer support are important for mental health recovery and reintegrating into society, and can be provided through shared virtual spaces.

Nevertheless, neurorehabilitation and mental healthcare based on the metaverse also have challenges concerning accessibility, privacy of data, and ethical governance. While adopting these AI-based interventions it is critical to ensure the safe management of sensitive neural data, avoid excessive dependence on artificial procedures, and mitigate the consequences of digital inequalities. With the ongoing convergence of immersive technologies, AI, and neuro-wearables, metaverse-guided therapeutic interventions will end neurorehabilitation and healthcare, moving episodic treatments to continuous, adaptive, and human–centred care modalities.

7. Closed-Loop Neural Feedback Systems

Closed-loop neural feedback systems constitute a decisive breakthrough in intelligent neurotechnology, as they allow having a continuous two-way engagement between the human nervous system and the adaptive digital or physical world. In contrast to open-loop systems that record neural signals passively, closed-loop systems monitor brain and physiological activity, interpret signals in real time, and provide immediate feedback or intervention depending on the state detected [15]. The cycle consists of dynamic feedback that enables systems to adapt to user cognition, behaviour, and physiological states on the basis of customized, responsive, and autonomous brain–body–virtual interactions as in Table 4.1.

Real-time neural sensing and adaptive decoding are fundamental elements of closed-loop systems. Brain signals obtained via BCIs (EEG, fNIRS, or hybrid neuro-wearables) are constantly processed using an AI-based model to identify cognitive states, motor intentions, or emotional reactions. Neural data are further contextualized by physiological biosignals, which increase reliability and robustness [16]. Decoding parameters continuously change in advance of neural variability and learning effects using machine learning algorithms to give the algorithm stable performance over time. This dynamic decoding allows closed-loop systems to operate successfully under real-world, non-stationary conditions.

The second important element of closed-loop neural systems is the delivery of feedback. The feedback may be in the form of visual, auditory, haptic, or somatosensory feedback, or by neuromodulation methods, such as transcranial electrical or magnetic stimulation. In full-immersion virtual worlds, feedback can be incorporated into the world, whereby users can experience the effects of their neural conditions or behaviours in real time. This embodiment-enhancing, neuroplasticity-enhancing, intention–action–perception sensory reinforcement boosts learning through a close association between intention and action, coupled with the perception.

Closed-loop neural feedback systems have shown a lot of impact in relation to neurorehabilitation, mental healthcare, assistive technology, and cognitive enhancement. These mechanisms in rehabilitation adjust therapeutic activities according to the processes of neural activity and fatigue, resulting in efficient recovery. Real-time feedback in mental health is useful for the self-regulation of stress, attention, and emotion. In virtual and metaverse spaces, closed-loop feedback creates a personalized experience that constantly changes with user cognition to increase the quality of immersion and interaction.

Closed-loop neural feedback systems have difficulties with latency, system stability, and ethical issues, as they have potential. The security of responsiveness in real time, without affecting accuracy, user autonomy, and the protection of sensitive neural information, are paramount issues. The future of explainable AI (XAI) is projected to be in future studies of explainable neuromodulation strategies and scalable architectures to enable long-term deployment. With these challenges resolved, closed-loop neural feedback systems will have a central role in mediating the brain, body, and intelligent virtual worlds with continuous, adaptive, and human interactive systems.

8. Ethical, Privacy, and Security Challenges in Neural Data

The high rate of BCI development, neuro-wearables, and AI-mediated neural interpretation has augmented negative concerns regarding the utilization of neural information, privacy, and the security of the data in an ethical manner. In contrast to

Table 4.1 Characteristics of Closed-Loop Neural Feedback Systems.

Aspect	*Description*	*Role in Brain–Body–Virtual Integration*
System Type	Closed-loop neural feedback system with bidirectional communication	Enables continuous interaction between neural activity and adaptive environments
Neural Signal Acquisition	EEG, fNIRS, and hybrid neuro-wearables	Captures real-time cognitive, motor, and emotional states
Physiological Context Signals	EMG, ECG, GSR, respiration	Enhances robustness and contextual understanding of neural data
Signal Processing & Decoding	AI-driven preprocessing, feature extraction, adaptive machine learning models	Interprets neural intent and physiological state in real time
Adaptive Learning Mechanism	Dynamic model updates to handle neural variability and learning effects	Ensures stability and personalization in non-stationary environments
Feedback Modalities	Visual, auditory, haptic, somatosensory, neuromodulation (tES/tMS)	Reinforces embodiment, learning, and neuroplasticity
Feedback Integration	Embedded within immersive virtual or physical environments	Allows immediate perception of neural actions and consequences
Core Applications	Neurorehabilitation, mental healthcare, assistive technology, cognitive enhancement	Supports personalized and adaptive therapeutic and interactive systems
Key Benefits	Real-time adaptation, personalization, autonomous interaction	Improves engagement, recovery efficiency, and interaction quality
Challenges	Latency, system stability, ethical and privacy concerns	Requires secure, explainable, and user-centric system design
Future Research Directions	Explainable AI, adaptive neuromodulation, scalable architectures	Enables long-term, ethical, and widespread deployment

traditional biometric data, neural data can demonstrate highly personal information about the way a person thinks, how he/she feels, and thinks. Informed consent and cognitive autonomy are among the greatest ethical issues [17]. The severity of how neural data can be analysed and inferred or repurposed might not be fully realized by the users, especially when the neural data are analysed using advanced AI models that extract latent cognitive or emotional states that were not originally intended by the data collection process. Wearable systems also make the process of consent more difficult since neural data can be passively recorded over time. Transparency of data practices, user control of data sharing, and the ability to revoke exemption are crucial to overall curb abuse or compulsive use of neural technologies.

There is also the issue of users being identified and the sensitivity of neural data, which increases the problem of privacy. Neural signals that have been anonymized might be re-identified or associated with individuals when they are combined with other datasets. The unifying of neural information on platforms in the cloud, metaverse, and AI-based analytics makes neural data more vulnerable to unauthorized access and data breaches. To reduce this risk, strong privacy-saving techniques such as encryption, secure edge processing, federated learning, and differential privacy are required to allow useful data-driven conclusions.

Security wise, the neural systems can be threatened by data interception, signal spoofing, and manipulation of AI models by adversaries. The manipulation of the neural interfaces without permission may create false interpretations or distort the feedback, which is very dangerous to physical and mental health. The frequency of ensuring neural communication pathways, signalling integrity, and the deployment of robust AI systems is fundamental in preserving the reliability of the system, especially in safety-critical infrastructures like the health sector and neurorehabilitation.

In addition to technical protection, there are other challenges in society and regulations that need to be tackled. Concerns about property, responsibility, bias in algorithms, and fair access to neural technologies have not been resolved. Responsible innovation requires the creation of ethical standard governance and interdisciplinary supervision. Considering neural data as a keystone of brain–body–virtual integration, ethical, privacy, and security issues will be critical concerns in ensuring that these technologies benefit the well-being of human beings without threatening the rights or values of society.

9. Future Directions of Wearable AI in Immersive Healthcare

Wearable AI in immersive healthcare has a great future, as this technology is bound to transform medical care delivery, experience, and personalization. With the ongoing evolvement of neuro-wearables, biosensors, and intelligent algorithms, healthcare systems are no longer doing reactive episodic interventions; instead, they are switching to continuous, predictive, and preventive care models [18]. This trend will continue as immersive environments (including VR, AR, and metaverse-based environments) become increasingly integrated with wearable AI to form adaptive therapeutic ecosystems that respond to the neural, physiological, and behavioural states of patients in real time.

A major direction for the future is the development of hyper-personalized digital therapeutics. The use of wearable AI systems will use long-term neural and physiological data to create personalized digital twins of patients to model accurately the progression of the disease, recovery process, and response to treatment. These digital twins will be used in immersive medical settings, where adaptive therapy protocols are directed by measuring real-time feedback and changing the intensity, timing, and modality of the intervention. This personalization is predicted to enhance neurorehabilitation, mental healthcare, and chronic disease management, in addition to minimizing the clinical burden [19].

Further developments in edge AI and low-power neuromorphic computing will increase the wearable system scale. Enabling direct real-time inference on wearable devices will shorten latency and improve privacy of data, as well as allow continuous operation in mobile and home environments in the future. Biological neuromorphic architectures will be energy efficient and capable of dealing with continuous streams of biosignals as these architectures are both sustainable and realistic in the long term. These innovations will prove to be effective in closed-loop therapeutic systems that demand immediate feedback and adaptation [20].

The other new direction emerges as immersive, multisensory, and embodied interaction in healthcare setting. The AI systems in wearables in the future will combine neural sensing with haptic feedback, eye-tracking, and gesture-recognition to develop more natural and richer therapeutic experiences. Virtual spaces built around AI will evolve visually, sensually, and emotively, making patients more engaged and encouraging greater embodiment. This intelligence will be used to aid motor relearning, cognitive training, and emotional regulation due to its close association with sensory feedback and neural and bodily responses.

These developments notwithstanding, such wearable AI as immersive healthcare must be informed by robust ethical, regulatory, and human principles. Fair access, openness of AI judgment, and adequate safeguarding of neural data will be essential as these technologies become ubiquitous. Responsible innovation will be defined as the collective work of clinicians, technologists, policymakers, and patients. Wearable AI has the possibility to transform healthcare to become a smarter, more empathetic, and adaptable system, as the convergence between wearable AI and immersive platforms opens up possibilities of connecting the brain, body, and virtual world in such a way that has never been done before.

10. Conclusion

This chapter has discussed how the cognitive and neural interface has undergone development to become a revolutionary interplay among the human brain, physiological processes, and the virtual worlds of immersion. The chapter reflects on the latest developments in sensing, computing, and smart adjustment of human–machine interaction, such as BCIs, neuro-wearables, multimodal biosignal acquisition, AI-based interpretation, and closed-loop feedback systems, by considering the underlying principles. All of these technologies, when combined, allow us to have systems that are no longer passive devices but active collaborators that can comprehend and react to real-time human cognition, emotion, and intent. The convergence of AI and neural and physiological data has become a key enabler of personalization, flexibility, and scalability. With the aid of AI-powered models, intricate biosignals are decoded with robustness, multi-modal fusion is supported, and immersive environments, such as VR and metaverse-based healthcare environments, are powered. These systems have tangible effects on society and have been used in both neurorehabilitation and mental healthcare, with applications to provide ongoing, accessible, patient-focused therapeutic solutions that transcend conventional clinical boundaries. Closed-loop neural feedback further improves these effects by strengthening neuroplasticity and embodiment by real-time and adaptive interactions. Although they are promising, cognitive and neural interface technologies present significant ethical, privacy, and security issues because neural data are more sensitive to interactions. The key to eliminating these questions and achieving a trustworthy and responsible implementation is to ensure clarity of governance, privacy-friendly AI, and human-focused design. The intersection of wearable AI, immersive experiences, and ethics provides an indication of the future of the medical field, where healthcare will be predictive, preventive, and highly personalized. With the responsible development of these technologies, cognitive and neural interfaces will have a major role in the development of intelligent ecosystems that can integrate the brain, body, and virtual worlds in a seamless manner and add to the well-being of humans.

References

[1] Donoghue, J.P. (2008). Bridging the brain to the world: A perspective on neural interface systems. *Neuron*, 60(3), 511–521.

[2] Xu, S., Liu, Y., Lee, H. and Li, W. (2024). Neural interfaces: Bridging the brain to the world beyond healthcare. *Exploration*, 4(5), 20230146.

[3] Zhu, H.Y., Hieu, N.Q., Hoang, D.T. et al. (2024). A human-centric metaverse enabled by brain-computer interface: A survey. *IEEE Communications Surveys & Tutorials*, 26(3), 2120–2145.

[4] Gholizadeh HamlAbadi, K., Laamarti, F. and El Saddik, A. (2024). Meta-review on brain-computer interface (BCI) in the metaverse. *ACM Transactions on Multimedia Computing, Communications and Applications*, 20(12), 1–42.

[5] Joshiraj, J.I. (2024). Brain-computer interfaces (BCIs) and AI: The future of human-machine symbiosis. *Journal of Science, Technology and Engineering Research*, 2(2), 58–65.

[6] Kaur, S., Acharjee, T., Das, D. et al. (2025). Switching on smart care: The ascendancy of wireless technologies in continuous health surveillance. *Smart Wearable Technology*, 1, A13.

[7] Nwagu, C., AlSlaity, A. and Orji, R. (2023). EEG-based brain–computer interactions in immersive virtual and augmented reality: A systematic review. *Proceedings of the ACM on Human–Computer Interaction*, 7(EICS), 1–33.

[8] Gatica-Rojas, V. and Méndez-Rebolledo, G. (2014). Virtual reality interface devices in the reorganization of neural networks in the brain of patients with neurological diseases. *Neural Regeneration Research*, 9(8), 888–896.

[9] Riva, G., Wiederhold, B.K. and Mantovani, F. (2019). Neuroscience of virtual reality: From virtual exposure to embodied medicine. *Cyberpsychology, Behavior, and Social Networking*, 22(1), 82–96.

[10] Zhang, H., Jiao, L., Yang, S., et al. (2024). Brain–computer interfaces: The innovative key to unlocking neurological conditions. *International Journal of Surgery*, 110(9), 5745–5762.

[11] Akhtar, Z.B. and Rozario, V.S. (2025). AI perspectives within computational neuroscience: EEG integrations and the human brain. *Artificial Intelligence and Applications*, 3(2), 145–160.

[12] Kumar, B. (2022). Integration of AI and neuroscience for advancing brain–machine interfaces: A study. *Integration*, 9(1).

[13] Calabrò, R.S. and Morone, G. (2025). Advancing rehabilitation medicine with the metaverse: Opportunities and challenges. *Brain Sciences*, 15(3), 321.

[14] Morone, G., Ciancarelli, I., Calabrò, R.S., et al. (2025). MetaRehabVerse: The great opportunity to put the person's functioning and participation at the center of healthcare. *Neurorehabilitation and Neural Repair*, 39(3), 241–255.

[15] Kanchan, A., Pawar, V., Polishi, D., et al. (2024). Neuro connect: Navigating the theoretical landscape of brain–internet integration and ethical considerations. *Grenze International Journal of Engineering & Technology (GIJET)*, 10.

[16] Huang, G., Chen, X. and Liao, C. (2025). AI-driven wearable bioelectronics in digital healthcare. *Biosensors*, 15(7), 410.

[17] Kim, K., Yang, H., Lee, J. and Lee, W.G. (2023). Metaverse wearables for immersive digital healthcare: A review. *Advanced Science*, 10(31), 2303234.

[18] Murala, D.K., Panda, S.K. and Dash, S.P. (2023). MedMetaverse: Medical care of chronic disease patients and managing data using artificial intelligence, blockchain, and wearable devices state-of-the-art methodology. *IEEE Access*, 11, 138954–138985.

[19] Shafik, W., Tufail, A., Apong, R.A.A.H.M. and Balasubramaniam, S. (2024). Future directions in cybersecurity, digital forensics and biometric systems. *In AI Based Advancements in Biometrics and its Applications* (pp. 238–263). CRC Press.

[20] Sumina, S., Kumar, K.S. and Prasanth, A. (2024). Machine learning based models for implementing digital twins in healthcare industry. In *Metaverse Technologies in Healthcare*, pp. 135–162. Academic Press.

5 Edge and Cloud Computing in Wearable AI Systems

Jeysi B.[1], B. Shanthini[2], B. Hariharan[3*], Manoj Jayabalan[4] and Wilfred Blessing N.R.[5]

The swift evolution of wearable artificial intelligence (AI) systems has significantly impacted continuous health monitoring, personalized healthcare, and human–machine interaction. At the heart of this revolution is the complementary convergence of edge and cloud computing models, which together facilitate scalable, real-time, and intelligent processing of the massive amounts of physiological and contextual data generated by wearable devices. This chapter presents a thorough review of edge-cloud architectures for wearable AI systems, focusing on their significance in real-time health analytics, adaptive intelligence, and immersive healthcare applications in both physical and virtual spaces. Wearable devices like smartwatches, biosensor-embedded clothing, neural interfaces, and implantable sensors continuously collect multi-modal data such as vital signs, activity patterns, biochemical signals, and environmental context. Cloud-based processing of this data alone is associated with latency, privacy concerns, and bandwidth issues, which are not amenable to time-critical and safety-critical applications in healthcare. Edge computing addresses these challenges by facilitating on-device or near-device intelligence, which allows real-time inference, anomaly detection, and adaptive feedback with negligible latency. In contrast, cloud computing enables massive storage, long-term analytics, model training, population-level insights, and platform portability across healthcare systems. This chapter reviews hybrid edge–cloud architectures, AI model splitting, federated learning, resource-constrained inference, security, privacy preservation, and regulatory support. New applications in digital twins, immersive telemedicine, and metaverse-based healthcare are also covered. The chapter concludes with a discussion of potential research avenues for scalable, secure, and intelligent wearable AI systems.

[1,2] Department of Computer Science and Engineering, St. Peter's Institute of Higher Education and Research, Chennai, Tamil Nadu, India.

[3] Department of Computational Intelligence, School of Computing, SRM Institute of Science and Technology, Chennai, Tamil Nadu, India.

[4] Bath School of Design, Bath Spa University, Bath, UK.

[5] College of Computing and Information Sciences, University of Technology and Applied Sciences-Ibri, Ibri, Oman.

* Corresponding author: hariharb@srmist.edu.in

DOI: 10.1201/9781003776291-5

1. Introduction to Wearable AI Systems

1.1 Evolution of Wearable Intelligence

From basic mechanical devices to intelligent, adaptive, and networked systems, the history of wearable intelligence reflects the general trend in computing technology. The majority of the first wearable systems were useful gadgets like pedometers and wristwatches that were made to provide simple measurements without any sort of computational intelligence. These self-contained systems lacked the capacity to learn, adapt, or interpret data in ways other than straightforward numerical interpretation.

The introduction of digital electronics and microcontrollers marked the first major advancement in wearable technology. Early digital wearables and fitness trackers incorporated basic sensors and embedded processors, enabling elementary data logging and rule-based analysis. Intelligence at this stage was confined to predefined thresholds and heuristic decision rules, resulting in limited personalization and static functionality.

Recent developments have led to a rise in the popularity of wearables with AI capabilities, such as strong inference engines and specialized neural processing units. These devices can perform deep learning on the device itself, allowing for real-time decision-making without requiring continuous cloud connectivity. Adaptive inference, quantization, and model compression have made it possible to deploy complex models within the strict energy and memory constraints of wearable technology. Because of this, wearable intelligence is now used for more than just tracking physical health; it can also be used for mental health evaluation, cognitive enhancement, and immersive human–machine interaction. Neural interfaces and brain–computer interaction systems are excellent examples of this convergence, illustrating the increasing demand for distributed intelligence architectures that can support adaptive, real-time intelligence at scale [1]. Fig. 5.1 illustrates the evolution of wearable intelligence from the 1990s to the 2020s and beyond.

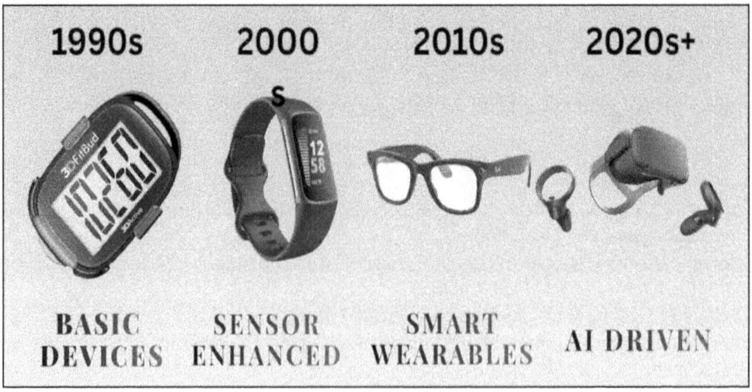

Fig. 5.1 Evolution of Wearable Intelligence.
Source: Author.

1.2 Role of Computing Paradigms in Wearable AI

Computing paradigms specify the structure, dynamics, and provision of computation, storage, and intelligence in a system. For wearable AI, the chosen computing paradigm has a direct impact on the system's responsiveness, energy consumption, scalability, and privacy preservation. Cloud computing has been the backbone of large-scale AI systems because of its theoretically unlimited computational and storage capabilities. In wearable ecosystems, cloud computing enables the training of complex models, health analysis over time, and integration of electronic health record systems.

In Fig. 5.2 hybrid edge–cloud computing combines the best features of both. Scalability and analytical capabilities are maintained while optimizing resource use. Resource-intensive tasks, such as deep learning model training for population-level health analysis, are performed in the cloud, and tasks requiring immediate response, such as anomaly detection and notification, occur in the edge [2].

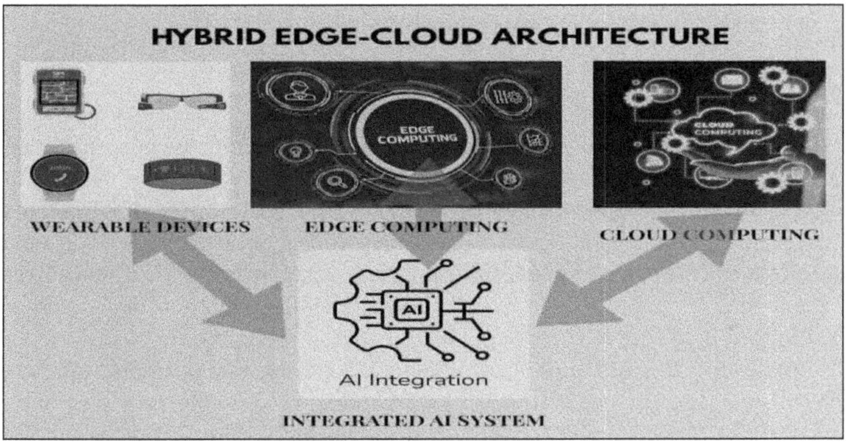

Fig. 5.2 Hybrid Edge–Cloud Architecture for Wearable AI.
Source: Author.

1.3 Motivation for Edge–Cloud Integration

The limitations of each paradigm when used independently are what motivate the necessity of integrating edge and cloud computing in wearable AI. Real-time communication, constant availability, energy efficiency, and strong privacy support are all necessary for wearable AI applications. Although edge computing can help with privacy and latency issues, it has processing, memory, and energy limitations. Conversely, cloud computing is scalable but has privacy and latency issues.

The current applications of digital twins, telemedicine immersion, and metaverse health care are all dependent on distributed intelligence platforms. The applications combine physical observations in real time with virtual environments and large-scale analysis. This means that edge–cloud integration is not only desirable but also necessary. The integration of local real-time interactions with large-scale intelligence makes edge–cloud integration the spine of the next generation of wearable AI health applications, which are personalized, adaptive, and trustworthy [3].

2. Fundamentals of Edge and Cloud Computing

Wearable AI systems come with a myriad of needs including, but not limited to, latency, power, privacy, and processing capability. To be successful in meeting the requirement to continuously and accurately monitor both physiological and contextual data, a responsive computing infrastructure is required to provide real-time processing of records while remaining secure. A centralized computing model cannot provide these requirements in the healthcare industry, where both on-time and reliable decision-making is critical. As such, wearable AI systems are rapidly moving towards distributed computing architectures including edge computing, cloud computing, and hybrid computing models.

2.1 Edge Computing Concepts and Architectures

Edge computing is a distributed system of computing that shifts the processing and intelligence of computations between the data source and end-user as opposed to relying on only one cloud computing location. In the context of wearable AI, the "edge" refers to the wearable device itself, smartphones, and edge nodes like home gateways and hospital servers. Edge computing works in healthcare as it resolves latency and reliability requirements that are time-dependent on the healthcare system.

Wearable devices continually generate exceptionally high-frequency physiological signals like heart rate, electrocardiograms, and motion. Forwarding all raw data from wearables to the cloud creates high and often unmanageable network latency, high bandwidth consumption, and high probability of connectivity issues. Edge computing meets these needs through processing data locally or semi-locally, providing real-time inference, anomaly detection, and feedback while not being tied to the network or requiring continuous connectivity to perform these functions [2].

From the point of view of the architecture, edge computing works on a hierarchical structure. Wearable devices can perform the minor preprocessing of information with embedded processors or neural processing units. Intermediate edge nodes will pool together information from multiple sources while performing more complex computing tasks. Edge computing also improves the confidentiality of sensitive patient information in the healthcare environment by allowing it to be processed nearby, as that meets regulatory compliance and protects against cyber threats [4].

2.2 Cloud Computing Models for Healthcare

Cloud computing provides an easy-to-scale infrastructure for storing, analysing, and managing artificial intelligence (AI) models utilized in wearable AI systems. Compared with edge computing, cloud computing offers more flexibility and the possibility for scalability to have larger amounts of computer power or data storage needed when performing deep learning, analysing health data across large populations, and storing extremely large amounts of health records. In the healthcare industry, cloud technology allows for greater data interoperability between healthcare providers and the implementation of evidence-based clinical decision support systems.

The classes of cloud computing are: Infrastructure as a Service (IaaS), Platform as a Service (PaaS), and Software as a Service (SaaS). IaaS has been used most commonly as a way to store longitudinally collected wearable sensor data at massive scale. PaaS has been used in many ways, but specifically, it has been used for the development, authentication, and management of AI pipelines; e.g., application of deep learning to wearable data for prediction of acute health crises. SaaS provides analytics platforms, platforms for clinical monitoring, and platforms for decision support for healthcare providers and patients [5].

One of the major strengths of cloud computing is its ability to aggregate data from various populations. Data aggregation facilitates the identification of global health patterns and the development of accurate AI models trained on multi-heterogeneous datasets. However, cloud computing–based systems are associated with latency, increased bandwidth usage, and privacy concerns when applied to real-time inference tasks. Therefore, contemporary wearable AI systems are increasingly shifting time-critical inference tasks to edge layers while using the cloud for training, management, and analytics [6].

2.3 Fog and Hybrid Computing Paradigms

Fog computing and hybrid computing models enhance the capabilities of edge computing and cloud computing by adding another layer of computation between the two. Fog computing refers to the addition of computing resources between edge computing and cloud computing, which is normally done within a local network such as a hospital or smart home. The fog nodes help in the aggregation of data.

In the case of wearable AI systems, fog computing is very useful in multi-user environments such as smart hospitals or rehabilitation centres. The fog nodes help in the orchestration of analytics of multiple wearable devices, thus encouraging collaborative intelligence with low latency. Additionally, fog computing reduces the need for redundant data transmission to the cloud.

Hybrid computing architectures are able to use all three types of computing models—edge, fog, and cloud—in one framework, allowing for computation to be distributed dynamically based on the requirements of the application. For instance, real-time inferencing computations that are highly time-sensitive will occur on the edge, collaborative analytics computations that are moderately time-sensitive will take place at the fog layer, and computationally intensive model training and archiving computations that are not time-sensitive will be processed at the cloud layer. In addition to dynamic distribution, hybrid computing architectures will also support privacy-preserving techniques, including federated learning, which is an essential requirement for healthcare applications [3].

3. Architecture of Edge–Cloud Wearable AI Systems

3.1 Sensor Layer and Data Acquisition

Wearable AI systems at the edge have the sensor layer as their foundational component, which allows for the ongoing collection of data on physiological, behavioural, and environmental factors. The intended purpose of each wearable sensor is to gather multiple types of signals including heart rate (HR), electrocardiogram (ECG), inertial movement (IM), temperature (T), and various biochemical markers (BM). The physical size (dimensions) and energy usage (battery/energy) required by these sensors are very tightly controlled but can also compromise their accuracy and reliability. Before data transmission to the next processing step, the data must be conditioned to improve quality or stripped of excess/noise, as well as synchronized with a time reference. The acquisition process is key to subsequent analyses; if the quality of signals received during this process deteriorates, then this deterioration will directly affect the results of analytic processes, including the built-in AI algorithms used to generate those results. The development of low-power sensors and embedded electronic technology has improved continuous real-time monitoring of health status for wearable devices [4].

3.2 Edge Intelligence and On-Device Processing

Wearables can process their own data at their location where the data is created, called edge intelligence. This helps with several aspects of decision-making, including anomaly detection and sending out notifications. Additionally, edge intelligence supports running smaller models on an embedded processor or a neural processing unit, reducing both latency and cost of communicating. The importance of edge intelligence is even more pronounced in healthcare, especially applications that require safety such as fall detection systems and cardiac monitoring devices. In addition, through the use of resource-aware scheduling and adaptive inference techniques [2], edge intelligence is able to enhance performance under conditions of limited energy and computational resources.

3.3 Cloud Analytics and Model Management

A cloud-based solution allows for a flexible platform for data; allows for the analytics and management of models (AI); provides the capability to gather data about large groups of people using multiple devices; is capable of population-wide analysis, trend analysis, and improving of models; and has the ability to train, validate, deploy, and version models, which are running on edge devices. Updating on the edge, AI model effectiveness and accuracy are improved over time. Although analytical in nature, the cloud's role is to provide assistance in terms of the five different types of analytics rather than entirely replacing them; therefore, if the cloud is used for long-term analysis of data and other analytical processes, it provides coordination rather than performing real-time analysis alone [5].

3.4 Communication and Middleware Frameworks

Middleware assists in creating integrated communication patterns among sensors, the edge, and the cloud. Routing, synchronization, and device discovery are among the types of data management for which middleware is responsible, and middleware will provide an interface to communicate across different types of hardware and software. Middleware also provides an abstract layer to hide the complexities associated with orderings found on a network. In wearables, middleware provides low latency for communication, fault tolerance, and secure data transfer, using protocol standards such as Message Queuing Telemetry Transport (MQTT) and Representational State Transfer Application Programming Interfaces (RESTful APIs) to transfer data in an adaptive manner according to network conditions and application needs [6].

4. AI Models for Edge and Cloud Environments

4.1 Lightweight AI Models for Wearables

The design of lightweight AI models focuses on operating in limited computational power resources of wearable devices. Efficient but also accurate models for tasks such as activity classification and anomaly detection will use models like simple neural networks, decision trees, and convolutional networks. These models allow for continuous processing of information with minimal battery drain; therefore, they are an ideal candidate for longitudinal health monitoring applications. Additionally, because of their simple structure, they can be rapidly deployed in wearable AI systems [5].

4.2 Model Compression and Optimization

There are model compression and optimization methods that help reduce the ability for the computational process to be completed on a wearable. The most effective method for transferring complex AI models for edge deployment preserves the original predictive tasks while reducing energy consumption and overall latency by approximately 12% through the use of auto-generated classifier tasks and transformer architectures.

This approach enhances the ability to execute AI tasks locally, ensuring improved privacy, lower latency, and efficient on-device intelligence, which are critical considerations for deploying AI solutions at the edge. Model compression methods are therefore a key contributor to bridging clouds with effective models, cloud implementation, and edge environments with limited sources [2].

4.3 Distributed and Collaborative Intelligence

Intelligent collaboration among various edge and cloud nodes to facilitate overall system learning and decision-making can be supported by distributed intelligence. The distributed intelligence model relies on a large number of devices to create a split between devices, which is a more scalable and robust model than the centralized model. Wearables can individually help in forming a shared insight for overall knowledge. The distributed intelligence model is also suitable for the adaptive healthcare application since the group will learn more about the adaptive trend of groups than the individual. The distribution of intelligence increases the robustness of intelligence since there are fewer points where failure can occur in the entire system. [3]

5. Federated Learning and Privacy-Preserving AI

5.1 Federated Learning Principles

Federated learning is a "decentralized approach to co-developing AI models simultaneously across multiple devices". This novel method of developing AI models maintains the privacy of the users with regard to their data. In federated learning, each wearable device updates its model training independently using the private data of the device. Then, at a central point the updates are aggregated into one or more models. By using a federated learning approach, an individual can enhance his/her privacy while also using his/her collective intelligence. Specifically, the development of federated learning algorithms for healthcare wearables is essential as the concern about the use of and access to patient data demands safe processing of the data. Moreover, by using federated learning to route processed data, the cost of sending raw data through traditional channels is cut by as much as 90% [3].

5.2 Secure Model Aggregation

Privacy protection is extremely important for participants in federated learning. Cryptography can be used to ensure privacy protection through either homomorphic encryption or by using secure multi-party computation (MPC). Using either of these two techniques will allow you to obfuscate your updates to your model(s) so that they cannot be reverse engineered by an attacker from the individual application of the update. In the healthcare area, secure aggregation of models is an important factor in creating mutual trust among users and cooperative wearable AIs. By providing secure aggregations of model(s), you can be sure that the data used to create your model(s) will not be subject to any unauthorized access or reproduction of any data that you have used to train your model(s) [3].

5.3 Privacy and Data Governance

Wearable devices illustrate examples of numerous technologies being utilized under prescribed formalized regulations and frameworks governing privacy and regulatory governance of data usage. Frameworks create guidance around how data collected through the use of wearable devices will be collected, processed, stored, and shared. The principle of data minimization is one way the goal of not storing sensitive data has been achieved through the use of edge intelligence and federated learning. Both concepts utilize localized storage of data as opposed to storing that data in centralized databases. Compliance with laws and ethical use of data to support the delivery of safe and secure healthcare, as well as establishing trust with the users of services, are all areas affected by governance of data. Policies that define how data is to be handled and effective means of obtaining user's consent create trust with those services. These types of practices will play an important part in the overall success of wearable AI systems [6].

6. Latency, Energy, and Resource Optimization

6.1 Real-Time Constraints in Health Monitoring

To ensure patient safety, the wearable AI systems deployed in the healthcare environment need to meet strict real-time constraints. For example, applications that involve cardiac arrhythmia analysis, fall analysis, seizure activity analysis, and glucose control require fast sensing, processing, and acting (within milliseconds). If the network latency or cloud processing introduces a delay in these applications, then the occurrence of critical events can be significantly delayed as a result. Consequently, an important requirement of wearable health monitoring systems is the use of latency-aware design principles.

In order to meet the real-time requirements of the applications we have listed above, the use of edge computing is very important because it will allow inference and feedback loops to be executed close to the data source. However, due to workload variability, wireless delays, and resource constraints, it is very difficult to have deterministic latency for these types of applications. Therefore, there must be scheduling techniques in place to schedule the sensing, processing, and communications tasks, giving higher priority to time-critical workloads. As a means of providing predictable system performance, real-time operating systems along with scheduling techniques are becoming increasingly popular.

Additionally, a comprehensive approach must be taken when optimizing end-to-end latency including all components involved in data movement throughout the process—from collecting sensory data through distributing alerts. The hybrid distribution of edge and cloud provides an excellent balance between minimizing latency while maximizing scalability through executing real-time, high-priority inference tasks at the edge and executing batch, low-priority analytics at the cloud level. Therefore, it is essential that all wearables deployed as AI in healthcare settings meet real-time performance requirement to ensure secure and efficient use [2].

6.2 Energy-Aware Computing Strategies

The AI device you wear will be efficient depending on how much energy it uses, because it runs off batteries, and therefore needs to be able to run for long periods of time. To achieve this, the design of the energy-efficient computing architecture must find a balance between the accuracy of the computation and the overall energy efficiency of the device. If the device is not energy efficient, then it will adversely affect how long the device will last, thus leading to a lack of system reliability and acceptance by users.

Adaptive sampling methods are a means to provide the flexibility to change the sampling rate of the information being "sensed" based on your user context and activity level. When there is lower risk, the sensors operate at lower rates and are energy efficient, while being able to meet safety standards as required.

Proper scheduling priorities for battery saving require that essential tasks are scheduled first, while all other tasks are suspended until essential task completion to save battery power. Cloud resources can be utilized for task optimization by offloading computational processes to the cloud, thereby conserving battery power. Overall, the use of cloud resources to offload power-hungry computations would lead to longer-lasting devices. All of this has resulted in significantly less time functionality compared to continuous operations for the end-user as it pertains to the success of implementing long-term health monitoring applications [4].

6.3 Dynamic Task Offloading

With the help of dynamic task offloading, intelligent decisions can be made regarding the distribution of computational tasks among wearable AI systems based on edge and cloud computing resources, taking into account real-time situational information. With regard to the decision of how and where to execute tasks, there are a number of factors that need to be considered, including the limitations imposed by latency, the amount of available energy, the network conditions, and the complexity of the computing requirements of the task. The most obvious example of this would be time-critical tasks such as anomaly detection, which are typically executed at the edge, and compute-intensive tasks such as executing an analytics task or updating a model, which are typically executed on cloud servers.

Adaptive task offloading algorithms are always monitoring the system in real time to dynamically change the execution plan as needed. For example, tasks can be executed when the network is stable and there is sufficient energy available to avoid the high computing requirements of the task.

In situations of connectivity issues or low battery power, the tasks will be performed locally. The dynamic offloading of tasks will improve the system response time; it will reduce energy consumption and will give the system more power to grow in terms of size. The dynamic offloading will help the wearables that employ AI to efficiently work in different locations such as hospitals and rural settings. Thus, intelligent offloading techniques are needed to help the wearable AI systems work at an optimal level [6]. Table 5.1 summarizes concepts from multiple studies latency, energy, task offloading, edge inference, etc.

Table 5.1 Optimization Objectives in Wearable AI Systems.

Objective	*Key Challenge*	*Optimization Strategy*
Latency	Network delays	Edge inference
Energy	Limited battery	Adaptive sampling
Resources	Limited compute	Task offloading
Reliability	Connectivity loss	Local autonomy

Source: Adapted from Satyanarayanan (2017) [2], Shi et al. (2016) [4], and Botta et al. (2016) [6].

7. Edge–Cloud Wearable AI in the Metaverse

7.1 Digital Twins and Virtual Health Avatars

A digital twin is the real-time representation of the changes that occur to a physical entity using sensor data, like a person, as it evolves. In wearable On-body Artificial Twin (OAT), digital twin of an individual can provide a detailed understanding of that individual through an analysis of their physiological and behavioural data, paving the way for a more accurate determination of how to best assess and simulate their health. The digital twin can be updated as frequently as necessary with the use of edge computing and the historical simulation and analysis of large volumes of data about that entity over time can be achieved with the use of cloud computing.

Extensions of the digital twin concept are referred to as virtual health avatars, which give both the patient and healthcare provider a more interactive way of visualizing health data through immersive environments. Doing so allows both the patient and the healthcare provider to analyses the patient's physiological state, simulate the effects of treatments, and track the progression of diseases. Digital twins are beneficial tools for the management of the following: chronic diseases, rehabilitation programmes, and preventive healthcare strategies, where ongoing surveillance and tailoring of solutions are of critical importance. The combined use of wearable OAT and distributed computing technology within digital twins will enable preventive and precision medicine [7].

7.2 Immersive Remote Monitoring

Remote monitoring of patients in an immersive environment is accomplished by combining wearable devices with AI and using cloud-based technology to create a comprehensive view of the patient while they are away from the hospital. The wearer's biomedical biosensor will allow real-time transmission of the patient's vital signs directly to the network edge to be processed and alerted instantaneously. The cloud-based analytics engine can also be used to identify historical trends over time, which will help to support future care decisions regarding the patient when all parties to the care process are working with the shared experience of an immersive remote-monitoring environment.

Healthcare providers will have a far more engaging and interactive experience in 3D space when accessing patient-related data than they would through traditional methods. In addition, by providing all parties to the healthcare process with the ability to create their own immersive experience while engaging in communication with one another, telemedicine services will be significantly enhanced. Immersive remote-monitoring solutions can be leveraged for monitoring older adults, post-operative surgical patients, and patients in rehabilitation at home by continuously monitoring their health and well-being without requiring the clinician or caregiver to be physically present.

7.3 Integration with Extended Reality (XR) Platforms

Wearable AI systems can have their data and information represented through immersive trips through augmented reality (AR) and virtual reality (VR) devices. The capabilities of XR combined with edge/cloud computing allow health data and simulations to be rendered in real time and viewed in immersive settings. Edge computing provides a solution for visualizing data while cloud computing supplies a platform for creating complex visualizations and conducting historical analysis on datasets.

The XR technologies are being utilized by medical professionals to improve their understanding of their patients and to boost patient participation in their treatment process. One way in which medical providers are doing this is by using digital twins to assist with surgical procedures; and patients are receiving feedback in real time when undergoing rehabilitation programmes. When wearables are combined with XR technologies and distributed systems, the ability to create personalized, immersive digital healthcare experiences has reached a new level of development [7].

8. Security, Trust, and Regulatory Challenges

8.1 Cybersecurity Threats in Wearable AI

There are many vulnerabilities in the cybersecurity of wearable AI systems such as data interception, unauthorized access to data, model inversion, and asynchronous attacks on the system. The capability of constant connectivity to edge devices through to cloud infrastructure, combined with the processing of sensitive health information, raises the attack surface and thus the likelihood of data breaches due to either a compromised device or reported breaches in the communication channels; thus, the likelihood of losing trust in the AI wearable system as a result of a data breach.

For a secure AI wearable system, there must be mechanisms related to security in place, i.e., encryption, authentication, and intrusion detection [8]. The use of edge security mechanisms can enhance resilience by offering the capability for threat detection at the edge and reducing dependence on centralized security. These assumptions are based on a good framework for cybersecurity to offer the required guarantees for the use of a trusted wearable AI system in the healthcare setting [5]. Fig. 5.3 represents the Optimization, Security, and Immersive Health in Edge–Cloud Wearable AI Systems.

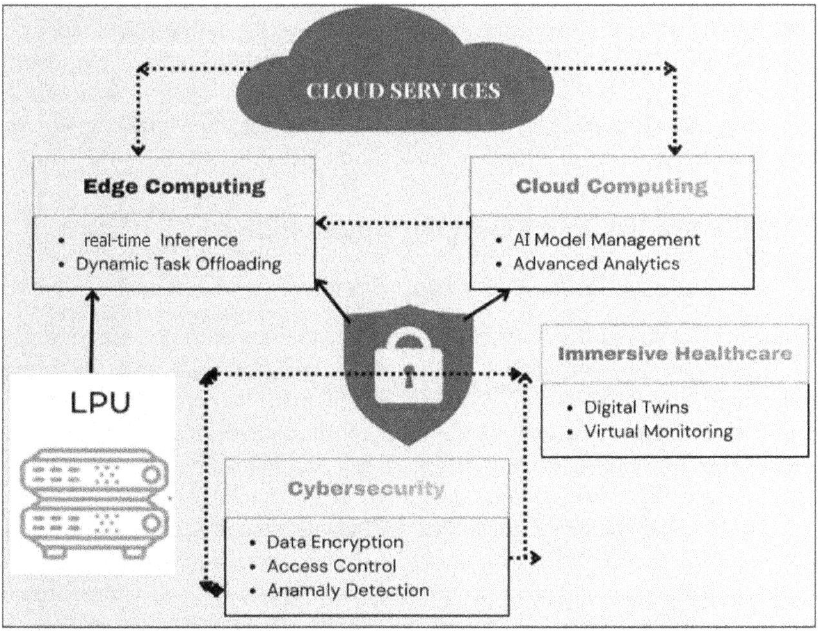

Fig. 5.3 Optimization, security, and immersive health.

8.2 Compliance with Healthcare Regulations

Healthcare regulations including General Data Protection Regulation (GDPR) and Health Insurance Portability and Accountability Act (HIPAA) require strict stipulations for the acquisition, retention, and processing of data. Wearable AI technology must comply with the principles of data minimization, that is, only collecting the minimum amount of personal data necessary to provide a service; effective access controls; and obtaining explicit consent from users. Edge computing supports compliance with healthcare regulations by reducing the amount of unprocessed data that must be sent across the network.

In addition to edge computing, cloud infrastructure supports compliance with healthcare regulations through audit trails, access logging, and policy enforcement solutions. Compliance with healthcare regulations is essential to legally deploy wearable AI technology, it builds trust between the user, healthcare provider, and healthcare institution [9].

8.3 Ethical Considerations

Regarding the development, use, and implementation of wearable AI technology, there are ethical considerations that must be taken into account. Wearable AI technology will impact health-related decisions in many ways; thus, it is important that the impact of wearable AI technology on health-related decisions must be explainable and unbiased. A person should have the capacity to comprehend what is being done with their own data, in addition to how that data will be used.

Apart from the ethical considerations of accountability, ownership, equity, and transparency, there are other ethical issues that are linked to wearable AI technology. All these ethical considerations are vital for the overall support and continued development of digital health technologies [10].

9. Case Studies and Emerging Applications

9.1 Continuous Health Monitoring Systems

Despite the fact that a lot of work has been done in the area of edge cloud wearables and AI, there are still many challenges that have to be addressed in order for them to be developed and used more widely. There are still many barriers to the widespread use of these technologies, including scaling for multiple devices, incompatibility of platforms, and the absence of standardized communication protocols. Equal performance of the models on all populations and scenarios is another challenge.

The technical challenge of achieving a balance among accuracy, speed, and power consumption is further complicated by the resource limitation of wearables. Because distributed systems are prone to security threats and data misuse, robust security mechanisms have to be employed. Finally, the ethical issues of fairness, user consent, and transparency have to be systematically addressed. These difficult problems will require a collaborative effort among the communities of AI, embedded systems, networking, healthcare, and ethics [2].

9.2 Smart Rehabilitation and Assistive Wearables

Wearable AI technology is being used in rehabilitation and assistive devices to assist with physical therapy, increase mobility, and regain function by providing feedback from motion sensors, electromyography, and inertial measurement units that analyse patient movement on the spot. Edge AI models of motion provide instantaneous analysis of motion patterns and give real-time feedback to help patients correct their posture or movement during therapy sessions, which reduces the need for continual supervision by clinicians. Cloud analytics provide long-term monitoring of progress, individualization of therapy modifications for patients, and supervision of therapy by clinicians.

Longitudinally collected rehabilitation data equips therapists with evidence to evaluate recovery trajectories, refine treatment plans, and predict rehabilitation outcomes. Assistive wearables (e.g., smart exoskeletons and orthotic devices) provide enhanced mobility by varying the amount of support provided according to real-time physiological data. Edge AI also facilitates real-time response, while cloud platforms enable customization by way of data analytics. Therefore, these systems provide enhanced rehabilitation outcomes, lower overall healthcare costs, and improve access to therapeutic services, particularly in home-based or remote settings [4].

9.3 AI-Driven Preventive Healthcare

Preventive healthcare uses AI to identify warning signs of risk (possible illness) early in the development of the condition and move the focus from problem solving to preventing the problem before it occurs. Wearable AI (device) collect real-time data for physiological and behavioural changes and help identify even small deviations from normal behaviour. Inference at the edge will enable notification of possible problems at the time the data is collected with the notification of population data being collected and analysed at a cloud-based server through comparative analytics.

These devices will identify early warning signs of heart disease, metabolic disorders, mental disorders, and lifestyle disorders. Combining intelligent edge with the cloud provides targeted assessment of risk and timely, accurate interventions. Therefore, healthcare costs will be reduced and quality of life improved through timely lifestyle changes and care. AI-enabled preventive care demonstrates the potential of wearable AI devices to undoubtedly transform healthcare systems when used in conjunction with a valid edge–cloud technology [3].

10. Future Research Directions and Conclusion

10.1 Open Challenges

Even with major progress in wearable intelligence , a few issues still stay unresolved in practice. Resource constrained wearable devices keep bumping into limits in processing power, memory, and especially battery runtime, so rolling out heavier AI models becomes quite hard. Then there is data privacy security and user trust, which is kind of hard to guarantee, because these devices keep collecting sensitive personal information , all day long. On top of that, getting dependable real time behavior while the surroundings change, and while networks vary between users or locations, is still not straightforward. Also, standardization, interoperability across different wearable platforms , and smooth integration with edge and cloud infrastructures , demand more investigation. Solving these problems matters a lot if we want scalable, energy efficient, secure , and user focused wearable intelligence systems that actually work at scale.

10.2 Vision for Edge–Cloud Wearable AI

The future success of wearable AI with edge–cloud services will rely upon its ability to easily interact across the physical, digital, and virtual environments. New advances in distributed intelligence will produce adaptive and context-aware systems that are always learning while also adhering to privacy laws. As a result, the interlinking of wearable AI and digital twins, immersive environments, and metaverse infrastructure will allow for a more personalized and predictive type of healthcare service delivery.

Furthermore, the use of the autonomously orchestrated distribution of resources over edge–cloud technology will lead to the auto-allocation of processing power based upon context, risk, and available computation resources. The consolidation of edge–cloud technologies within the healthcare ecosystem will occur via the creation of standardized frameworks and platforms for edge–cloud systems. Support for developing intelligent and human-centred systems with the purpose of improving human wellness while maintaining trust, security, and ethics with respect to data will be paramount [2].

10.3 Concluding Remarks

The rise of edge–cloud computing has created new opportunities for intelligent, scalable, and reliable functionality of wearable AI. Wearable AI has the potential to improve healthcare delivery systems because of its use in monitoring, rehabilitating, preventing, and delivering immersive healthcare.

Edge–cloud wearable AI has an essential role within the next-generation digital healthcare ecosystem by overcoming the barriers presented by technology, regulation, and ethical considerations. The edge–cloud wearable AI will support real-time intelligence while providing a global view, making it a key enabler for delivering personalized, preventive, and immersive healthcare services.

References

[1] Patel, S., Park, H., Bonato, P. et al. (2012). A review of wearable sensors and systems with application in rehabilitation. *Journal of NeuroEngineering and Rehabilitation*, 9, 21.

[2] Satyanarayanan, M. (2017). The emergence of edge computing. *Computer*, 50(1), 30–39.

[3] Rieke, N., Hancox, J., Li, W. et al. (2020). The future of digital health with federated learning. *NPJ Digital Medicine*, 3, 119.

[4] Shi, W., Cao, J., Zhang, Q. et al. (2016). Edge computing: Vision and challenges. *IEEE Internet of Things Journal*, 3(5), 637–646.

[5] Kuo, A.M.H. (2011). Opportunities and challenges of cloud computing to improve health care services. *Journal of Medical Internet Research*, 13(3), e67.

[6] Botta, A., de Donato, W., Persico, V. and Pescapé, A. (2016). Integration of cloud computing and Internet of Things. *Future Generation Computer Systems*, 56, 684–700.
[7] Wang, X., Xu, L. and Zhang, Y. (2022). Digital twins in healthcare: A review. *IEEE Access*, 10, 13772–13789.
[8] Balasubramaniam, S. and Kavitha, V. (2013). A survey on data retrieval techniques in cloud computing. *Journal of Convergence Information Technology*, 8(16), 15.
[9] Floridi, L. and Cowls, J. (2019). A unified framework of ethical principles for AI. *Harvard Data Science Review*, 1(1).
[10] Balasubramaniam, S. and Kavitha, V. (2015). Hybrid security architecture for personal health record transactions in cloud computing. *Advances in Information Sciences and Service Sciences*, 7(1), 121.

6 Remote Patient Monitoring in Immersive Health Platforms

C. Valarmathi[1*], Anitha Velu[2],
Rashad G. Abaszade[3] and F.G. Abaszadeh[4]

Remote patient monitoring (RPM) has evolved to be one of the ground-breaking approaches in the current healthcare sector since it enables the monitoring of the patient 24/7 and in cases other than when the patient is in the typical clinical environment. RPM in combination with immersive health technologies like virtual reality (VR), augmented reality (AR), and mixed reality (MR) is transforming the process of providing personalized, patient-centred care. This chapter considers how the idea of RPM can be developed into the world of immersive health setting where cloud-edge computing infrastructures, wearables sensors, and Internet of Things (IoT) devices would have the ability to introduce a seamless system in data collection, visualization, and interaction. The chapter also considers factors of user experience focusing on engagement and ease of human–computer interaction of the patients and medical professionals. In order to reveal the practical impact, such significant spheres of application as the management of chronic diseases, care of old age, rehabilitation, and monitoring of mental health are investigated. This chapter provides an in-depth summary of how immersive RPM systems can improve the healthcare outcomes, efficiency, and accessibility in next-generation digital health ecosystems by describing current trends and future research objectives.

1. Introduction

The healthcare delivery is shifting its paradigm whereby the episodic, hospital-focused care is being replaced by continuous and patient-focused models of monitoring. The driving force behind this shift is the rise in chronic illnesses, increase in old age population as well as the need to deliver personalized healthcare services. One of the most significant solutions is remote patient monitoring (RPM) wherein it is possible to monitor physiological and behavioural health parameters at all times in a nonclinical settinhg [1]. The wearable devices, wireless

[1] Department of Computer Science and Engineering, Sri Sairam College of Engineering, Bengaluru, India.
[2] Department of Electronics and Communication Engineering, Sri Sairam College of Engineering, Bengaluru, India.
[3] Electrical and Electronics Engineering, Turan International Research Institute, Baku, Azerbaijan.
[4] National Aviation Academy, Baku, Azerbaijan.
* Corresponding author: vinmathi20@gmail.com

DOI: 10.1201/9781003776291-6

communication with smart analytics, can help doctors monitor in real time the condition of the patient, allowing the reduction of readmission rates and improving clinical outcomes.

At the same time, the immersive digital spaces, including the virtual reality (VR), augmented reality (AR), mixed reality (MR), and metaverse-based ones, are reinventing the way healthcare data is presented, analysed, and acted upon. This virtual desk allows many dimensions of interaction settings within which patient data could be examined, simulated, and placed within the context in a manner unconfined to traditional dashboards. When applied to RPM, immersive technologies can offer improved care delivery through shared care, patient experiences, and patient clinical decision-making processes. The convergence of artificial intelligence (AI) of wearables, remote monitoring systems, and immersive environments is also one of the key elements of the future healthcare ecosystem. In this chapter, the authors discuss the essence of monitoring parameters in healthcare, the development of RPM systems, and the emergence of immersive health platforms as the revolutionary facilitators of continuous health monitoring in the metaverse period [2, 3].

1.1 A Run-Through of Healthcare Monitoring Parameters

Remote patient assessment and clinical intervention are based on healthcare monitoring parameters. These parameters can be generally divided into physiological, behavioural, biochemical, and contextual parameters that do not offer an equal amount of information about the well-being of a patient. The vital signs that are included in the physiological parameters are heart rate, blood pressure, respiratory rate, oxygen saturation, and the temperature of the body. Recent developments in wearable biosensors have made these measurements accessible to be recorded continuously at a clinical level of resolution. Long-term monitoring of body parameters such as electrocardiographic signals, photoplethysmography-based pulse measurements, and respiratory motion sensing is becoming a part of unobtrusive wearable devices, only to interfere with everyday activities.

Parameters of behaviour and activity offer different viewpoints on health. Physical activity level, gait pattern, postures, and sleep duration and quality are some of the metrics that are especially useful in the management of chronic conditions, rehabilitation, and geriatric care. Changes in activity patterns that are not baseline activities are usually among the first symptoms that signal a deterioration of functions or the development of a disease. Whereas biochemical parameters have been traditionally obtained using laboratory technologies, there is an incremental trend in the non-invasive or minimally invasive wearable technologies that allow access to these parameters. An example of this trend includes continuous glucose monitoring, electrolyte sensing via sweat, and newer biomarker detection methods. These parameters are used to make timely interventions, particularly in metabolic and cardiovascular disorders.

Situational awareness through contextual and environmental parameters such as ambient temperature, humidity, location, and patterns of social interactions contributes to improved interpretation of physiological data. Such multi-modal parameters, in combination with AI-powered analytics, will enable customization of health profiling and prediction of risk. All these parameters are no longer available in the form of numerical figures in the immersive health platforms. Instead, they will be transformed into interactive visual aids, timelines, and predictive models, allowing clinicians and patients to assess the health courses and effects of interventions [4, 5].

1.2 Evolution of RPM

Patient follow up outside the clinical setting is not a recent development, but as time has changed, its method and advanced levels have changed tremendously. The early systems of RPM were characterized by many constraints in terms of telephonic follow-ups and intermittent transmission of manually digitized measurements. These systems were mostly involved in post-operational treatments and general chronic illness management, and provided limited real-time information [6].

The establishment of digital sensors and wireless communication technologies became a turning point. The ability to record physiological data frequently and reliably (through portable devices) was realized. Mobile health (mHealth) applications continued to open the door to RPM by using smartphones as a means of data aggregation and delivery.

Then, RPM was turned into data-driven and scalable ecosystems by cloud computing and Internet of Things (IoT) architecture. Wearable devices now could store, process, and analyse continuous data in real time. The use of machine learning (ML) algorithms had started receiving the primary role in anomaly detection, adverse events prediction preclusion, and the stratification of the risk of patients [7].

In more recent times, RPM is now not only reactive but also rather proactive and predictive care model. AI-driven systems currently acquire individual baseline patterns and change the monitoring strategies. This development justifies early intervention, individual treatment planning, and health management on population levels [8].

1.3 Emergence of Immersive Health Platforms

Immersive health platforms have appeared as a reaction to the increased complexity and amount of care data produced by the system of constant monitoring. The conventional two-dimensional interface may frequently be ineffective in presenting the multidimensional health data, and cognitive overload as well as omitted clinical information will ensue. Immersive technologies overcome this limitation through the possibility to visualize spatial, interactive, and experience data.

The VR and AR technologies enable clinicians to investigate patient data in simulated settings, where time variations, associations, and forecasting results may be intuitively studied. As an illustration, longitudinal RPM data may be displayed as changing physiological landscapes and allow finding trends and anomalies in a short time. This may be of special use in the treatment of multi-parameter, complex conditions.

Immersive platforms improve engagement and health literacy for the patient. Patients are able to communicate with customized avatars, visualize the effect of lifestyle change, and engage in virtual consultations which generate a sense of presence and relatedness. The experiential style has been demonstrated to enhance the compliance to treatment regimens and self-management practices.

These capabilities are further expanded through the introduction of metaverse-based healthcare environments, which facilitate a virtual environment of persistent and shared space. In this case, clinicians, patients, and caregivers will be in a position to collaborate in real time regardless of geographical boundaries. With wearable AI and RPM systems, immersive platforms would provide an easy transition between the physical and the digital world of healthcare sector which shifts under predictive, preventive, and participation systems. The ability to put RPM data in contexts related to interactive systems is one of the enabling agents of next-generation healthcare systems, which are patient-centric.

2. Nitty-gritties of RPM

Remote patient monitoring is a total transformation of the model of healthcare services delivery, where the episodic and facility-digitalized model of care provision gives way to the patient-centred and round-the-clock care provision. The immersive health platform grounded on AI and metaverse technologies uses RPM as a basis of real-time clinical decision-making, proactive disease management, and personalized interventions. The section addresses building blocks, operations, and data forms, which are the components of the RPM systems, and how they could be leveraged to contribute to the next-generation immersive healthcare ecosystems.

2.1 Definition and Scope of RPM

Remote patient monitoring refers to a systematic collection, transmission, estimation, and clinical translation of patient-generated health data in atypical clinical contexts. Unlike the traditional telemedicine where virtual consultations are given the reign of authority, RPM is coverage that spans across the preventive, chronic disease care, post-operative care, geriatric care, mental health assessment, and rehabilitation care.

Combining AI in wearables with immersive platforms makes RPM more than the active work of data collection in order to support contextual, responsive, and predictive health services. RPM data do not appear in immersive health ecosystem only, but are rather embedded in VR or AR in order to give clinicians and patients the perception of the physiological conditions in a manner that is intuitive and meaningful. Moreover, RPM enables population analyses alongside maintaining personalized care directions, thereby being a scalable solution to the challenges of modern healthcare systems, including workforce shortages and an increase in the number of chronic diseases.

2.2 Key Components of RPM

The components of an RPM system are interdependent and guarantee the reliable data acquisition, safe communication, intelligent analysis, and feedback that can be taken into action, as represented in Figure 6.1. Body-worn or ambient sensors used in sensing and wearable devices can be used to measure physiological and behavioural parameters. Current developments in miniaturization and wearable AI enable the devices to take the form of continuous operations devices that are also conducive and compliant to the user. Data obtained are exchanged using wireless communication devices [Bluetooth Low Energy (BLE), Wi-Fi, or cellular networks]. Data transmission layer guarantees the provision of timely and continuous data flow in the patient environment to the backend systems. Health data volumes on time-series are stored on cloud-based infrastructures. Data integrity and confidentiality require the use of secure storage systems, encryption systems, and adherence to standards of healthcare data.

The ML models are utilized to process incoming data to reveal anomalies/predict health risks and provide clinically relevant insights. AI-generated signals can be converted into real-time visual information or prompts in virtual settings in immersive platforms. RPM insights are made available to healthcare providers using dashboards, decision-support systems, or immersive interfaces. Feedback to patients is delivered as a mobile app, wearable display, or virtual coaching avatars, and this bridges the gap between monitoring and intervention.

2.3 Architecture of RPM Systems

An RPM system has an architecture that is designed to be scaled, interoperable, and resilient through a layered and modular design. Perception layer is made up of the sensors and wearable devices that record the raw messages of physiology and behaviour. To increase data reliability and minimize noise, sensor fusion techniques are commonly used. Communication layer allows transfer of data between the patient and the backend systems. It integrates network management, latency optimization, and fault tolerance features, which are especially important when managing real-time monitoring applications. Processing and intelligence layer involves preprocessing and normalizing raw data and analysing them with the help of AI algorithms. At this stage, feature extraction, pattern recognition, and predictive modelling are done. In high-level architectures, edge computing is used to do the initial analysis nearer to the source of data and this slows down the latency and bandwidth consumption. Application and visualization layer is the one

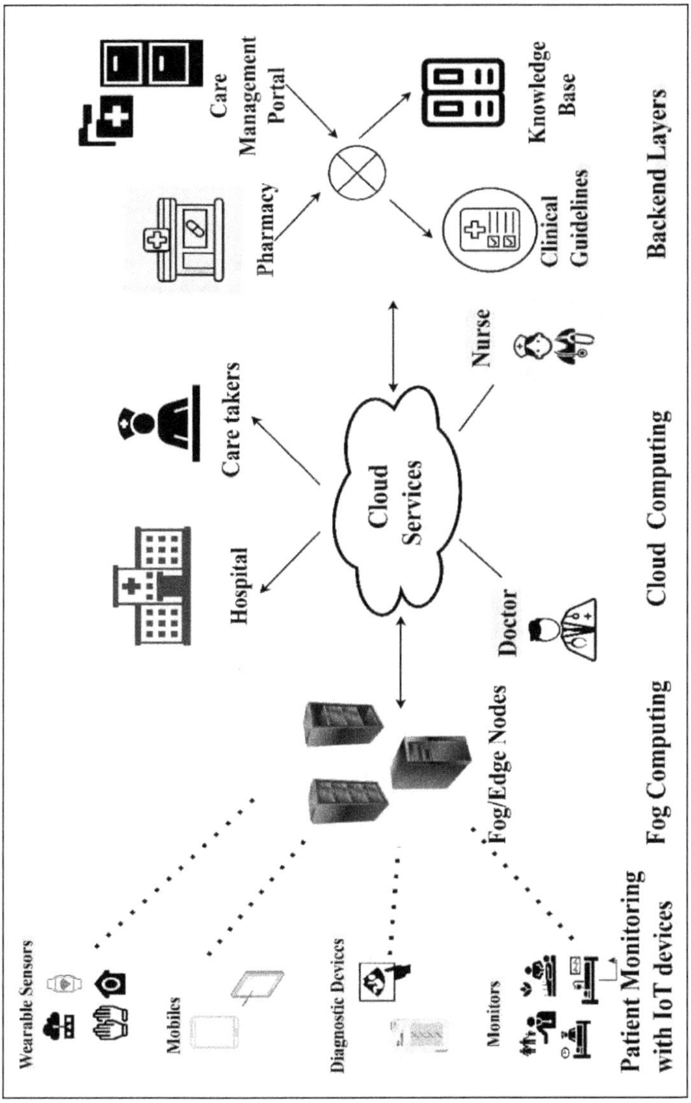

Fig. 6.1 Components of RPM.

that will offer the user-facing application to the clinicians and patients. It consists of virtual dashboards, digital twins, and 3D health visualizations in metaverse environments in immersive health settings that enable more effective situational awareness and clinical comprehension.

2.4 Types of Physiological and Behavioural Data in RPM

The RPM systems process a wide range of data that would deliver the comprehensive picture of patient health.

2.4.1 Physiological Data

Physiological responses are signs of the bodily internal activity and are used significantly during the clinical assessment. The numerous regularly measured data include cardiovascular parameters such as heart rate, heart rate variability, and blood pressure; respiratory parameters such as breathing rate and oxygen saturation; metabolic parameters such as the glucose concentration and body temperature; neurological parameters, with the help of the electroencephalography (EEG) or the movement patterns. All these data streams would be helpful to identify clinical deterioration in its early stages and help in the individual treatment plan.

2.4.2 Behavioural Data

Behavioural data will be represented in lifestyle and activity patterns that define the outcome of health. It manifests itself in the intensity of physical work, the state of sleep, the posture, drug adherence, and activities. The contextual information gathered through immersive settings, including spatial movement, patterns of interaction, and cognitive involvement can be combined to augment clinical interpretation. Wearables have accelerometer and gyroscope sensors that can count the number of steps, how intensively the person moves, change in position, and detect falls, which can be used to measure daily activity or motor symptoms in diseases like Parkinson's.

Behavioural markers usually involve sleep duration, sleep stage distribution and disturbances, particularly in chronic and mental health monitoring. The levels of stress, alterations in mood, or cognitive deterioration can be detected as passive sensing based on phone data including mobility patterns, frequencies of phone use, and measure of social interaction. Patient-reported data, including mood scores, pain levels, medication adherence, and quality-of-life questionnaires are some of the examples of RPM studies that enrich behavioural understanding.

Physiological and behavioural data are combined to enable RPM systems to transition to predictive and preventive healthcare, rather than reactive monitoring, which is consistent with the overall vision of AI-based immersive health platforms based on wearables.

3. Immersive Health Platforms: A Recapitulation

Immersive health technologies are a combination of advanced digital environments and healthcare services that are used to improve the care, education, and monitoring of patients. They make use of the VR, AR, MR, and extended reality (XR) technologies in order to develop interactive, engaging, and realistic simulations or perspectives on patient data and healthcare situations. When combined with RPM systems, immersive technologies can have a considerable positive impact on clinicians watching, evaluating, and communicating with patients beyond conventional clinical environments.

3.1 Concept of Immersive Technologies

Immersive systems can allow clinicians to view patient data in 3-D formats or engage with the virtual environment of a realistic simulation of a clinical situation. As an example, vital sign or imaging outcome overlay on an AR interface can enhance remote decision-making and clinician awareness without the need to visit patients in person. Patients participate in guided rehabilitation exercises, while the RPM program supports and monitors the rehabilitation process or therapeutic routines. These environments have the capability to modify levels of difficulty, give real-time feedback, and motivate the patients more than traditional screens or wearable dashboards. Immersive platforms are used to help patients in the self-management of their conditions through the provision of interactive educational programmes, simulated physiological experiences, or virtualized medication compliance instructions. The tools enhance comprehension, active participation, and adherence to chronic condition monitoring in the long term. Immersive tools can be used by caregivers and other healthcare teams engaged in RPM to train remotely on either procedural skills, emergency scenarios, or handling patients. This is particularly applicable to the case of decentralized healthcare based on RPM data and digital diagnostics. Immersive health solutions are best used along with the Internet of Medical Things (IoMT) devices, edge computing, AI and secure data frameworks like blockchain. These integrations can be real-time data streaming, contextual visualization, and safe distance interaction enabling safe, accurate, and fast RPM care.

3.2 Virtual Reality, Augmented Reality, and Mixed Reality

Virtual Reality is an immersive technology that places the user in a completely digital setting where there is a limited knowledge among real-world awareness. VR is widely used in training and therapeutic stimulus, with the assistance of the Head Mounted Displays (HMDs) and spatial audio, it offers an interactive simulated environment that enables the establishment of experiential engagement and training.

The AR is the overlay of the real world with the digital information which is not replacing the view of the user but integrating it. AR systems are based on smartphones, tablets, or smart glasses that display visual, audio, or haptic contextual data in line with the environment. To give an example, wearable biosensors experiencing live data about heart rate, blood pressure, or glucose level could be made available to AR interfaces to enhance the understanding of physiological conditions between clinician and patients (e.g., to plot trends onto a body image of a patient, which can be seen through AR glasses). This integration creates a hybrid framework that combines physiological data with immersive visualization, representing an emerging area of research.

Mixed reality is a combination of VR and AR, and is able to have both digital and real objects co-exist and interact in real time. In MR, virtual objects are spatially anchored to the real-world environment, enabling context-aware interaction between users and both physical and digital elements: such as the use of holographic glasses. VR, AR, and MR are changing the interface between the human body, data, and digital experiences. The comparison of VR, AR, and MR in healthcare and remote monitoring is depicted in Table 6.1. These immersive technologies can expand receiving care to the edge of wearables and remote treatment, to augmenting surgical education and patient education, to mesh with digital technologies.

As connected care increasingly develops, starting with the innovations in sensors, machine learning, and real-time data processing, XR is becoming a component of healthcare ecosystems in the future, affecting how clinicians and patients interact with health data and environments.

Table 6.1 Comparison of VR, AR, and MR in healthcare and remote monitoring.

Aspect	*Virtual Reality (VR)*	*Augmented Reality (AR)*	*Mixed Reality (MR)*
Concept	Replaces the real world with an entirely computer-generated environment	Enhances the view of the real world by adding digital components	Integrates the real and virtual worlds to enable dynamic interaction between them
Interaction with Physical World	No direct interaction with real objects	Minimum interaction; digital overlays are aligned with real-world scenes	Robust interaction; virtual objects react to and anchor to real-world spaces
Typical Hardware	Head-mounted displays with motion tracking and spatial audio	Smartphones, tablets, smart glasses	Advanced headsets with spatial mapping and environmental sensing
Example use case	Virtual rehabilitation programmes or exposure therapy	Visualizing heart rate or glucose trends directly on the patient's body	Virtually guiding a patient during physical tasks
Immersion Level	Very high immersion	Low to moderate immersion	Moderate to high immersion with environmental awareness

3.3 Role of Digital Twins in Healthcare

In medical care, a digital twin can be defined as a dynamic digital model of a particular patient or clinical system that integrates real-time measurements of sensors, wearables, medical imaging, genomics, and electronic health records (EHRs). It offers virtual models on which clinicians can recreate diagnostic scenarios and treatment choices without exposing patients to harm. The digital twins offer multi-modal data including genetic profiles, imaging, and wearable real-time data, which allows clinicians to predict what the patient will do upon treatment, as well as its efficacy, side effects, and optimal dose. In the case of chronic illnesses, such as diabetes or cardiovascular disease, the model of a digital twin can be used to recreate dynamic changes in the state of glucose or the hemodynamic variables in response to additional medication or diet or to changes in activity, and to make comparable predictions ahead of time, before the disease progresses. The unification of EHRs, IoT sensors, imaging systems, and genomic platforms in heterogeneous data streams is complicated. In the absence of the process of the coordinated exchange of data, twin models can be incomplete or false. Digital twins work with sensitive personal data on health. Strong data governance, encryption, and access controls will be important in ensuring confidentiality and patient autonomy. The explainable AI and inter-platform advances will be critical to implement the digital twin application responsibly in clinical settings.

4. Integration of RPM with Immersive Technologies

In the past, RPM has been based on wearable devices, mobile applications, and telemetric monitoring to record vital signs, patient-reported outcomes, and physiological trends, thus increasing continuity of care and patient autonomy. Simultaneously, VR, AR, and XR become an increasingly popular aspect of immersive technologies in healthcare due to their applications in the field of rehabilitation, training clinicians, engaging patients, and conducting behavioural therapy. Immersive technologies can also be applied in transforming patient monitoring, when combined with RPM, into an active, interactive interface to healthcare. When combined with RPM sensor data, AR/VR systems, in the context of post–acute care or physical rehabilitation, offer real-time feedback of an adaptive nature with respect to the movement, posture, or gait. This will enable clinicians to remotely adjust the therapy regimens and patients will undergo immersive visual directions, resulting in more accurate rehabilitation outcomes.

4.1 System Architecture and Workflow

An ideal process of system workflow of RPM integrated with immersive technology can be simplified into four significant steps.

Data Capture and Transmission: Wearable sensors and IoMT devices constantly track the symptoms of physiological indicators and context (e.g., activity levels, vital signs) on the site of the patient. They are QoS-enabled wireless infrastructure

(Bluetooth, Wi-Fi, cellular) to communicate information to the intermediate gateways or local hubs safely and then relay it to cloud/edge servers [9].

Data Mining and Preparation: The gateway devices process and store the received information prior and after, which they pass to cloud/edge servers. Cloud networks can offer storage that is scalable, but edge compute units provide the ability to run low-latency analytics in cases where time is critical. The more advanced processing tiers comprise AI/ML models—predictive analytics, anomaly detectors, etc.—to consider risk profiles and deliver actionable information. False alarms are also minimized by the integration of AI, and the clinically significant trends are easier to notice, which reduces the burden on clinicians.

Clinical Integration and Interface Augmentation: Processed data is provided on clinical portals, mobile apps, and immersive interfaces. The clinicians can achieve communication with patient portfolio in VR/AR space or two-dimensional screens. Immersive workflows could offer 3D displays of patient wellness patterns, even distant physical therapy, or modelling care experiences, offering more rigorous patient–clinician interaction [10].

Feedback and Intervention Delivery: The system provides patients with feedback, alerts, personalized recommendations, and immersive therapy modules. This feedback can be provided in immersive systems either in the form of VR sessions to rehabilitate patients or as AR overlay that can take the patients through therapeutic activities at home. In addition to monitoring, this bidirectional loop also assists in virtual execution of treatment, enhancing the interests and adherence of patients.

4.2 Data Acquisition, Transmission, and Visualization

Acquisition of various health signals is the central point of RPM. The data are recorded using a variety of wearable devices in the form of physiological sensors (heart rate, activity, respiration), smart phones which capture behavioural metrics, and new biosensors which extract digital biomarkers synonymous with health conditions (pattern of movement or sleep) [11, 12].

The most useful type of digital biomarkers, i.e., quantifiable behavioural or physiological data gathered using digital devices, are especially helpful in passive monitoring (e.g., mobility patterns, circadian rhythms, speech markers) [9]. After capturing health data, they should be reliably and securely delivered to endpoints at remote servers or clinicians. Current RPM systems utilize wireless networks like Wi-Fi, cellular, and Bluetooth to provide real-time information of patient devices to cloud-based repositories or fog/edge computing layers that process information prior to full uploading. Raw data as it comes in at remote servers needs processing and contextualization. Layers of analytics purify, partition, and decipher streams of data to identify significant trends or signal notifications. More sophisticated systems are frequently based on machine learning to identify an anomaly, anticipate risk, and rank clinical interventions. The results of these analyses are later inputted into visualization systems to support operating processes as well as clinical logic.

The last layer is the interpretation which is known as visualization which converts complex data into actionable data for the users. Traditional RPM dashboard offers trends, alerts, and status of measurements represented in line charts, heatmaps, and colour-coded indicators. Immersive virtual reality (IVR) environments have also been investigated in Journal of the American Medical Informatics Association (JAMIA) research as environments in which users can be provided with the opportunity to interactively explore dense landscapes of health information, which can help in self-management of care [13].

4.3 Real-Time Monitoring and Feedback Mechanisms

Heart rate, blood pressure, and oxygen saturation are some of the signals that are collected by biosensors on wearable devices in advanced RPM systems. Such physiological inputs are sent to networked systems, typically, with the help of IoT, edge computing, or cloud computing to guarantee low-latency data exchange [14]. Real-time monitoring implies that clinicians and computerized systems are able to identify variations in health metrics in real time, instead of periodically (i.e., checking in), and this is essentially what widens the scope of early warnings on the worsening of the state.

Notably, it is not only the clinicians who can receive real-time feedback of an intervention. Unlike conventional RPM systems, new products provide immediate feedback to the patient. An AR system can be used a guide in the rehabilitation setting by having the user follow a given exercise with real-time performance statistics and corrective feedback based on sensor data. VR platforms also can give instantly relevant prompts in contexts where physiological limits are exceeded, reminding users to follow the therapeutic regimen or encouraging them to seek medical assistance. The timely clinical decision-making, personalized care, and health outcomes of the chronic conditions or postoperative care and preventive healthcare management are enhanced, and patient self-management practices are reinforced with the help of the amalgamation of the real-time data streams and communicative technologies of the interactive character. The wearable tools like smart watches or arrays of biosensor units are employed to monitor physiologic signals and transmit the data through wireless networks. Such sensors enable constant measurements of the health parameters when engaging in daily activities. Such sensors are also connected to the IoT platforms that are then connected to cloud services that then store their data, process them, and make them available to the healthcare practitioners on-the-fly. The real-time health information that has been previously collected and relayed to the subjects must be processed to meaningful outputs. Real-time monitoring systems take advantage of edge processing to perform real-time processing near the sensor, whereas cloud analytics can aggregate and attach more longitudinal trends. Pattern classification and anomaly detection (e.g., arrhythmias or signs of early heart failure) are done faster than traditional rule-based systems with advanced algorithms, which aid in predictive and proactive care. To promote adherence and self-management, feedback is provided to patients directly by smart devices: (i) visual displays with daily trends; (ii) text or application notifications about the abnormal readings; (iii) individualized instructions on how to change medications or modify activities [15, 16].

These direct feedback mechanisms enhance the interaction and also give patients more power to take charge of their health. Team-based dashboards facilitate real-time data access, trend visualization, and instant messaging among healthcare providers. Shared virtual clinical rooms enable physicians to guide patients through visualized health data and remote consultations.

5. Wearable and Sensor Technologies for Immersive RPM

Wearable sensors are small electronic gadgets that are fastened by the user to their body or clothing to constantly measure physiological signals. These are photoplethysmography (PPG) of heart rate, accelerometers of motion, electrocardiography (ECG) patches of cardiac monitoring, and biochemical sensors of glucose or sweat.

5.1 Wearable Sensors and IoT Devices

The key components include Wireless Body Area Networks (WBANs) as shown in Figure 6.2, where the multiple connected sensors form a network around the body that synchronizes measurements and reduces latencies in communication. Wireless connectivity that includes Bluetooth Low Energy (BLE), Wi-Fi, and cellular links enables seamless data transfer from wearables to processing systems and the IoT architectures that consist of the components of local edge computing filter sensor data and reduce noise before transmitting data to save bandwidth and battery life. Recent reviews emphasize the fact that IoT wearables are needed in order to have continuous and long-term monitoring of health parameters like heart diseases, breathing patterns, movement disorders, and metabolic changes [17].

Computer-based machine intelligence trained using this type of data is able to identify trends that are not easily visible and forecast negative occurrences in advance compared to the limited nature of clinical visits. Although technology has improved, there are still issues such as striking a balance between energy use and sensing as well as user comfort, among other concerns, to deploy the technology sustainably in a real-life healthcare setting.

5.2 Smart Implants and Ambient Sensors

Smart implants are futuristic biomedical instruments that can be implanted within the body in order to record key physiological indicators at the location. In contrast to external wearables, implants have high fidelity to deep tissue signals, including intracardiac electrical activity or neurochemical concentrations.

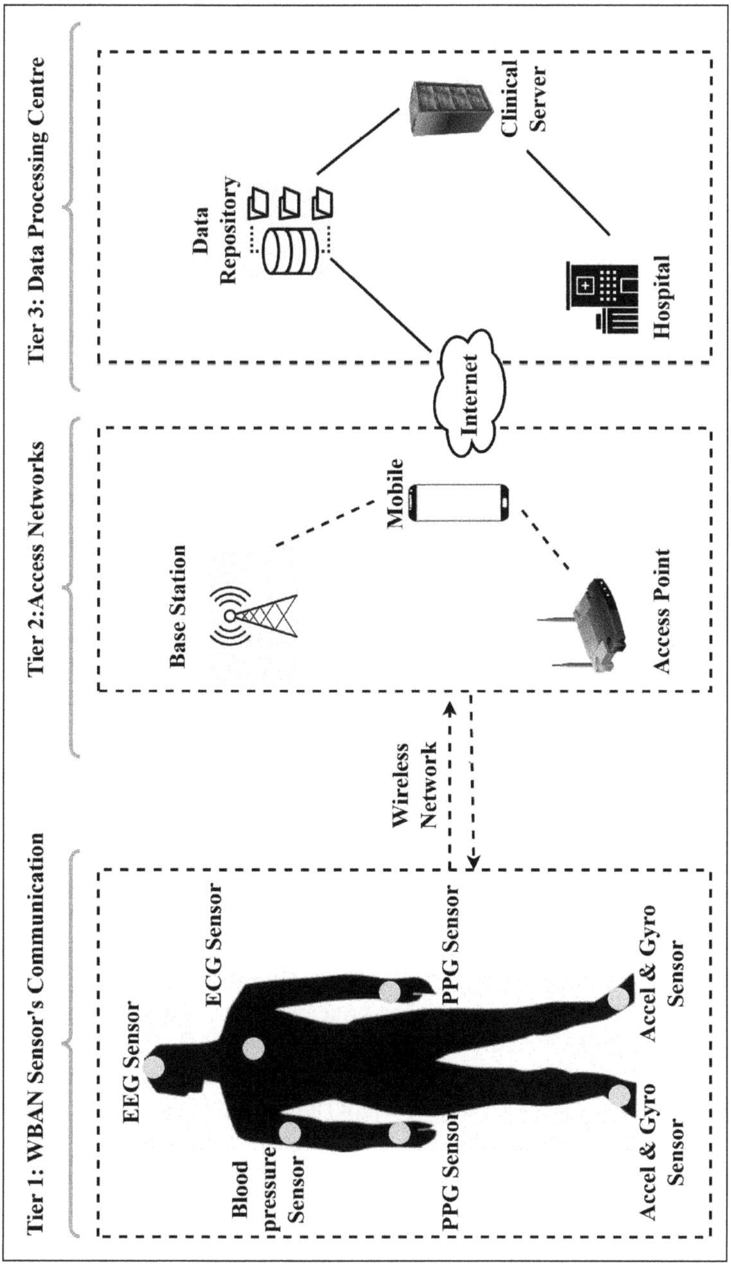

Fig. 6.2 Structural overview of a Wireless Body Area Network (WBAN).

Examples are a pacemaker with sensing abilities and biosensors-enabled implants that identify warning signs of inflammation or metabolic imbalance. The 2022 book *Nanosensors for Futuristic Smart and Intelligent Healthcare Systems* explains that implantable sensors take advantage of miniaturized nanomaterials to provide increased sensitivity in cellular terms and have the ability to work synergistically with wearables to provide comprehensive insights into patients [18].

5.2.1 Ambient Sensors

Environmental sensors or ambient sensors are sensors that are positioned in the living or clinical area of the patient. They track the context-related parameters which include temperature, humidity, air quality, motion, and occupancy patterns, which can affect the health status or warn about the risk of falls among the elderly people.

The RPM systems are augmented with ambient sensor frameworks that work by putting physiological data into perspective (e.g., relating heart rate variability to room temperature variations); identifying environmental health hazards (e.g., poor air quality causing respiratory problems); and promoting assistive living–related applications with the help of pattern recognition (e.g., gait tracking as a mobility assessment).

5.3 Interoperability and Standards

With the spread of sensor technologies, it is important to make sure that the data flows smoothly among devices, platforms, and care systems. Interoperability allows: (i) uniform information transfer among wearables, implants, ambient systems, and health records; (ii) integrated understanding of health indicators in all clinical tools and analytics platforms; (iii) lower integration cost and complexities of implementation by healthcare providers [19].

5.3.1 Standards and Protocols

Health devices are required to adhere to the ISO/IEEE 11073 family of communication standards in order to exchange vital sign data safely and to interoperatively implement heterogeneous systems. The H.810 Connected Health Recommendation on connected health devices defines the principles of design and interoperability standards to facilitate the personal health systems and device connection. The Electronic Medical Records (EMR) integration interfacing standards like Fast Healthcare Interoperability Resources (FHIR) are now being used more frequently to mediate wearable and sensor information into clinical health records to provide longitudinal tracking of patients and support decision-making.

6. Data Analytics—Security, Privacy, and Challenges

The use of data analytics continues to spur decision-making, predictive modelling, and contextual awareness, but all these faculties present distinct challenges that must be considered with due caution in terms of technical, ethical, and organizational aspects of these tools.

6.1 Big Data Management and Cloud-Edge Computing

The intersection of the big data analytics with cloud and edge computing paradigms has transformed the manner in which large-scale data are processed and consumed. Conventional centralized cloud technologies provide storage scalability and high-performance analytics capabilities, yet may cause latency, bandwidth constraints, and system failure points.

Practically, hybrid cloud–edge designs intelligently distribute computing loads: operations that are sensitive to latency are run at the edge whereas long-term storage and sophisticated analytics are restricted to cloud platforms. Nevertheless, the control of data consistency, synchronization, and resource distribution among the heterogeneous nodes is still technically complicated [20].

6.2 Artificial Intelligence and Machine Learning Techniques

New enablers of data analytics are AI and ML. Such methods are the basis of classification, grouping, anomalies, and prediction modelling in industries. The latest progress in the field of deep learning models in the form of transformer-based frameworks and graph neural networks has enhanced the possibility to extract meaningful patterns in large data streams with high dimensions. ML algorithms help in early identification of health deviations and response systems in remote patient monitoring.

In spite of the power, AI/ML models have been challenged by interpretability, can be affected by noisy data, and are vulnerable to adversarial manipulation. The reason is that the black box nature of most sophisticated algorithms makes it difficult to comply with regulation and clinical trust, which has led to the exploration of explainable AI (XAI) techniques. Moreover, lightweight models and the optimization of computation and memory footprint are needed to have the real-time deployment on resource-limited edge devices [21].

6.3 Data Security and Privacy Preservation

Sensitive data protection is also a core component of an analytics ecosystem that manipulates personal, financial, or health data. Data security involves confidentiality, integrity, and availability which guarantee that unauthorized access is avoided, data is not modified, and the services are still available even under attack. Minimum measures include encryption, well-developed authentication protocols, and access control policies [22].

Security is not limited to privacy preservation, which is to make sure that the identity and other sensitive features of individuals are not compromised even in the case of aggregation of data to aid analytics. Differential privacy, homomorphic encryption, and secure multi-party computation are some of the techniques that are currently being developed to enable the computation on encrypted data without disclosing raw records. Privacy risks in healthcare and remote monitoring are increased because data streams are continuous and they can be re-identified by matching with auxiliary datasets.

6.4 Ethical Issues in Immersive Remote Monitoring

Immersive remote care like constant monitoring of physiological activities or behaviour patterns provides new possibilities of personalized care and operational efficiency. At the same time, it also introduces the ethical aspects related to autonomy, informed consent, and surveillance. While constant surveillance offers advantages, it may also raise concerns regarding invasive monitoring, especially when the users do not know how their information will be accessed or what conclusions will be made and who will have access to this information. The moral theories ought to be directed on transparency, agency among the users and proportions: users want to be aware of how the information is being collected, how inferences will be made, and with whom will such information be discussed. Also, the use of analytics systems should be guided by the importance of fairness and non-discrimination, which implies that automated judgment processing should not inevitably promote discrimination and victimize vulnerable groups [23].

6.5 Technical and Infrastructure Challenges

A large-scale deployment of data analytics indicates certain technical and infrastructure difficulties. The heterogeneity of devices, communication protocols, and data formats makes interoperability a challenge. Edge devices tend to possess a smaller number of computational resources, and are forced to compromise between hard work in analytics and power constraints. It can result in the blockage of the data flow (through unstable networks, particularly in remote ones or poorly resourced ones), thus causing incomplete or delayed insights. Scalable infrastructure must also include a competent fault tolerance strategy to address node failure, data corruption, or cyberattacks. The architectural designs that enhance resilience are some of the containerization, microservices, and software-defined networking which require proper configuration and maintenance. Finally, seamless integration with the previous systems is a pervasive issue, and there is a necessity to have flexible middleware systems that have the ability to bridge the past technology stack and the current technology stack.

6.6 Cost, Scalability, and Sustainability Issues

The advanced analytics systems are not free of cost despite the value they provide. The preliminary cost of equipment, software licence, and expert staffing may be high. The cloud services also effuse certain costs in the form of pay-as-you-go models; however, data egress charges, storage charges, and computation charges might mount up quickly with large datasets and high-frequency analytics.

Scalability shall be attained without growth in cost, which is linear. This will require the efficient consumption of compute resources, including elastic scaling, serverless functions, and model compression methods. In addition to the economic cost, sustainability-related issues are also increasing: the large-scale analytics and AI training require a lot of energy, which adds to environmental footprint. Green computing practices, energy-sensitive scheduling, hardware acceleration, and energy consciousness are essential towards long-term sustainability.

7. User Experience and Human–Computer Interaction

Human–computer interaction (HCI) is a critical component of the current healthcare technologies as it determines the experience and use of the systems by their users, whether patients or clinicians. When interacting with immersive and complex environments, e.g., in XR or analytics dashboards, user experience (UX) is as important as algorithms behind the scenes. High HCI concentration guarantees that the digital health tools are user-friendly, effective, and human cognition–informed, thus enhancing the adoption and results. Studies in the field have continued to increase tremendously, and they have identified trends, challenges, and evidence-based practices to design on behalf of the user in the healthcare settings.

7.1 Patient-Centred Design in Immersive Environments

Patient-centred design places needs, behaviours, and experience of the patients at the centre of the system development as opposed to focusing on technical features alone. This philosophy of design is based on empathy, access as well as meaningful interaction to ensure that immersive environments such as VR, AR, or sensor-based interface in reality facilitate patient interaction and well-being.

Contrary to conventional interfaces which consider the data in a tabular or textual form, immersive environments can provide information in a three-dimensional and interactive representation in which the patient can be more interactive with their health information. As an example, a VR within the framework of home care or rehabilitation can give contextual information closer to the experience of its users and it can help them perceive intricate health-related information in a more instinctive manner. This has further been shown to happen when nurses and other professionals in the field play a role in the task of defining design requirements as far as immersive patient environments are concerned where the resulting systems are less realistic in user requirements and more rewarding in user feedback during the evaluation process itself.

A patient-centred approach to design is generally characterized by the repeated use of user research, prototyping, and user testing to make sure that design choices are constantly tested against user expectations. The benefits of patient-centred care approach are illustrated in Figure 6.3. It especially needs to be done among older adults or digitally illiterate people; in this case, simplicity, transparency, and clarity are key. Methods such as contextual inquiry and co-design workshops help uncover patients' nuanced preferences, emotional responses, and concerns related to cognitive load—issues that might otherwise go unnoticed.

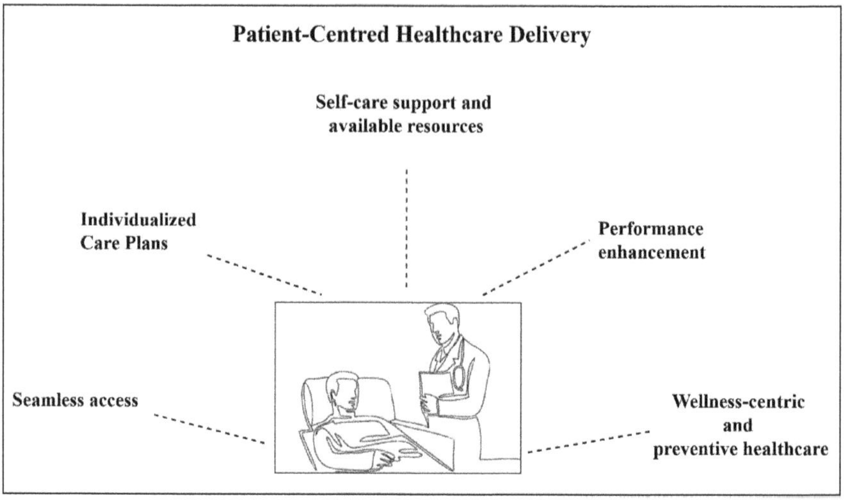

Fig. 6.3 Overview of patient-centric care benefits.

In addition, the immersive systems should be capable of providing useful feedback and control to users—information they ought to receive includes what the technology is doing with their data, what interactions do and should control the output, and how system failures or performance issues can be identified and resolved. This openness will generate confidence and foster an investment that is necessary in the long-run usage of interventions.

7.2 Clinician Interfaces and Visualization Dashboards

The data streams of the modern health analytics tools are based on the clinician interface and visualization dashboard that links the complicated data streams to clinical actionable information. Unlike ordinary consumer-based software, clinician dashboards ought to be capable of displaying intensive information concisely as well as allow a rapid decision-making process in a time-pressured clinical environment. High-quality interface design has a direct conversion to the skills of clinicians with respect to patient-data interpretation, prioritizing actions, and coordinating care activities. Powerful dashboards are the involvement of understanding, relevancy, and awareness. Instead of having the raw numbers with overwhelmed clinicians, they package them into curated summaries and trend lines, which provide meaningful trends with time passage. Through experiments with clinicians as participants in the process of designing dashboard prototypes, it has been revealed that visual representations (as consolidated daily trends relative to raw data) are far more understandable and satisfactory.

The key design principles of clinician interface are:
Prioritization of relevant insight: Clinicians would desire dashboards on the clinically important thresholds and trends rather that enjoy big volumes of raw data. This will reduce the load on the mind and help to make quick decisions.

Personalized visual metaphor: Well-known visual representations such as line charts, colour-coded status indicators, and comparative graphs would play a useful role in helping the clinicians to quickly assess the status of patients. Its legends and annotations too enhance clarity without the need of going through a long training.

Controllability and customization: The adaptability of the tool to different clinical settings (e.g., ICU, outpatient settings) can be good through the application of dashboards allowing clinicians to filter data, set a time range, and create views.

Health systems research too contentiously brings to the fore that health information dashboards being built improperly will inadvertently result in the aggravation or inaccuracy of a healthcare professional. The adequate interface designed according to the principles of HCI can not only increase usability but also the apparent security or the quality of the care outcomes.

8. Applications and Use Cases

Currently, analytics, digital health systems, and immersion-based monitoring systems are ready enough to be a possible solution to the process of delivering care to a large population. The research has been applied in the field of clinical and community practices, where they make a difference in enhancing better outcomes, reducing caregiver burdens, as well as offering remote and personalized support.

8.1 Elderly Care and Assisted Living

The assistance to aging individuals to enable them to live as independent and healthy citizens is one of the basic applications of digital technologies. The sensor networks, wearable devices, and AI-powered analytics observations of vital signs, mobility, and daily routine are introduced to the assisted living and independent home setting to eliminate such abnormalities as falls, abnormal gait, or aberrant behavioural patterns. The caregivers and clinicians receive the alerts and longitudinal trends through the systems which assist them in preventative care and timely intervention. Constant monitoring can improve the safety and confidence of adults. In addition, full-fledged smart home environments use the Internet of Medical Things (IoMT) to enable real-time environmental control, continuous data monitoring, and rapid response to emergencies. These systems (along with predictive analytics) help predict a decline in health before clinical incidents occur. Additionally, the studies imply the significance of such assistive devices as social robots, voice assistants, and interactive electronic companions to reduce the isolation of elderly population and enhance their psychological comfort.

8.2 Rehabilitation and Mental Health Monitoring

One such shifting directions is rehabilitation and mental health where the impact of the digital solutions is quantifiable. It is possible to employ wearables, computer vision, and AI to assist in physical rehabilitation by tracking the movement of the patient, compliance during the exercising process, and bio-mechanical data of recovery. These systems create feedback mechanisms that complement other current therapies, enable clinicians to customize interventions, and self-programme them through self-monitoring. New platforms combine imperative information and neural networks to evaluate the performance and dynamically change difficulty levels.

Mental health mobile apps, telepsychiatry, and digital therapeutics bring care out of the clinic. Scalable support interventions, including tools with cognitive-behavioural exercises, mood tracking, or chatbots, provide support in case of anxiety, depression, and early cognitive change. Systematic reviews suggest that digital mental health apps have the potential to provide more nursing care and improve therapy engagement; however, the results provide evidence of the need to develop robust design and data privacy measures, and incorporate them into workflows.

8.3 Postoperative and Home-based Care

The common practice of postoperative care has been based on the routine follow-up visits and physical assessments which might not spot the complications or factors delaying recovery. Electronic health programmes such as smart phone–based monitoring systems and home-based communication systems are associated with effective and continuous measurement of pain, healing, functional mobility, and self-reported outcomes. Clinical trials prove that mobile apps can enhance quality of recovery and enable early identification of complications after surgery in comparison with the standard care routes.

The digital health interventions that include home-based, structured systems, telerehabilitation, clinician feedback loop, and educational support programmes can improve the outcomes of functional recovery and independence among older adults who have undergone surgery, including hip fracture repair. Meta-analytic data demonstrates a substantial enhancement in the mobility and performance of daily activities with the implementation of such interventions that are smooth during post-discharge treatments.

9. Future Trends and Research Directions

The future trends show that the upcoming wave of digital health system will be more personalized, multi-modal, predictive, and ethically cognizant.

- **Predictive and Personalized Analytics**
In addition to descriptive surveillance, the modern machine learning and AI algorithms should be able to foresee health events and tailor care recommendations in accordance with one's unique biological, behavioural, and environmental data. Such models will progressively highlight the social determinants of health in order to finetune predictions of various populations.

- **Multi-modal and Context-Aware Systems**
The next platforms will combine various streams of data—physiological markers and activity patterns, indicators of mental condition, and environmental situations—in order to create more appropriate models of health condition and risk. These multi-modal architectures would be more instrumental in understanding the inter-relationship between physical and mental health, especially in chronic conditions and rehabilitation efforts.

- **Inclusive Usability and Accessibility**
The studies on the design of digital health will focus on supporting older adults, neurodiverse people, and persons with sensory impairment. Participatory design and adaptive utility attempt to decrease the obstacles to technology adoption and improve interaction by adapting modalities of interaction to user inclinations.

- **Ethical AI and Data Governance**
The explainability, accountability, and the transparency models in AI will be highly important since they will perform more functions in supporting decisions. The technologies that they regulate should also vary and so should data sharing, consent control, and fair access strategies.

- **Integration with Healthcare Systems**
Being closely interoperable with electronic health records, clinical decision support tools and care coordination systems will contribute to scalability. Research is likely to support standardized data formats and models that help in providing secure and enlarged information transfer within the care environments.

10. Conclusion

The application of data analytics, immersive monitoring systems, and the availability of digital technologies in healthcare are changing the context of care delivery. These innovations become more effective in such areas as elderly care, rehabilitation, mental health, and postoperative care since they enhance the degree of safety, facilitate independence, and bridge the gaps in traditional care. However, to fully utilize the potential of these technologies, one should consider the importance of attention to usability, an ethical approach to data processing, inclusiveness, and smooth integration of such technologies into the current clinical and caregiving processes. Future research must bring the technological opportunities at the same level as the capabilities offered by humans, taking into consideration the fact that innovations must not be simply technologically sophisticated, but they must also be just and reasonable, available, and supported by solid evidence. With the increasing digitization of healthcare, interdisciplinary collaboration among clinicians, engineers, designers, ethicists, and users would become the key to sustainable and human-centred health systems.

References

[1] Wettstein, R., Sedaghat-Hamedani, F., Heinze, O. et al. (2024). A remote patient monitoring system with feedback mechanisms using a smartwatch: Concept, implementation, and evaluation based on the activeDCM randomized controlled trial. *JMIR mHealth and uHealth*, 12, e58441.

[2] Mann, D.M. and Lawrence, K. (2022). Reimagining connected care in the era of digital medicine. *JMIR mHealth and uHealth*, 10(4), e34483.

[3] Lawrence, K., Singh, N., Jonassen, Z. et al. (2023). Operational implementation of remote patient monitoring within a large ambulatory health system: Multimethod qualitative case study. *JMIR Human Factors*, 10, e45166.

[4] Vallée, A. (2024). Envisioning the future of personalized medicine: Role and realities of digital twins. *Journal of Medical Internet Research*, 26, e50204.

[5] Bouabida, K., Malas, K., Talbot, A. et al. (2022). Healthcare professional perspectives on the use of remote patient-monitoring platforms during the COVID-19 pandemic: A cross-sectional study. *Journal of Personalized Medicine*, 12(4), 529.

[6] El-Rashidy, N., El-Sappagh, S., Islam, S. et al. (2021). Mobile health in remote patient monitoring for chronic diseases: Principles, trends, and challenges. *Diagnostics*, 11(4), 607.

[7] Shah, S.S., Gvozdanovic, A., Knight, M. and Gagnon, J. (2020). Mobile app–based remote patient monitoring in acute medical conditions: Prospective feasibility study exploring digital health solutions on clinical workload during the COVID crisis (Preprint). *JMIR Publications Inc.*

[8] Boikanyo, K., Zungeru, A.M., Sigweni, B., et al. (2023). Remote patient monitoring systems: Applications, architecture, and challenges. *Scientific African*, 20, e01638.

[9] Shaik, T., Tao, X., Higgins, N., Li, L., Gururajan, R., Zhou, X. and Acharya, U.R. (2023). Remote patient monitoring using artificial intelligence: Current state, applications, and challenges. *WIREs Data Mining and Knowledge Discovery*, 13(2), e1485. HYPERLINK "https://doi.org/10.1002/widm.1485?utm_source=chatgpt.com"https://doi.org/10.1002/widm.1485".

[10] Dinh, A., Yin, A.L., Estrin, D., et al. (2023). Augmented reality in real-time telemedicine and telementoring: Scoping review. *JMIR mHealth and uHealth*, 11, e45464.

[11] Arun, S., Sykes, E. R. and Tanbeer, S. (2024). RemoteHealthConnect: Innovating patient monitoring with wearable technology and custom visualization. *Digital Health*, 10, 20552076241300748. https://doi.org/10.1177/20552076241300748.

[12] Annis, T., Pleasants, S., Hultman, G., et al. (2020). Rapid implementation of a COVID-19 remote patient monitoring program. *Journal of the American Medical Informatics Association*, 27(8), 1326–1330.

[13] Shea, S., Weinstock, R.S., Starren, J., et al. (2006). A randomized trial comparing telemedicine case management with usual care in older, ethnically diverse, medically underserved patients with diabetes mellitus. *Journal of the American Medical Informatics Association*, 13(1), 40–51.

[14] Uddin, R. and Koo, I. (2024). Real-time remote patient monitoring: A review of biosensors integrated with multi-hop IoT systems via cloud connectivity. *Applied Sciences*, 14(5), 1876.

[15] Leo, D.G., Buckley, B.J.R., Chowdhury, M., et al. (2022). Interactive remote patient monitoring devices for managing chronic health conditions: Systematic review and meta-analysis. *Journal of Medical Internet Research*, 24(11), e35508.

[16] Seshadri, D.R., Davies, E.V., Harlow, E.R., Hsu, J.J., Knighton, S.C., Walker, T.A., Voos, J.E. and Drummond, C.K. (2020). Wearable sensors for COVID-19: A call to action to harness our

digital infrastructure for remote patient monitoring and virtual assessments. *Frontiers in Digital Health*, 2, 8. https://doi.org/10.3389/fdgth.2020.00008.

[17] Vahdati, M. (Monica), Laamarti, F. and El Saddik, A. (2025). Meta-review of wearable devices for healthcare in the metaverse. *ACM Transactions on Multimedia Computing, Communications, and Applications*, 21(7), 1–36.

[18] Kim, K., Yang, H., Lee, J. and Lee, W.G. (2023). Metaverse wearables for immersive digital healthcare: A review. *Advanced Science*, 10(31), 2303234. https://doi.org/10.1002/advs.202303234.

[19] Huang, G., Chen, X. and Liao, C. (2025). AI-driven wearable bioelectronics in digital healthcare. *Biosensors*, 15(7), 410.

[20] Ashwini, A., Chirchi, V. and Shah, M.A. (2025). Bio inspired optimization techniques for disease detection in deep learning systems. *Scientific Reports*, 15(1), 18202.

[21] Yammouri, G. and Ait Lahcen, A. (2024). AI-reinforced wearable sensors and intelligent point-of-care tests. *Journal of Personalized Medicine*, 14(11), 1088.

[22] Rashid, Z., Folarin, A.A., Zhang, Y., et al. (2024). Digital phenotyping of mental and physical conditions: Remote monitoring of patients through RADAR-base platform. *JMIR Mental Health*, 11, e51259.

[23] Balasubramaniam, S., Kadry, S., Manoj Kumar, T.K. and Kumar, K.S. (Eds.). (2025). *Bio-inspired Algorithms in Machine Learning and Deep Learning for Disease Detection*. CRC Press.

7 AI-Guided Fitness and Wellness in the Metaverse

B. Hariharan[1*], P.G. Om Prakash[2], Mohakk Harshal Malvankar [3], Manoj Jayabalan[4] and Wilfred Blessing N.R.[5]

The fusion of artificial intelligence (AI), wearable technology, and the metaverse is transforming fitness and wellness. However, when combined, these technologies are redefining fitness and wellness to offer a better experience. Indeed, combination of AI and wearable technology has offered smarter guidance and comprehensive wellness experience through virtual or augmented reality. The conventional fitness technology is only concerned with data collection and analysis. In that regard, AI-related wearable technology, along with the metaverse, offers a dynamic, contextual, adaptive, and interactive wellness experience compared to conventional fitness technology. These experiences are also real-time, based on the physiological state, health status, and wellness needs of each individual user. This chapter discusses AI-related models for motion detection, physiological state estimation, affective computing, coaching, digital twins, avatars, and ethical, psychological, and social issues, where AI-related wearable wellness is considered a fundamental part of preventive healthcare within the metaverse.

1. Introduction to AI-Guided Fitness and Wellness

Artificial intelligence (AI)–based fitness and wellness solutions are an intelligent way of improving health wherein AI, in collaboration with wearable technology, helps in continuous monitoring and analysis. Unlike traditional fitness, which is a one-time activity, AI-based wellness solutions consider wearable technology is a long-term adaptive process that changes according to the physiological state, behaviour, and goals of the user. Wearable technology records real-time signals like heart rate activity, movement patterns, sleep quality, and stress levels, which are interpreted by AI algorithms to estimate effort, fatigue, recovery, and well-being, helping in timely interventions [1]. Due to modern lifestyles characterized by irregular schedules, sedentary behaviour, and high stress, AI has helped digital fitness evolve from passive observation to an active wellness companion that helps in long-term health improvement [2].

[1-3] Department of Computational Intelligence, School of Computing, SRM Institute of Science and Technology, Chennai, Tamil Nadu, India.

[4] Bath School of Design, Bath Spa University, Bath, UK.

[5] College of Computing and Information Sciences, University of Technology and Applied Sciences-Ibri, Ibri, Oman.

* Corresponding author: hariharb@srmist.edu.in

DOI: 10.1201/9781003776291-7

Shi et al. [15], for example pointed to edge computing as the part that keeps latency low and processing close to where the data is produced, more or less in real time. Then Kuo [16] talked about how cloud computing can be a game changer for delivering healthcare services at scale, and not only that, it can keep things flexible when demand rises. Botta et al. [17] also showed that once IoT and cloud computing are tied together, you can get ongoing data exchange and more than basic analytics, which makes personalized health applications easier to run. All in these layers form the base for adaptive, AI-guided wellness and immersive fitness experiences, especially inside the metaverse.

1.1 Evolution of Digital Fitness Technologies

There are several levels in the development of digital fitness technology. As a result, digital fitness technology has developed from simple step-tracking devices to more complex systems that are health-focused. Initially, fitness technology involved manual entry, pedometers, and heart rate monitors. Although able to track physical activity output and offer some contextual and personalization elements, these devices were not individualized [1].

The development of smartphones led to the development of consumer wearables, which involved automation, activity tracking, motion detection, and body detection. These devices included exercise libraries, summaries, and sleep trackers, which suggested a retroactive approach to fitness that tracked past activity but did not promote improvement [2].

Currently, the technology has developed to an intelligent adaptation level. These tools learn from the most recent moments down to long-established patterns using AI. They devise strategies on training, recovery, and overall wellness—managing fitness tech to morph from simple trackers into smart decision-makers.

1.2 Role of AI and Wearables in Wellness

Wearable technology has the potential to be used as a continuous sensing layer for wellness because of its ability to sense real-world signals in real life. These signals include cardiovascular signals, stress responses, sleep patterns, and locomotion dynamics. This allows for a complete understanding of the body's response to training and real-world stimuli. Without interpretation, sensor data has little use in making decisions for wellness [1].

Artificial intelligence adds the intelligence layer to this information to create the personal experience through wearable technology. This is achieved through a series of ready levels that can recognize fatigue trends as well as abnormal patterns that could signify inadequate rest or excessive strains. AI hopes to reduce the dependency on generalized guidelines by achieving individualized recommendations by developing individualized baselines [3].

With this capability, wellness can now advance beyond the performance development stage and move towards the prevention and stability stages. This would assist the user in a better way through AI, which would provide a pathway towards a secure option for training, habits for stability, and habits for pro-wellness through the development of health monitoring feedback [2, 4].

1.3 Emergence of the Metaverse for Health

The metaverse provides an immersive environment through which humans can experience the concept of health and fitness as an activity rather than just watching a screen in order to do a workout, rehab, or focus on activities through the mind. This is a new way of experiencing a change in health, as health becomes a social experience even when working remotely.

An AI-driven coach in the metaverse can provide personalized feedback to students using avatars or other agents. The role of avatars as personalized agents is further amplified by the fact that the users are provided with a visualization of their progress using such options to understand their movements [5, 6].

Despite these benefits, metaverse-based wellness creates new concerns related to privacy, digital identity, and psychological effects. Since immersive platforms may capture sensitive health data alongside behavioural interaction patterns, and so responsible system design becomes essential. When implemented ethically, the metaverse can serve as a scalable platform for preventive, personalized, and immersive health support [7].

2. Wearable Technologies for Fitness and Wellness

2.1 Physiological and Biomechanical Sensors

Physiological and biomechanical sensors provide the foundation of an integrated system of senses in an "AI-guided" system of fitness and wellness since they directly provide an insight into the "physiological state of the human body at any given" instance itself. An intelligent system is also aware of "heart rate characteristics, oxygen saturation, breathing patterns, skin temperature", and is also "capable of detecting an increase in perspiration rates" in order to "estimate the amount of exertion required" [1].

The identified parameters from biomechanical sensors relate to movement quality, including posture, gait patterns, repetition form, important joint motions, and balance stability. These parameters are frequently extracted with the help of an inertial sensor used to calculate acceleration and angular velocity. This recognition is then used to determine potential activity patterns in the presence of dangerous movement. The fusion of the aforementioned parameters into the final solution facilitates personalization by linking inner effort with outer movement [2].

2.2 Smart Textiles and Body Area Networks

Smart textiles enable sensing in wearables to extend past watches and bands by embedding sensors into textile fabrics in a way that is indistinguishable from normal clothing. This process is natural, seamless, and can be done while achieving comfort in daily use. Smart fabrics can sense movement, muscular activities, respiration, expansions, and even postures in alignments. Because they maintain skin contact on larger body surfaces, smart garments often yield more stable movement and biomechanical signals than single-point devices, thus enhancing AI analysis of form, asymmetry detection, and deepened training feedback.

Body area networks (BANs) connect multiple wearable nodes across the body to create a coordinated sensing ecosystem. Instead of relying on one device, a network distributes sensing tasks across different locations such as wrists, chest, legs, and shoes, allowing richer coverage of both physiological and biomechanical signals. The distribution of sensing enhances the stability and reliability of movement reconstruction as a team is unlikely to have a noisy sensor placement problem [8].

Collectively, smart textiles and BANs provide a scalable and precise well-being tracking solution with improved efficiency. Additionally, they provide complex AI application support, such as rehabilitation tracking, sports analysis, and metaverse-based training, for which accurate body knowledge is critical for successful training [5, 7].

2.3 Data Acquisition and Quality Challenges

In AI-assisted wellness, high-quality data collection is essential, but wearable sensing is prone to issues that affect data accuracy and dependability. While motion artifacts, poor skin contact, environmental factors, and sensor drift can affect physiological data, incorrect positioning or movement variations can compromise biomechanical data [1].

Because real-world movement and environmental factors differ from those in training environments, real-world variability also affects the quality of data, making it challenging for models to generalize. A metaverse wellness system must have appropriate preprocessing and system design, including signal fusion, noise reduction, calibration, and confidence-aware decision systems, in order to be dependable. If not, AI models might produce inconsistent wellness recommendations that are risky and untrustworthy [2, 9].

3. AI Models for Personalized Fitness and Wellness

3.1 Activity Recognition and Motion Analysis

The capability for activity recognition and motion analysis enables an AI-assisted fitness platform to recognize what the user is doing and how well they are doing it by analysing data from wearables for various types of motion activities such as acceleration change, angular velocity, and change in orientation during the execution of activities like walking, running, weight training, or even stretching. This makes it easier to convert raw sensor data into useful workout data, thus allowing coaching systems to provide exercise-specific advice rather than general advice [10].

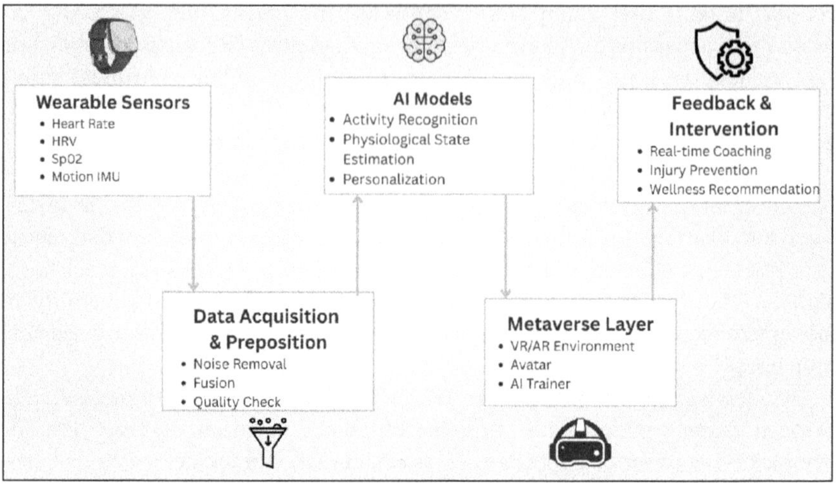

Fig. 7.1 Metaverse wellness system architecture.
Source: Authors

Motion analysis is especially useful for safety and optimization because it has the capability to identify inefficient motion, imbalance, and fatigue-induced motion degradation. In metaverse-based training, accurate motion analysis enables more immersive experiences through better avatar alignment and realism, as well as real-time corrective feedback [5, 7]. As such, activity recognition is the key component of adaptive coaching that depends on the type and quality of the exercise being performed.

3.2 Physiological State Estimation

Hence, physiological state estimation involves understanding internal physiological signs to measure exertion, stress, readiness to improve, state of recovery, and potential health risks. Using measurements like heart rate variability, oxygen saturation, respiration rate, heart rate dynamics, and skin temperature allows for a continuous understanding of how a human reacts to various training or state conditions. AI would be used to estimate intensity levels, abnormal stressful situations, and fatigue levels, even if invisible through motion [1, 2].

These are traits which allow the well-being systems to tailor the guidance provided through training sessions, depending on the level of activity to match user attention levels—allowing the level of activity appropriately to the user level of preparation [5]. Through the estimation provided by the physiological states, users gain adaptability, particularly through immersive sessions designed for real-time adaptation, like easier training when a person is strained and recovery-oriented when a person does not sleep well [3].

3.3 Behavioural and Lifestyle Modelling

Behavioural and lifestyle modelling helps to understand long-term patterns affecting wellness outcomes, which incorporate consistency, sleeping patterns, sedentary lifestyles, stress patterns, and overall adherence to routines and lifestyles. AI comes to understand how daily living affects performance and recovery, and provides recommendations on how to learn and incorporate long-term habits beyond mere workouts [4]. In the metaverse, this might aid user engagement through motivation patterns and dropout prevention [3, 7].

Table 7.1 AI Modelling Techniques for Wearable Data in Personalized Fitness and Wellness

Wearable Data Type	*AI Modelling Approach*	*Application Context*
Heart rate, Heart Rate Variability (HRV)	Physiological state estimation	Adaptive workout planning
Motion Inertial Measurement Unit (IMU) Data	Activity recognition, motion analysis	Real-time feedback
Sleep Metrics	Behavioural modelling	Long-term wellness optimization
Multi-modal Signals	Reinforcement learning	Metaverse training

Source: Compiled by the authors based on Patel et al. (2012) [1], Rieke et al. (2020) [2], Eiselt et al. (2025) [3], Kim et al. (2023) [5], Alarfaj et al. (2024) [10], Lauffenburger et al. (2024) [13], and Jayaraman et al. (2024) [14].

4. Metaverse Platforms for Immersive Wellness

4.1 Virtual and Augmented Reality Foundations

Virtual reality (VR) and augmented reality (AR) form the experiential foundation of metaverse-based wellness by turning fitness into an immersive, interactive activity rather than a screen-based routine. VR places the user inside fully simulated environments where workouts, mindfulness sessions, or rehabilitation exercises can be guided through spatial cues and real-time interaction. This perception of presence enhances engagement due to the experience of taking part in a constructed environment instead of only following a set of rules. Therefore, VR can facilitate consistency better since wellness activities become more engaging, organized, and less monotonous, compared to traditional digital fitness programmes [11].

Augmented reality has different support mechanisms for wellness in that it augments instead of changing the real world. In AR, elements of virtual coaching, such as moving, alignment of positions, repetition of steps, or breathing exercises, are forced into one's real surroundings [3, 7]. AR increases the accessibility of wellness experiences for regular use by being combined with home exercise routines, outdoor activities, and office recovery sessions without the need for full immersion. By design, AR maintains a balance between usability and engagement, which allows for regular practice regardless of lifestyle conditions.

With the integration of wearable sensing and AI analysis, the VR and AR environments become dynamic rather than static. Physiological readiness, fatigue cycles, and motion quality affect the intensity and cadence of a session in an extremely adaptive way [5]. This interface design provides realistic feedback because it allows the environment to react to the user's physiological state, thus enhancing safety. Moreover, it has the potential to greatly aid long-term compliance by offering experiences that maintain an effective feedback loop [1].

4.2 Digital Avatars and Personalized Trainers

Digital avatars are the physical interfaces for well-being in the metaverse, which are representations of users as interactive and responsive figures that enable movement-related interactions. When integrated with wearable sensing and motion analysis, avatars enable more realistic simulations of posture, exercise, and trend dynamics, thus enhancing the immersion and interactivity of training [5]. This representation also enables users to have a better understanding of their progress, as improvements in stability, range of motion, or consistency can be represented both numerically and graphically. Highly customized trainers, enabled by AI, offer scalable yet personalized training.

Not only do they provide advice regarding exercise, proper body positioning with biomechanical inputs, or intensity control in accordance with individual indicators of physiological readiness such as fatigue or recovery cycles, they also differ from video methods in that they provide real-time responses in order to facilitate safety/motivation and varied coaching methods in order to take into account individual progress with time along various wellness paths [3].

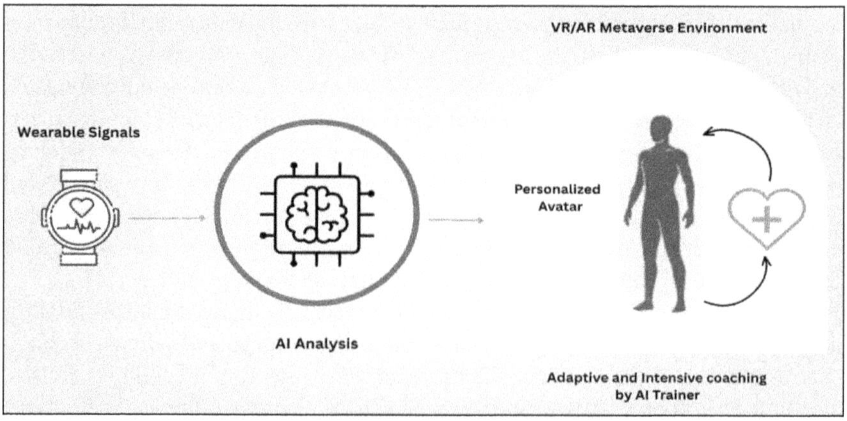

Fig. 7.2 Avatar-based AI coaching loop.

4.3 Social and Community-Driven Wellness

Social wellness in the metaverse promotes user motivation through activities such as shared learning, avatars, and virtual classes, independently of physical locations or places of origin. Such engagements reinforce healthy habits via enhanced responsibility, rivalry, or emotional support mechanisms provided through interactions in digital societies or communities [6, 7]. Hence, it is important that social wellness is carefully managed without exposing associated risks of comparison, invasion of privacy, or addiction issues, since it can otherwise be an effective motivational force in sustaining healthy habits or lifestyles in the long term [3, 12].

5. AI-Guided Coaching and Adaptive Training

5.1 Intelligent Workout Planning

Intelligent training systems can also offer customized training programmes that are designed according to the training objectives, fitness level, and recovery ability of an individual using AI. Currently, these systems can also vary training programmes not according to fixed plans but according to patterns derived from wearable data related to training, sleep, and levels of fatigue [3]. This is very useful in ensuring consistency in training while avoiding the possibility of overtraining. In the metaverse, intelligent training can also enhance engagement by organizing training programmes into experiences that are progressively designed [6, 7].

5.2 Real-Time Feedback and Injury Prevention

Feedback will, therefore, make any pending changes in movement easier, thus being advantageous in ensuring that the risks associated with injury to the actively participating users are kept to a minimum. Additionally, based on the analysis of patterns associated with movement, the system will aid in the monitoring of deterioration, imbalance, and instability, thereby helping to predict strains before they happen, thus ensuring safety for the user [1, 10]. Moreover, there are advantages associated with safety that can also be achieved based on the support provided by the feedback and physiological signals, which may prevent over-exertion and sub-optimal preparation towards recovery, especially in an ideal virtual training environment. Additionally, performance quality and sustainability will also be improved by providing immediate corrective feedback for errors, as is the case with the trainer, avatar, and visual feedback [5].

5.3 Reinforcement Learning for Coaching

Through its application called reinforcement learning, reinforcement learning allows coaching systems to automatically improve themselves as it becomes aware of the types of actions that lead to better outcomes for a particular user. It no longer strictly acts according to templates or perfectly defined courses of action, but instead reads signs such as training progress, fatigue patterns, and ease of following an action, and then responds accordingly. This is important in order to make the coaching more personalized as it becomes aware of the particular type of action required for a user in terms of intensity and recovery [13, 14].

In metaverse-based health and wellness environments, using reinforcement learning enables greater immersion because virtual trainers can act more naturally. Reinforcement learning can also enable trainers to be less likely to risk overtraining an individual while maintaining motivational factors. Over several interactions with an individual, reinforcement learning can also enable optimization for effective decision-making for safety while seeking progress, thus resulting in coaching that is consistent and supportive [7].

6. Mental Health, Mindfulness, and Well-Being

6.1 Stress and Emotion Detection

Stress/emotion recognition is one of the most important functions for AI-assisted wellness management because mental status affects physical performance, recovery quality, and health behaviour on long term. Wearable devices enable continuous monitoring of physiological patterns associated with stress, including changes in heart rate, heart rate variability (HRV), respiratory patterns, and electrodermal activity (EDA) [1]. These can then sum with other diagnostic information, such as activity level, sleep patterns interrupted by stress, and day-to-day inconsistency caused by stress, to inform AI estimations of whether or not a user is under stress/emotional pressure.

Emotion awareness extends wellness systems well beyond basic stress scoring to include awareness of patterns associated with mood shifts, decreases in motivational levels, and behavioural retreats. This allows interventions to become supportive rather than purely performance-focused, enabling coaching systems to recommend recovery sessions, lighter workouts, or mental health activities at appropriate times [7]. In a metaverse-based environment, emotion detection can improve immersion and experience since the environment can react accordingly, such as by showing soothing images and reducing the degree of competitiveness.

Nevertheless, to estimate human emotions accurately, it must handle differences between individuals while not over-interpreting signals. Good systems will interpret the detected stressful states as probabilistic signals but not necessarily truths, in order to provide helpful yet respectful interventions while supporting human well-being holistically [4, 7].

6.2 AI-Guided Meditation and Cognitive Training

The AI-powered meditation and cognitive training utilizes adaptive AI, which enables the personalization of mental wellness practices according to "real-time" physiological data and associated user patterns. Traditional mindfulness practices, within applications, tend to offer pre-defined sound-based practices, together with "general" reminder practices that might not adequately correlate with user-defined real-time stress requirements or attention capacity. This is where AI-powered practices can personalize meditation length, respiratory rate, and meditation type according to readiness inferred from heart rate variance, respiratory regularity, and user trends tracking [2, 4].

In wellness scenarios, cognitive training programmes are geared towards reinforcing skills for enhanced attention control, emotion regulation, and stress resistance. The model continuously monitors the enhancement of stable concentration and response-behavioural patterns, increasing intensity for appropriate challenge while minimizing mental weariness. For meditation and cognitive training scenarios in the metaverse environment, immersion can also be enhanced with less distraction by the environment.

Such systems are best implemented in such a manner that allows personalization to occur in conjunction with the level of simplicity required. In this regard, the adaptation of an AI-aided mental wellness framework would enable the promotion of sustained conditions of calmness, directed focus, and proper coping behaviour in daily living [3].

6.3 Emotional Resilience in Virtual Environments

Emotional resilience in the virtual environment means the ability to assess the psychological stability of a user despite the immersive experience. Within the metaverse, immersive environments can strengthen users' emotional well-being through community support, helping reduce perceived stress, foster a sense of belonging, promote therapeutic recovery, and enhance their ability to cope with psychological challenges [7]. However, the stress may be generated by designing an unfavourable virtual environment, which may translate to negative images of the user's avatar or the stress created by excessive competition within the environment [6].

7. Digital Twins and Predictive Wellness Models

7.1 Personalized Health Avatars

Health avatars are undergoing transformations from simple identification icons to complex and data-intensive representations of an individual's fitness condition and physiological readiness. Contrary to static avatars that are used for identification purposes and are not updated, health avatars can be updated regularly to indicate levels of fatigue, recovery, fitness, and behaviour trends [5]. This enhances the virtual presence of the user, as the avatar acts as an interface between the user and the wellness system. When used with motion analysis tools, health avatars are used to monitor postures and efficiency of movements in training sessions, ensuring users engage in safe and informed training sessions [7].

During metaverse training, health avatars are used to promote immersion by presenting users with the results of their efforts and performances. A user could be training with a coach, with the avatar adjusting and changing due to the precision or limitations put behind the motions, including the intensity or recovery limitations [6]. Moreover, avatars help in personalizing the training and coaching processes through the adaptive nature.

However, personalized avatars have to be cautiously designed so as not to create negative psychological outcomes, such as unrealistic self-comparison or an overemphasis on visual transformation. An ethical avatar system should be transparent and refrain from harmful representation biases and sensitive health information disclosure. If designed responsively, a personalized health avatar powerfully bridges wearable sensing, AI interpretation, and immersive wellness engagement [3, 6].

7.2 Predictive Analytics for Fitness Outcomes

Predictive analytics would help an AI-based system to become more efficient by transforming an otherwise reactive decision-making system into a more proactive decision-making system, utilizing its historical data to inform it about a more predictable future fitness. Rather than simply presenting historical workout data, AI systems can utilize past trends to anticipate future performance, recovery, and potential risks. These risks may include alterations in training load consistency, sleep stability, heart rate variability, and shifts in stress and movement patterns, all of which are derived from data gathered via wearable devices [2].

Some examples of such predictions in fitness could include improvements in endurance, rates of strength progression, trends in body composition, and stability in adherence. It becomes more reliable in those models that use individual baselines instead of population averages, given the high impact of personal physiology and lifestyle pattern variations on how training responses unfold. Predictive analytics also provides goal planning through the detection of whether current habits will yield a target outcome within a specified time frame and changes that would improve the likelihood of success.

In the metaverse, predictive insights can be integrated with interactive experiences to enable users to see the progress that will be made in the future using predictive outcomes. On the other hand, predictions should be communicated in a manner that does not result in the development of false certainty or anxiety [7]. A good system should focus on awareness of uncertainty, autonomy, and framing to ensure that predictive analytics has a positive effect on motivation and safety without burdening users psychologically [6].

7.3 Long-Term Wellness Optimization

To optimize wellness in the long term, there is a need to ensure that these benefits are sustained by finding the right balance between training and recovery. This strategy aims at finding a balance among training intensity, recovery, stress management, and lifestyle habits over a longer period of time [2]. This is made possible by AI models, which learn continuously about how people react to different levels of training and life conditions, ensuring that the recommendations always align with the changing goals, fitness levels, and life conditions.

Success, as far as the end-user is concerned, is defined not only by the training programme but also by the quality of sleep, the timing of meals, the quality of activity, and the quality of the mental state. The AI system ensures that all of these are considered while ensuring that training programmes are provided that are realistic within the schedule of the end-user but still enable progress to be made [7]. Long-term wellness optimization can be achieved within the metaverse platforms by providing immersive experiences in the development of habits, storytelling, and community designs that are not too aggressive [4].

8. Ethical, Psychological, and Social Implications

8.1 Digital Identity and Self-Perception

Digital identity in the context of the metaverse enables the development of wellness experiences through self-expression, interaction, and presence. The concept of identity is beyond the confines of social presence since the avatar of the user represents not just their social identity but also their performance and wellness. This is a flawless feedback loop since the user is involved in the training process and at the same time feels as though they are undergoing training in a virtual way. Well-developed digital identity can thus play a vital role in the enhancement of motivation. This is because the user is more likely to try new experiences in the virtual world due to the training they receive in the virtual environment.

However, self-perception can also be influenced negatively when avatars promote unrealistic standards or when users associate worth with performance metrics. The overemphasis on visual transformation, unrealistic morphs of the virtual physique, and comparative competitions can create anxiety and undermine positive healthy body acceptance. AI personalization might contribute to such negative consequences inadvertently if it is outcome-based without regards to emotional well-being and self-image stability [3].

To support healthy self-perception, wellness systems must design avatars and identity features with psychological sensitivity. Representation must promote authenticity, progress framing should centre on capability rather than appearance, and systems must avoid reward schemes that promote unhealthy behaviours. Following these guidelines on balanced design, digital identity can be a positive force in wellness, rather than an instrument of distortion, in the digital world [6].

8.2 Privacy, Consent, and Data Ownership

Privacy is an underlying ethical principle for AI wellness technologies, particularly because, in most cases, data from wearable devices tend to be rather personal and sometimes even never-ending. The physiological signals, behavioural patterns, and contextual information integral to AI wellness technologies all convey useful information about stress, recovery, routine, and risk. In the metaverse, however, issues regarding data privacy become even more alarming, considering the integration of data with other aspects of interaction, identity, and participation. The combination of biometric signals and avatar-based identity can create unique risks if data is shared without control, stored insecurely, or used for secondary purposes such as advertising, profiling, or behavioural manipulation.

Therefore, the consent mechanism should be active, transparent, and flexible. Users should clearly understand what data are being collected, why they are collected, how long they will be retained, and whether they are processed locally or in the cloud.

Another consideration is data ownership. In some cases, data ownership decreases the level of control over personal data in the wellness platforms. Ethical frameworks emphasize the ownership of the wellness data by the user; this is where access, portability, deletion, and limits of third-party sharing come into play. Without proper data privacy, trust is lost as it becomes unsustainable [6, 12].

8.3 Inclusivity and Accessibility

Inclusivity and accessibility play an indispensable role in ensuring that metaverse wellness systems cater to a wide range of users or, conversely, limit their access. Physiological care technologies, for example, may fail to consider a normed body type, movement patterns, and ease of access to devices for all users, which may ultimately eliminate or limit those who may be physically disabled, elderly, or less privileged in their access to resources [3].

Accessible design should enable different interface types, avatars, and wellness services to cater to different levels of mobility and sensory requirements. Affordability, hardware, and language requirements must also be factored into the accessibility dimension to make metaverse wellness accessible to all [7]. Everyone will benefit if AI-based wellness focuses on fairness and accessibility; thus, it will transcend the digital privileged domain [6].

The major ethical risks associated with AI-guided wellness in the metaverse, including privacy, digital identity, fairness, accessibility, and psychological well-being, are summarized in Fig. 7.3.

9. Applications and Case Studies

9.1 Virtual Fitness Studios

Virtual fitness studios in the metaverse offer the same services as physical fitness studios, but the members are not limited by geographical factors. The members engage in fitness sessions with the system, where wearable sensing is used to dynamically adjust the workout sessions [7]. The virtual fitness studios also promote user engagement and commitment by offering 24/7 workout routines, social training, and gaming, thereby reducing dropout rates.

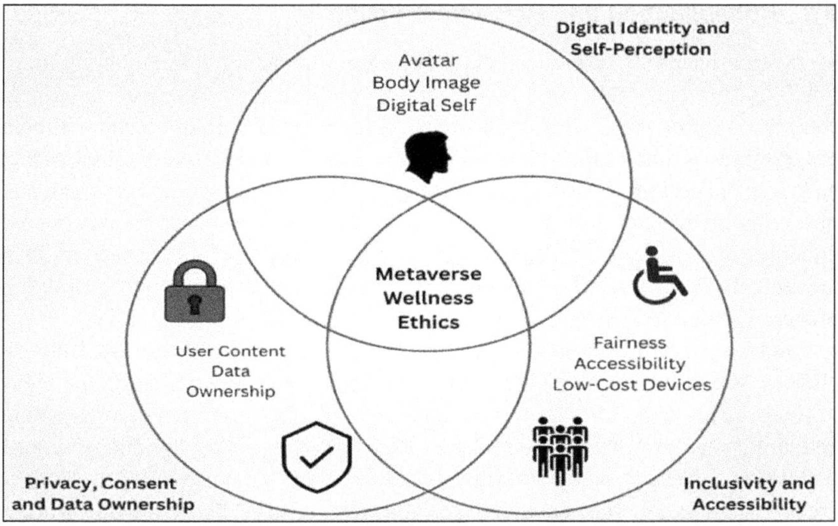

Fig. 7.3 Ethical risks in metaverse wellness.
Source: Adapted from Dwivedi et al. [7] and Vahdati et al. [6].

The analysis of motions and feedback mechanisms involved with biomechanics can enhance the resultant quality of fitness sessions by identifying any movement irregularities in real time [5]. However, virtual fitness studios should also ensure an encouraging environment is maintained by immersive fitness experiences while addressing safety issues and offering appropriate recovery advice at the right time [10].

9.2 AI-Driven Corporate Wellness

The AI-based corporate wellness programmes utilize the potential of wearable devices and behavioural analytics to enhance the health, productivity, and happiness of employees in the corporation. This is in contrast to the conventional method of corporate wellness, which relies on specific challenges and occasional check-ins with the employees [7]. This AI-based method is more prevalent because it is based on noticeable signs of stress, sleep, and fatigue patterns in the daily routine of the employees. By incorporating metaverse technologies, these AI-based programmes can easily blend in relaxation activities, rejuvenation, and even group activities in the work routine of the employees without hampering the flow [6].

The success of employee wellness programmes depends on trust and ethics as well. If employees feel that their monitoring or data usage is a concern, then the engagement levels will drop drastically. So, privacy policies must be taken care of as well, as all the above aspects will be fruitful if well-executed for the enhancement of wellness programmes as unique support rather than basic support for mental stability and calmness among employees [6].

9.3 Rehabilitation and Preventive Health

Metaverse-based AI wellness platforms are increasingly being applied to rehabilitation and preventive healthcare by providing personalized guidance, continuous monitoring, and support for adherence to rehabilitation and wellness programmes. Rehabilitation involves a set of repetitive and harmless activities that an individual needs to perform, such as appropriate technique, gradual progress, and observing the progress [1]. Wearables and movement algorithmic monitoring are undoubtedly beneficial for rehabilitation, as this would allow for the observation of movement execution and facilitation to ensure correct movement while the training process is hands-off [3].

In the case of prevention, AI has the ability to search and investigate lifestyle choices, stress levels, sleeping patterns, and lack of activity to identify the signs of illness. This creates a platform for low-risk interventions to foster long-lasting health. Further, the metaverse has the ability to improve preventive care solutions by making such solutions more enjoyable and socially supportive, as long as they are both valid and flexible enough to accommodate all clinical needs in the process [3, 7].

10. Future Directions and Conclusion

10.1 Challenges and Research Opportunities

One of the challenges of AI-based well-being in the metaverse is the sensing and modelling of the real world. Apparently, the use of wearable sensors in metaverse well-being has difficulties in motion noise, placement, and environment, which could affect the precise level of how well we sense the physiology and movement of the users of the wearable devices [2].

The second major challenge is to achieve actual personalization without any bias. The fact is many AI technologies have been trained on small and biased datasets, and these datasets do not tend to include all sorts of body types, ages, fitness, and conditions. The truth is, this will result in biased results and recommendations [3].

Finally, ethics and governance are important factors to consider, especially since the information being collected by the metaverse wellness platforms includes biometric data, behavioural data, and identity data. In this case, the role of privacy-preserving machine learning, consent, and data ownership is of paramount importance in the development of trustworthy wellness platforms [6].

10.2 Vision for AI-Guided Wellness in the Metaverse

Wellness in the context of AI in the metaverse is geared towards creating a health environment that is always adapting and engaging users through immersive experiences. Wearable sensing is always-on health, and AI interpretation of this data is used to provide recommendations for workout routines, relaxation, and dynamic habit-building strategies, amongst others [5].

In this regard, digital twins and health avatars are critical components for applying progress visualization and motivational assistance for sustainable behavioural change. Users can then apply simulation assistance for training choices, while metaverse platforms can provide assistance for comprehensive wellness experiences that can increase engagement and compliance with interactive and socially enabled experiences [6].

Wellness platforms must be built with a future in mind that is transparent, safe, and autonomous. AI coaching with explanatory features must be able to communicate, be autonomous, and not employ manipulative strategies to retain users [3]. With these ethical pillars in mind, the metaverse can be a platform for preventive healthcare to provide accessible and personalized wellness to mitigate health risk and build resilience for its user [6].

10.3 Concluding Insights

Fitness for AI combines the best qualities of wearable technology, smart modelling, and participation. It offers timely adaptation, allowing individuals to change from routine physical activities to a highly personalized dynamic routine that meets the levels of preparedness, fatigue, tension, and behavioural patterns through the preventive health benefits offered in a way that enhances consistency, safety, and both physical and mental health [5, 7].

However, in order for the technology to flourish in the long term, there is a need for its responsible integration. The issues of privacy, consent, fairness, and psychological well-being need to be at the top of the agenda. Sometimes, this will be the case especially where the metaverse technology is responsible for handling bio-data. In this case, wellness in the context of AI will have created a long-lasting layer [3, 6].

References

[1] Patel, S., Park, H., Bonato, P., et al. (2012). A review of wearable sensors and systems with application in rehabilitation. *Journal of Neuroengineering and Rehabilitation*, 9, 21.

[2] Rieke, N., Hancox, J., Li, W., et al. (2020). The future of digital health with federated learning. *NPJ Digital Medicine*, 3, 119.

[3] Eiselt, A.-K., Kirkendall, S., Xiong, E., et al (2025). Achieving clinically meaningful outcomes in digital health. *Frontiers in Digital Health*, 7, 1713334.

[4] Bucher, A., Blazek, E.S. and Symons, C.T. (2024). How are machine learning and artificial intelligence used in digital behavior change interventions? A scoping review. *Smart Health*, 2(3),375–404.

[5] Kim, K., Yang, H., Lee, J., et al. (2023). Metaverse wearables for immersive digital healthcare: A review. *Advanced Science (Weinh)*, 10(31), e2303234.

[6] Vahdati, M., Laamarti, F. and El Saddik, A. (2025). Meta-review of wearable devices for healthcare in the metaverse. *ACM Transactions on Multimedia Computing, Communications and Applications*, 21(7), 1–36.

[7] Dwivedi, Y.K., Hughes, L., Baabdullah, A.M., et al. (2022). Metaverse beyond the hype: Multidisciplinary perspectives on emerging challenges, opportunities, and agenda for research, practice and policy. *International Journal of Information Management*, 66, 102542.

[8] Fadhel, M.A., Duhaim, A.M., Albahri, A.S., et al. (2024). Navigating the metaverse: Unraveling the impact of artificial intelligence—A comprehensive review and gap analysis. *Artificial Intelligence Review*, 57, Article 264.

[9] Satyanarayanan, M. (2017). The emergence of edge computing. *Computer*, 50(1), 30–39.

[10] Alarfaj, M., Al Madini, A., Alsafran, A., et al. (2024). Wearable sensors based on artificial intelligence models for human activity recognition. *Frontiers in Artificial Intelligence*, 7, 1424190.

[11] Reshmi, L.B., Vipin Raj, R., Balasubramaniam, S. and Kumar, K.S. (2024). 12 generative AI and LLM: Case study in finance. In Balasubramaniam, S., Kadry, S., Prasanth, A., & Dhanaraj, R. K. (eds), *Generative AI and LLMs: Natural Language Processing and Generative Adversarial Networks*, pp. 231–252. Berlin, Boston: De Gruyter.

[12] Arishma, M. (2024). Prediction of breast cancer using ensemble learning and boosting techniques. In *2024 International Conference on Communication, Computer Sciences and Engineering (IC3SE)*, pp. 513–519. IEEE.

[13] Lauffenburger, J.C., Yom-Tov, E., Keller, P.A., et al. (2024). The impact of using reinforcement learning to personalize communication on medication adherence: Findings from the REINFORCE trial. *NPJ Digital Medicine*, 7(1), 39.

[14] Jayaraman, P., Desman, J., Sabounchi, M., et al. (2024). A primer on reinforcement learning in medicine for clinicians. NPJ Digital Medicine, 7, 1316.

[15] Shi, W., Cao, J., Zhang, Q., et al. (2016). Edge computing: Vision and challenges. *IEEE Internet of Things Journal*, 3(5), 637–646.

[16] Kuo, A.M.H. (2011). Opportunities and challenges of cloud computing to improve health care services. *Journal of Medical Internet Research*, 13(3), e67.

[17] Botta, A., De Donato, W., Persico, V. and Pescapé, A. (2016). Integration of cloud computing and Internet of Things: A survey. *Future Generation Computer Systems*, 56, 684–700.

8 Rehabilitation and Neurotherapy through Immersive Environments

Vanajaroselin Chirchi[1*], Emmanvel Raj M. Chirchi[2], Jagatheesan K.[3], Azrour Mourade[4] and Ciro R. Rodriguez[5]

The way that virtual reality and artificial intelligence (AI) and the metaverse are coming together is changing the way we do rehabilitation and neurotherapy. We used to do rehabilitation and neurotherapy in clinics and only sometimes. Now they can be done all the time. It changes based on what the person needs. This chapter discusses how engineers design systems for rehabilitation that use reality. It talks about how to design these systems and how to make them work well. It also talks about using machine learning and looking at data in time to make rehabilitation and neurotherapy better. The systems for rehabilitation that use reality are very important and this part of the book presents an engineering point of view on these systems. It emphasizes the design of algorithms and the architecture of the systems and the pipelines, for machine learning and the analytics that happen in time. Rehabilitation and neurotherapy are changing because of virtual reality and AI and the metaverse. Recent advances in virtual reality (VR), augmented reality (AR), mixed reality (MR), wearable sensing, and AI-driven personalization are analysed with respect to physical rehabilitation, neurotherapy, and cognitive rehabilitation. The role of the metaverse as a persistent computational layer for continuous health monitoring, digital twins, and remote therapy orchestration is discussed. Challenges related to scalability, data security, model generalization, and ethical deployment are highlighted, followed by future research directions.

1. Introduction

The initial models of rehabilitation engineering were structured on tedious repetitive tasks guided by the therapist with very little quantitative feedback or adaptation introduced to the controller. Thanks to modern technology which

[1] Department of ISE, Dayananda Sagar Academy of Technology and Management (DSATM), Bengaluru, Karnataka, India.
[2] Department of Information Science & Engineering and Artificial Intelligence and Data Science, East-West Institute of Technology, Bengaluru, Karnataka, India.
[3] Department of Electronics and Communication Engineering, M. Kumaraswamy College of Engineering (Autonomous), Karur, Tamil Nadu, India.
[4] Department of Computer Science, Faculty of Sciences and Technologies, Moulay Ismail University of Meknès, Morocco.
[5] Software Engineering Department, Universidad Nacional Mayor de San Marcos, Lima.
* Corresponding author: dr.vanajaroselin-ise@dsatm.edu.in

DOI: 10.1201/9781003776291-8

enables the automation of the learning and training processes of rehabilitation, from top-down design, across intelligent design of rehabilitation communication interfaces and then adaptive control system design, and real-time, continuously monitored, and updated system design with increased opportunities for learning. Immersive settings, by definition, provide controlled, repeatable, and motivating rehabilitation, while wearables provide highly tensile measurements in the full domain of kinematic, physiological, and neurophysiologic signals.

Each system must have interaction devices involved in the already well-defined manner of structural anatomy at large-degree interaction level. At even a higher level, these interaction devices must be proceeding beyond previously learned experiences and must therefore produce a new realm of artificial intelligence (AI) interpretation. A collection of corresponding bioinformatics technologies growing in the working present context of a given project can vary in value due to these approaches. Lower-level AI accentuates this intersection by bringing forth new forms of therapy.

2. Immersive Technologies and Wearable AI in Healthcare

New technologies such as virtual reality (VR), augmented reality (AR), and mixed reality (MR) are playing a significant role in many industries, especially in healthcare industry. Providing interactive and reprogrammable environments further enhances many advanced therapies with less complexity. The advanced precision innovations are with the computational interfaces that blend sensing, analysis, feedback, correction, and exact execution. Wearable AI integration makes the environment go further than visualization to form intelligent, adaptive healthcare systems capable of providing support for personalized monitoring like neurotherapies and rehabilitation [1].

2.1 Immersive Technologies: VR, AR, and MR

Immersive technologies, such as VR, AR, and MR, have proven their significance in the healthcare industry by providing manipulatable, interactive, and reprogrammable environments, enhancing the Attend–Experience Radius for therapy. By "technology", an immersive environment means the computational interfaces that blend sensing, analysis, and feedback. When used together with wearable AI, these environments go further than visualization to form intelligent [2].

Augmented reality is a digital content that is overlaid onto the actual world and therefore maintains the real-world context but offers guidance through computation. AR-based rehabilitation systems have been found to be effective especially in task-oriented therapy, gait training, and activities of daily living. AR can be viewed as having engineering advantages by minimizing sensory conflict and enhancing ecological validity over full-virtual environments, and still capable of providing real-time feedback and task adaptation [3].

Mixed reality builds upon AR and allows both way communication between the physical and the virtual worlds. Virtual objects are spatially attached to the real physical world and dynamically react to user interventions. The given characteristic is essential when it comes to upper-level rehabilitation activities that require manipulating objects, coordination, and group therapy. But MR systems pose other engineering issues, such as the spatial mapping accuracy, occlusion management, and real-time synchronization between the physical and virtual coordinate system [1].

2.2 *Wearable AI: Sensing and Embedded Intelligence*

The main layer of sensing in immersive healthcare is wearable devices. The most frequent modalities of common sensing include inertial measurement unit (IMU), surface electromyography (sEMG), electroencephalography (EEG), electrocardiography (ECG), photoplethysmography (PPG), and force or pressure sensors. These devices produce multi-modal time-series data of high frequency, which records kinematic, physiological, neurophysiological conditions of concern in rehabilitation and neurotherapy [4].

Recent advancements in edge and embedded AI have allowed processing the data collected by wearable sensors on the device, eliminating latency and dependency on cloud computing resources. Activity recognition, gait phase detection, tremor assessment, and fatigue monitoring are typically performed with the use of lightweight convolutional neural networks (CNNs), long short-term memory (LSTM) networks, gated recurrent units (GRUs), and temporal convolutional networks (TCNs) [5]. Most recently, transformer models and graph neural networks (GNNs) have shown an increase in long-range temporal dependence and inter-joint correlation in complex rehabilitation data [6].

Engineer-wise, wearable AI systems need to be deployed with rigid requirements of power usage, memory footprint, and real-time inference. Pruning, quantization, and knowledge distillation are thus model compression methods that are necessary to facilitate incessant health monitoring without affecting the battery life or system responsiveness [7].

2.3 *Integration of Immersive Systems and Wearable AI*

By combining immersive technologies and wearable AI, closed-loop rehabilitation architectures are made possible, where sensor-based information is constantly used to adjust the system. Wearable devices transmit real-time data to AI systems which approximate user conditions like motor performance, cognitive load, or neural engagement. Such estimates are used to dynamically control immersive environments with the modulation of the difficulty of the task, visual or haptic feedback intensity, and pacing parameters [3, 6].

Kinematic measures (movement smooth, movement symmetry, and joint coordination) derived using IMU data can be overlaid using adaptive VR task parameters to achieve an optimal challenge point that matches each user, in motor rehabilitation. Biomarkers obtained through EEG such as spectral power, event-related potentials, and measures of functional connectivity can be used in cyber-physical therapeutic loop through real-time neurofeedback applied in immersive cognitive tasks [1, 4].

2.4 Engineering Challenges and Opportunities

Immersive and wearable AI systems despite their potential also have a number of engineering challenges. They are multi-modal data synchronization, hard latency constraints of the closed-loop control, sensor drift, and poor generalization of AI models in different patient populations. The domain shift due to the change of sensor locations, user behaviour, and environmental factors further complicates the deployment in the real world of rehabilitation environments [4].

However, the progress of spatial computing, low-power AI accelerators, and metaverse infrastructures can be highly promising. Digital twins, longitudinal analytics, and collaborative rehabilitation can be home to persistent virtual environments, which places immersive technologies and wearable AI as core elements of the next generation of intelligent healthcare systems [1].

3. System Architecture for Immersive Rehabilitation and Neurotherapy

There is an immersive rehabilitation engineering reference architecture that consists of five layers, including sensing, edge intelligence, communication, immersive interaction, and cloud/metaverse services.

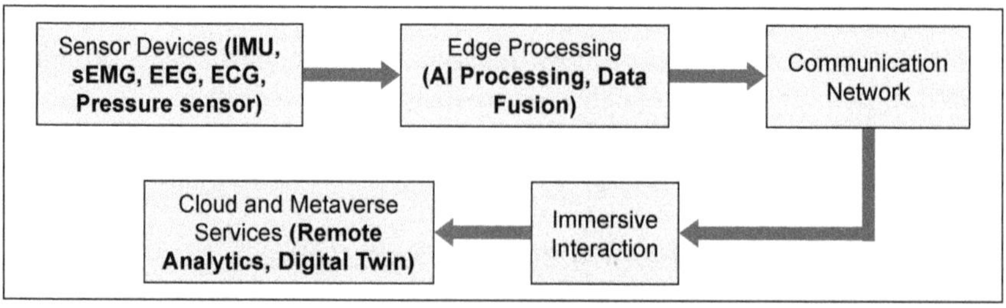

Fig. 8.1 Reference architecture for immersive rehabilitation integrating wearable sensors, edge AI, immersive interaction, and cloud services.

Wearable and ambient sensors that produce high-frequency multi-modal data make up the sensing layer. The edge intelligence layer conducts the preprocessing, features extraction, and simple inference models, including gait phase detection or estimation of cognitive load. Web Real Time Communication (WebRTC) and

Message Queuing Telemetry Transport (MQTT) real-time streaming have low-latency protocols used as communication layers.

The layer of immersive interaction makes the VR/AR/MR environments and incorporates the haptic feedback devices. On the cloud and metaverse layer, longitudinal analytics, patient clustering, and simulation of digital twins are done by large-scale machine learning models. Adaptive difficulty scaling is enabled with closed loop control mechanism on real-time performance measures.

4. Rehabilitation Applications Using Immersive Environments

4.1 Overview and Rationale

Computer-generated immersive environments made feasible through VR, AR, and MR have become the new revolution in the current rehabilitation process. Such technologies enable simulating the real-world tasks in a controlled way, but also provide the accuracy in tracking the patient performance by installing wearable sensors. Combined with AI, the work of immersive rehabilitation takes the form of an adaptive intervention based on the data, being adaptable and focused on individual patients [1, 2].

Conventional rehabilitation is characterized by a lack of personalization, low level of patient engagement, and subjective evaluation of the outcomes. The use of immersive, smart, interactive environments removes barriers to traditional forms of therapy; through a combination of real-time motion capture, AI analytics, and sensory inputs, brain remodelling will be promoted and patients will be fully engaged at all times in their recovery journey.

4.2 Motor Rehabilitation Using Immersive Systems

4.2.1 Post-Stroke and Neuromotor Recovery

Repetitive, task-oriented, motor training is necessary as part of post-stroke rehabilitation to induce cortical reorganization. The customizable tasks can be developed in the context of immersive environments that include reaching, grasping, and manipulating objects in virtual environments. There are wearable IMUs and EMG sensors that constantly receive data about kinematic and muscle activity. An assessment pipeline comprising of standardized motor assessment entails:

- Wearable signal acquisition
- Feature extraction
- This is based on AI to classify motions
- Feedback and adaptation of therapy

Let $x_t \in \mathbb{R}^n$ is a feature vector based on sensor signals at time t, which may consist of joint angles, angular velocity, and EMG amplitude. An example of

Table 8.1 Rehabilitation applications enabled by immersive environments.

Rehabilitation Domain	*Immersive Technology*	*Wearable AI Components*	*AI Functionality*	*Targeted Outcomes*
Post-stroke motor rehabilitation	Virtual Reality (VR)	IMUs, EMG sensors	Movement quality assessment, adaptive task difficulty	Improved range of motion, motor coordination
Gait and balance training	VR with motion tracking	IMUs, pressure sensors	Gait pattern analysis, fall-risk detection	Enhanced balance, reduced fall risk
Upper-limb rehabilitation	VR/Mixed Reality (MR)	IMUs, joint angle sensors	Compensation detection, performance feedback	Improved fine motor control
Cognitive rehabilitation	VR-based serious games	EEG wearables	Cognitive state classification, neurofeedback	Improved attention and executive function
Pain management	VR distraction environments	Heart rate, skin conductance sensors	Stress and pain level inference	Reduced perceived pain and anxiety

a supervised learning model, e.g., a support vector machine (SVM), is used to classify the quality of movements:

$$f(x_t) = \text{sign}\,(w^T x_t + b)$$

where w and b are learning parameters. The result of the classification is to detect compensatory movements and provide corrective feedback [3].

4.3 Gait and Balance Rehabilitation

4.3.1 Immersive Gait Training

Immersion-based gait rehabilitation combines head-mounted display and wearable pressure sensors and IMUs. The virtual terrains, obstacles, and visual flow control improve balance control and walking adaptability. Such systems are especially useful with patients having Parkinson's disease as well as age related mobility impairments [4].

4.3.2 AI-based Gait Analysis

Machine learning models analyse temporal gait parameters such as stride length, cadence, and stance duration. A common approach employs recurrent neural networks (RNNs) to capture temporal dependencies:

$$h_t = \sigma(W_h h_{t-1} + W_x x_t)$$

$$h_t = W_y x_t$$

where h, t represents the hidden state encoding gait dynamics. Deviations from normative gait patterns trigger adaptive modifications in the immersive task difficulty [5].

4.4 Upper-Limb and Fine Motor Rehabilitation

Upper-limb rehabilitation benefits from immersive environments that support repetitive, goal-directed movements with immediate visual feedback. AI-driven pose estimation algorithms evaluate joint coordination and movement smoothness.

A commonly used metric is jerk minimization, defined as:

$$J = \int_0^T \left(\frac{d^3 x(t)}{dt^3} \right)^2 dt$$

Lower jerk values indicate smoother and more coordinated movements. AI models track improvements in this metric over time to quantify motor recovery [6].

4.5 Neurotherapy and Cognitive Rehabilitation

4.5.1 Cognitive Training in Immersive Environments

Neurotherapy immersive environments are being used more and more in the treatment of cognitive disorders associated with traumatic brain injury, dementia, and attention disorders. The exercises that address memory, executive function, and visuospatial awareness are incorporated in gamified virtual scenarios. The computer interfaces to the brain through EEG interfaces allow monitoring of the cognitive state in real time. EEG signal feature vectors are then used to predict cognitive workload or level of attention through deep learning models [7].

The EEG time frequency representations are used in a CNN:

$$z = \text{CNN}(X_{EEG})$$

where X_{EEG} denotes spectrogram inputs and z represents inferred cognitive states.

4.6 Pain Management and Psychological Rehabilitation

Immersive environments can be effective in the reduction of perceived pain and anxiety through the redirection of attentional resources. Personalization is done by AI that alters the visual intensity, the complexity of the task, and auditory signals, depending on physiological indicators (such as heart rate variability [HRV]).

An Reinforcement Learning (RL) framework can maximize therapy parameters:

$$Q(s, a) \leftarrow Q(s, a) + a\left[r + \gamma \max_{a'} Q(s', a') - Q(s, a)\right]$$

where the reward r measures decrease in the measures of pain or stress. This dynamic method improves the effectiveness of therapy and the comfort of the patient [8].

4.7 Tele-rehabilitation and Home-based Therapy

The cloud-based immersive setups have eliminated remote rehabilitation monitoring. Wearable AI technologies, sending encrypted data to cloud servers, translate into predictive modelling for progress-based evaluation and clinician dashboard display. These are regarded as prospective therapies and can serve as a core principle for interim treatment. Tele-rehabilitation improves access to healthcare services and diminishes their prices in settings without resources [9].

4.8 Clinical Outcomes and Advantages

Rehabilitation with exciting components supplants the traditional non-engagement conditions. Mostly in clinical research, here was contrasted with recovery-enhancement as of-isolation therapeutic intervention with poorer outcomes, augmented dropout rates, self-intrinsic motivation, and overall program adherence with the patients in truly immersiveness. Objective tracking tools, running as AI solutions, avoid the situation where the therapist's judgment is overly shaped by subjective inferences.

5. Neurotherapy and Cognitive Rehabilitation

The theme of neurotherapy deals with the direct functioning of the brain. This involves precise stimulation, signals, and adaptive training in order to enhance cognitive behaviour so as to also enhance various reasoning skills. On some occasions, cognitive therapy is implemented within a fully immersive environment (VR or MR) that seems practically real and allows long-lasting interest from the patient. This is where such set-ups will aim to test memory, attention, executive functions, spatial functions, etc., in many well-designed scenarios. At the end of the day, the patients undergo an even longer, more coherent, and high-intensity learning session which goes well beyond the demand for generic cognitive therapy.

5.1 EEG-based Neurofeedback in Immersive Environments

Physiological signal recordings collected from infants, such as EEG and wearable sensor data, are processed to extract meaningful features, including power spectral density and synchronization across different brain regions. These extracted features are channel-specific and analyzed using machine learning techniques to support real-time therapeutic decision-making. This approach enables timely and personalized interventions, improving the effectiveness of therapy and patient outcomes.

Defining $x_i(t)$ as the EEG signal recorded from channel i is necessary. For a given frequency band f, a power spectrum density (PSD) of an EEG signal is computed, defined as:

$$P_i(f) = \frac{1}{T}\left|\int_0^T x_i(t)e^{-j2\pi ft}\,dt\right|^2$$

The feature vectors extracted from different EEG channels are combined and provided as input to a supervised learning model, such as a Support Vector Machine (SVM) or a deep neural network. These models analyze brain activity patterns to identify whether the individual is focused, relaxed, or experiencing stress. Based on the detected cognitive or emotional state, the system dynamically adapts the immersive environment by adjusting task difficulty, modifying the activity, or changing the audio stimuli to enhance user experience and therapeutic effectiveness.

5.2 Graph Neural Networks for Functional Connectivity Analysis

Graph neural networks have only recently been adopted for mapping the interconnectivity between different parts of the brain in the context of neurofeedback.

In this setting, there are nodes, each corresponding to different EEG channels, that send and receive information to each other as coherences or phase-locking values. This set-up is a way to capture spatial and temporal brain patterns while performing a given task or thinking.

Let $G = (V, E)$ denote the brain graph, with V representing all the EEG channels and E denoting all connections between them.

The graph convolution operation reads as follows:

$$H^{(l+1)} = \sigma\left(D^{-\frac{1}{2}} A D^{-\frac{1}{2}} H^{(l)} W^{(l)}\right)$$

in which A is the adjacency matrix, due to the presence of an edge between two nodes, D represents the degree matrix, $H^{(l)}$ is the node feature matrix at layer l, and $W^{(l)}$ indicates the trainable weights. Techniques have outperformed all other heuristics so far by their ability to discover individualized neural signatures for customizing neurotherapy interventions.

5.3 Attention-based Models and Cognitive State Inference

Neurofeedback, refined through attention structures, enables pharmacological therapy. Such mechanisms direct the model to learn from the most important patterns of neural activation. In an attention-based neural network, the model learns to weigh differently important EEG channels and frequency bands.

$$\alpha_i = \frac{\exp(e_i)}{\sum_k \exp(e_k)}, \; e_i = w^T \tan h(Wh_i)$$

where α_i refers to the weight of attention accorded to the h_i feature. Thus, not only is the model made interpretable, but in case of increased complexity, feedback may also help the model decide which direction to adapt appropriately while in the environment.

5.4 Brain–Computer Interfaces and Closed Loop Neurorehabilitation

Bringing brain–computer interfaces (BCIs) to immersive environments is a big step in neurorehabilitation. The real-time feedback loop enhances the training and facilitation of desired activity patterns in your brain.

A closed-loop control formulation may be stated as:

$$u(t) = f(\hat{s}(t))$$

where, $\hat{s}(t)$ is the estimated cognitive state derived from EEG data, and u(t) represents an adaptive stimulus applied by the immersive system. The brain's real-time interaction leads to neuroplasticity and, hence, accelerates the pace of cognitive recovery.

- **Clinical Impact and Future Potential**

Clinical studies have shown that combining immersive neurotherapy with AI-assisted neurofeedback significantly improves neurocognitive performance, attention, and executive functioning in patients with neurological disorders. AI-assisted immersive neurotherapy is increasingly regarded as a key component of future digital healthcare due to its potential to deliver personalized, adaptive, and effective therapeutic interventions.

6. Continuous Health Monitoring in the Metaverse

Wearable AI devices that are immersed in AI ecosystems provide sustained data streams for health-monitoring possibilities through the metaverse around the clock. This makes it possible to provide ongoing observation of the physiological, behavioural, and cognitive states, unlike the episodic clinical assessments [10, 11], thus enabling the delivery of services for proactive and personalized healthcare. The digital metaverse provides an essential digital layer where data collection, analytics, visualization, and interaction across physical and virtual domains take place together.

In the context of therapeutic sessions and daily living, wearable devices continuously capture multi-modal data (e.g., motion patterns, physiological signals, and neural activity). Edge intelligence conjoins early-stage processing with latency and bandwidth reduction, and cloud-based analytics offer long-term trend analysis on unprecedented amounts of data. All streams are time-synchronized by metaverse and displayed by clinicians and patients on aesthetically immersive dashboards and avatar-based frames.

Artificial intelligence–driven anomaly detection mechanisms offer significant opportunities for identifying abnormal patterns in patient health data. Changes in biological signals that deviate from normal patterns or established recovery profiles can indicate early signs of deterioration, noncompliance, or adverse events. Such early detection enables timely intervention and improves patient monitoring, particularly in chronic rehabilitation and home-based therapy settings, where direct supervision by hospitals or healthcare professionals is limited.

Scalability, interoperability, and data governance are required under any effective metaverse for continuous monitoring application from the point of view of engineering. Systems are to integrate heterogeneous devices, secure the data exchange, and indeed comply with health laws [12], finding ways to bypass India's medley of harsh restrictions on the location of health data. When properly designed, the continuous monitoring promises to remodel the end-of-the-line model of care from reactive and clinic-centred to proactive, individualized, and distributed.

The AI-powered wearable devices collect all kinds of imaginable data on our bodies, the pulse, movements, and brain activity via sensors they have strapped on board. Streams of data never stop coming; they get analysed to be seen and used by chained entities. Doctors and patients together with AI in the metaverse thus see to healthcare 24/7, jumping in whenever their assistance is needed, not just ad hoc, whenever patients find their way to a clinic.

- **AI Wearables and Continuous Data Streams**

Different ranges of signals are captured all the time by wearables—biosignals like heart rate variability, EMG, EEG, and motion, and electro-skin conductance. This cleaning up process happens with high-speed processing inside the actual device itself, preserving valuable processing resources and bandwidth by pre-qualifying these data by uploading them off METASOURCES.

Let $x_t \in \mathbb{R}^d$ denote a multivariate sensor observation at time t. Edge-level preprocessing performs normalization and feature extraction:

$$\hat{X}_t = \frac{X_t - \mu}{\sigma}$$

where μ and σ represent running estimates of mean and standard deviation. This enables stable downstream learning and analytics.

- **Metaverse-based Visualization and Interaction**

These data are deep linked to immersive dashboards in the metaverse where, in real time, patient states can be visualized using avatars, timelines, and interactive overlays. The users, or clinicians, can (together) examine physiological trends and replay motion paths and test treatment scenarios. The interactive interface facilitates the awareness of environment and the decision at a distance in telerehabilitation.

- **Digital Twin Models for Personalized Monitoring**

Digital twins treat the patients as computational entities, whose internal states are updated based on received sensor data and prediction. A patient digital twin can be considered, from a computational viewpoint, as a state–space system:

$$s_{t+1} = f(s_t, x_t, u_t)$$

where s_t—patient's current rehabilitation state,

x_t—sensor/biological data collected from patient

u_t—therapeutic intervention decided by AI.

Machine learning models, such as RNNs and transformer-style architectures, approximate the unknown state transition.

Digital twins support what-if simulation, where clinicians can inspect the effect of changes in therapy before applying them to the patient, including increased safety and personalization.

- **Time-Series Analytics and Predictive Modelling**

Continuous monitoring can be performed through scalable time series databases that are designed for high throughput ingestion and query. Models using AI scrutinize historical patterns to spot deviations from normal activity.

$$h_t = LSTM(x_t, h_{t-1})$$
$$\hat{y}_t = Wh_t + b$$

where $\hat{y}_t$ may represent predicted risk scores or functional performance metrics.

- **AI-Driven Anomaly Detection**

Functional deterioration or unwanted incidents are detected early with the help of anomaly detection algorithms applied on normal behaviour patterns. Reconstruction-based models such as Autoencoder reconstruct the input signals and detect anomalies:

$$L = ||x_t - \hat{x}_t||^2$$

If the model can provide reconstructions of the volume using the principal component analysis (PCA) coefficients, then for a random dataset generated using the same parameters, it will likely fail to reconstruct it and generate an error.

- **Scalability, Security, and Interoperability**

While interventions shall remain on the safe side in administering health monitoring concerning metaverse, various vital steps must be taken including the use of distributed architectures, secure data exchange protocols, and interoperability standards. Federated learning (FL) allows training of a model over the decentralized source of data without sharing patient-level sensitive information, thus maintaining privacy and ensuring compliance with regulations. Reliable identity management and encrypted communication channels can establish confidence among metaverse participants.

- **Clinical and Societal Impact**

Metaverse health allows for the continuous monitoring of health in place of episodic care, leading to a more proactive system and better outcomes at lower costs. Through wearable AI, digital twins, and immersive interaction, it enables early warning personal therapy and long-term physical connection between doctor and patient. It puts metaverse as a core platform for the next generation of digital healthcare.

7. Clinical Outcomes, Engineering Challenges, and Case Studies

7.1 Clinical Outcomes of Immersive Rehabilitation and Neurotherapy

Clinical trials show time after time that wearable AI-supported immersive rehabilitation systems enhance functional recovery, patient motivation, and therapy compliance more than traditional rehabilitation methods. Patients who receive immersive motor therapy show physical gains in degrees of joint movement, motor coordination, and speed at which they carry out the task. The multisensory character of the virtual surroundings facilitates brain plasticity changes by strengthening the sensorimotor loop and encouraging the repetition of the practice that is focused on goals. Immersive treatments have been reported to lead to better concentration, improved executive function, greater working memory, and better control of emotions in patients with neurological and cognitive difficulties. Neurofeedback via EEG combined with virtual settings allows patients to regulate their brainwaves voluntarily; thus, benefits in cognition can be retained after several therapy sessions. Most importantly, the monitoring that goes on continuously makes it possible for the doctors to use metric-based evidence to track progress over time rather than depending on their subjective observation only. From the point of view of patients personally, immersive rehabilitation boosts their mood and keeps them from dropping out. In particular, gamified therapy settings help reduce the feeling of being tired and the fear factor with children and the aged. These results underline the clinical feasibility of immersion and AI, powered rehab systems for patients of different kinds.

7.2 Engineering Challenges in Immersive Rehabilitation Systems

The equipment or system may need to be checked eventually to determine if it can provide any immediate clinical benefit, despite the challenges put forth by the interface to be overcome, and with limited engineering logic being applied in the process. The issue is identifying the right sensor hardware producing high fidelity logs. Powered sensors restrict their application with impediments of motion artifacts, drifting signals, and the behaviour of non-cooperative users, contributing cumulatively to some inaccurate AI-based evaluations. Hence, the information magic has to be initiated with quality signal preprocessing and fault-tolerant system designing.

Latency and synchronization are mounted as problems that are directly related to closed-loop systems of neurotherapy. These feature sets of real-world portable systems and holding an acceptable real-time feedback demand a deemed synchronization of wearable sensors, some edge AI, the immersive interface, and also cloud services. High latency will intimidate the patience of the individual and have a largely negative impact on the efficacy of that therapy. Scalability and interoperability should not be overlooked either. It is important for immersive rehabilitation platforms to be able to work with heterogeneous devices, software frameworks, and data formats. If there is a lack of standard interfaces, then it may become difficult to roll out large, scale deployments across healthcare institutions. Privacy and data security are two of the most critical issues that may stand in the way of adoption. Continuous health monitoring produces very sensitive personal data, and these data should be protected by using secure communication protocols, access control mechanisms, and regulation-compliant data governance frameworks. Gaining the trust of patients, clinicians, and platform providers is an important engineering as well as ethical challenge.

7.3 Case Study: Immersive Post-stroke Upper Limb Rehabilitation Using Wearable AI

7.3.1 Background and Clinical Context

Stroke is the main cause of long-term motor disability. One of the common strokes is upper-limb dysfunction that severely limits the patient's ability to carry out daily living activities. Traditional post-stroke physiotherapy usually involves performing the same exercises repetitively which might become dull and also lacks customization to the individual's condition. This chapter reports on a case study of the introduction of an immersive rehabilitation system combined with wearable AI for upper-limb motor recovery of post-stroke patients.

7.3.2 System Configuration

The rehabilitation system is made up of a VR world that patients can be a part of and it has wearable motion sensors that are attached to the patient's arm that is hurt. These sensors have IMUs that keep track of how the patient's joints are moving, how fast they are moving, and how they are doing with the tasks they have to do during their therapy sessions. The VR world is like the real world and it has things in it that the patients must do, like reaching out for things, picking them up, and putting them down so that they can practice doing everyday things in a safe place. The rehabilitation system, the VR world, and the motion sensors all work together to help the patients get better. During real-time movement data analysis, upon which edge-level AI processing was based, performance quality was assessed and compensatory strategies were detected. Based on this analysis, the system dynamically adjusted task difficulty, including target size, movement speed requirements, and environmental complexity.

7.3.3 Therapy Protocol

The patients were asked to have therapy sessions only with a frequency of five visits per week for a total of six weeks. Each session had a duration of 30 minutes. The patients were motivated because the therapy sessions involved repetitive arm-movement tasks designed to help them achieve their specific rehabilitation goals. Positive feedback further enhanced motivation, as patients could visually and audibly track their progress during each session. In addition, effective communication between the patient and therapist helped clarify concerns and improved engagement throughout the rehabilitation process. After the last session, they all attended a session with their clinician. The doctors provided an overview of all the visits if they were going into the immersive treatment overnight. The visit summaries helped the patients gain awareness from the visit to the clinician. The study was carefully administered to manage changes in the neurorehabilitation program therapy (NPT) and similar programmes (telehealth). The patient's care and status helped to fully engage in the immersion of this technology with precise data to direct the therapy. The software ensured the patient's care and was used in the derivatives to observe the therapist's activity in a remote manner from the dashboard. The therapy had to be variable. We designed therapy programmes in the correct order for each person.

7.3.4 Clinical Outcomes

There was a noticeable improvement in the degree of movement of their hands and feet. They now moved them better/properly than before. There was a noticeable improvement in the mobility of the participants' hands and feet. They were able to move their limbs more effectively than before and relied much less on compensatory body movements when performing tasks outside of the prescribed exercises. The patients also improved in terms of task performance ability. They were able to achieve a given task at a quicker rate, with a greater measure of accuracy. Participation and adherence by the patients were greater than those in conventional therapy, somewhat due to the interactive, enjoyable nature of the immersive environment. Participants reported that they were less frustrated and had increased self-efficacy in performing daily activities.

7.3.5 Engineering Observations and Challenges

Indeed, the sensors required accurate calibration in addition to negligible glitches in motion to ensure the system was functioning the way it was designed to. Real-time feedback only functioned properly if the sensors communicated with the situational context quickly as any delay in the system marred the immersive experience. For components that still require some data while being converted to the web, such as scanners, they will create a self-contained module that can be communicated using the appropriate web services in the future, with the implementation of more developed camera-based classification systems. Since data fusion is vital, researchers intend to use the intelligence of adaptive decision mechanism in integrating data and protecting its security.

7.3.6 Implications for Future Rehabilitation Systems

According to the narrative, it believed that, besides an immersive rehabilitation experience, wearable AI systems can offer certain levels of treatment as per the patient's requirements. The experience's enhancement and the clinical significance of the hurdles overcome mean the approach can be scaled. This, then, fits into the bigger approach of the extension of targets, which includes app-at-home rehabilitation in terms of therapy or long-distance therapy. Also, given the innovations in neurotechnology, AI applications, and standards, these immersive rehabilitation solutions are likely only expected to become more effective and accessible.

8. Neurotherapy and Cognitive Rehabilitation

Neurotherapies and cognitive rehabilitation are concerned with the improvement or restoration of cognitive functions through structured stimulation, feedback, and training. The interactive, controlled, ecologically valid environments make better sense and engage a patient as opposed to the ordinary clinical setting. Immersive neurotherapy systems, when coupled with wearable technologies informed by AI software, enable the implementation of tailored, adaptive, data-driven interventions, which can be dynamically altered according to the cognitive and neural status of each individual [7, 11, 13, 14].

Cognitive rehabilitation guided in immersion rests on the neurosensing devices worn, in particular the EEG headsets; these record neural signals for processing in real time related to mental workload, attention, memory load, and emotional control. Using machine learning models digesting these mental states from operated signals, we adapt the immersion tasks, e.g., memory games, attention training exercises, and executive function challenges. This closed-loop feedback mechanism, by adjusting the difficulty of the therapy moment by moment and regulating sensory stimuli based on the mental capabilities of the patient, sustains engagement and ensures reliable learning [15-17].

Neuro-interface integration enhances immersive neurotherapy by allowing direct interaction between neural activity and the virtual environment. By using neurofeedback, the patient is able to control some aspects of the immersive environment based on his brain activity, such as object movement, task progression or visual feedback, when positive neural patterns are being reinforced due to the brain's activity. These procedures could be most efficacious in any situation involving a neuropsychiatric disorder, attention deficits, and cognitive impairment following a neurological injury, where conventional therapy protocols may lack tools for direct feedback.

The most tenable result of advanced analytic brain connectivity has been the possibilities now present for more detailed neurotherapies. The computer simulations are modelling functional connectivity across different regions of the brain. The treatment approach of the future will no longer be based on population averages, but rather on a patient's own neuro-connectivity. This personalized neuromodulation, which includes behavioural interactions undergoing individualization through male or female gender, should deplete dissatisfaction and cognitive stagnation and increase therapeutic efficiency. In a broader field, deep neurotherapy shows hope for moving beyond traditional cognitive exercises to an adjusted, engaging, and easily representative therapeutic framework. Wearable AI, immersive experiences, and intelligent feedback lead to a bright future for capitalism: quick-paced rehabilitation and real cognitive enhancement in the guise of infecting the social will rather than being solely a medical prescription proper [11, 12, 18, 19].

9. Ethical, Legal, and Social Considerations

Integrating wearables with AI and with immersive rehabilitation and neurotherapy is not only about exciting technologies. Concrete ethical, legal, and social questions are also raised, and these cannot be ignored. In order to remain safe, fair, and truly responsible, these must be addressed. The stakes are much higher in these systems: they do not merely passively collect data; they continuously siphon the most private and sensitive information about people's health, habits, and their daily lives. They are also capable of making decisions on their own, sometimes without an influential human being, thereby altering ways to establish complicatedly semantic relationships with technologies. Therefore, a lot of this has to be taken very seriously. The introduction into real-world situations would bring a sense of responsibility to all participants: procedures must be exposed as much as possible, facilitating clear communication to disclose information on data handling and decision-making, and setting up for acceptable oversight. Further, the last mile must have a watchman, someone explicitly standing guard for the rights, privacy, and well-being of patients, ensuring that innovation does not compromise trust and ethical standards [18].

9.1 Data Privacy and Security

These devices remain on all the time, tracking various types of parameters like your pulse or your gait, and maybe even what is running through your mind. Again, that is an immense treasure trove of sensitive data. Privacy and security are not voluntary. They are the essence where information storage is concerned. That means getting everything encrypted, using secure channels to disseminate this information, and giving access only to those who can contribute positively in this dark globe. The part of keeping data secure during use is easily met. Now, considering how long we store data and how we safely and perhaps totally delete it when it is no longer needed has moved centre stage in engineering design philosophy. A small error and privacy in its entirety hovers on the head of a pin.

9.2 Algorithmic Transparency and Accountability

The AI-based rehabilitation tools do not only follow instructions but also learn; thus, they come with a decision. However, this decision-making process is invisible to everyone involved, making it problematic for the doctors to trust such a system. AI designers must provide information on how their AI solution works; if a clinician has to get into the AI's grandmotherly shoes (as they must do, at the end of the day), they must see why AI came to its decision and they must also get the proof. In this sense, the actual transparency means explaining why the algorithms work, where the training data came from, and where the system might fall short. People should be able to zoom into how that network had created the suggestion as soon as they perceive that something has gone wrong, not hide behind the excuse of complicated code [12].

9.3 Bias and Fairness in AI Models

The AI systems were provided with the data that only represent a limited number of scenarios, so different results can be expected in the real world. This is not a technical error, but a serious moral issue. For this reason, an ethically prejudiced dataset could magnify health disparities and social inequities. Therefore, there is a need to embrace a broader spectrum of datasets, reflect on the data to see if there is any bias, and build systems useful for all types of people, and not just for the few who fit the criteria of the computer initially. They also need to monitor the reliability of temporal algorithms so as not to embed any form of outdated biases.

9.4 Compliance with Regulation and the Law

Immersion rehabilitation systems, given their categorization as medical devices, have to comply strictly with safety, performance, and quality prescriptions. When developing features or implementing the tools, the regulations for medical software, wearables, or AI clinical support must be seriously taken into consideration. Only through these rules are patients kept safe, and doctors and clinics develop trust in and with the technology, with reduced risk of litigation slipping across from anywhere.

9.5 User Autonomy and Informed Consent

The dynamic interaction provided by the immersive therapy experience makes user autonomy and informed consent significant issues. Patients must be duly informed so that they know about all the data collected, how the AI processes it, and also the risks and benefits involved in therapy. This consent cannot be considered as a permanent sign-off considering the long-term monitoring involved [18] as well as the possibility of an evolving situation. The discussion should remain open to all, not just at the detailed informed consent stage, but throughout the care processes.

9.6 Social Impact and Accessibility

According to societal standards, or rather with less ethnographic points of view, internet-based rehabilitation facility support is easier to manage for friends and family members, both in close proximity and from a long distance. The problem here is when everybody does not share the same internet and computer skills or even invariably do not have functioning connections or tablets or laptops. Expense, efficiency, and the potential to benefit mankind form cherished considerations, as not addressing these issues implies the rehabilitation systems shall become tools for but a few and lead to a cumbersome legacy for the less fortunate [19]. Such technologies must be made affordable for the public and available for conventional use.

10. Future Direction

The AI-embedded wearables will support an interface with immersive extended gaming for many purposes, primarily for rehabilitation and the neurosciences. The convergence between small sensors, longer-lasting batteries, and newer materials is making possible the manufacture of more amiable, wearable, and continuous monitoring devices for several rehabilitation applications. This type of therapy system will begin to govern early-life set-ups rather than be limited to clinic walls.

The role of AI and human-like intelligence will increase in the days ahead. Personalized and decision-making systems are the ones to looked forward to. The emerging systems are expected to incorporate methods to proactively treat or prevent the so-called chronic diseases by monitoring the early signs of functional mobility, and presenting interventions as advised according to the predictions made by AI. The use of digital twins with real-world patient datasets all combined on a single large-scale and sophisticated platform could provide intervention options for drug design, devising protocols, and management that are physiologically better informed than the present conventional methods. The full-scale adoption of immersive rehabilitation solutions depends on technology integration and continuous innovation, which are supported by the right infrastructure. In this light, organizational, institutional, standard, and data attributes entirely enable supporting open architectures and healthcare data interoperability. A range of healthcare wearable devices, training systems, and clinical systems—even secondary in nature, using some cutting-edge "cloudification" app support—can integrate with each other not merely within one institution, across multiple organizations. This enables collaboration among enterprises that come together for consortium-based research, large-scale multi-site clinical trials, and population health analytics.

Further studies must rely mostly on large-scale longitudinal studies in accordance with future developments to ensure the long-term safety and efficacy of VR therapy. It will be critical to implement evidence-based design frameworks to turn technological innovations into salient therapeutic outcomes. Also, hybrid models—perhaps with the therapeutically more potent coalescent form of combining on-site care and immersive telerehabilitation system as remote assistance—might soon become the typical practice. In other words, these models will magnify services as they administer them and promote access while maintaining good [=high] quality clinical oversight. Hence, ethical and regulatory frameworks should keep pace with prevailing technologies. The systems of the future should necessarily come with robust mechanisms for ensuring transparency, data protection mechanisms having clout, and inclusive design possibilities to maintain fairness and trust over the long term. Additionally, the issues of accessibility, affordability, and digital literacy are barriers to removing the disparity in the adoption of immersive rehabilitation technologies.

It is, therefore, expected that the future development of neurotherapy and immersive rehabilitative technologies will be intensified by AI-engineering advancements, with significant strides in AI interoperability, medical legitimacy, and addressing ethical concerns. With this, there could be possible disruptions in rehabilitation services with AI-driven healthcare enterprises that could bring forth a new patient-centric approach.

11. Conclusion

The integration of AI with metaverse-oriented technology and other immersive environments and systems could thus enable the development of some potentially powerful systems for the benefit of rehabilitation and neurotherapy. Such systems can also operate differently in terms of gathering information, in that they are capable of listening, assessing, and tailoring themselves to treatments designed specifically for a unique individual rather than for a model of "generic" patients presented in a set standard. This, in fact, is a major step away from the usual rehabilitation route laid down for other treatments. With the wearable sensors and smart devices operating on-premise and in cloud set-ups and coming with interactive interfaces, patients are continuously monitored and immediately supplied with feedback at any given time. All this data for continuous monitoring is not kept idle, but it assists clinicians in making better decisions, as well as in keeping the therapy process monitored throughout. This increases the interactivity of the therapy, supports brain health, and provides the clinicians with some real data instead of just their gut feelings. The integration of digital twin models with feedback-controlled systems can facilitate the development of self-adaptive treatments that are personalized and predictive, allowing interventions to be optimized before symptoms appear. The engineers sense a big opportunity here, especially with telerehabilitation and systems that people can adopt for home use. Hence, more people have access to healthcare services even if they have fewer resources and without requiring big hospitals. Surely, there are still battles of technology issues, concerns for privacy, and making sure that everything is legitimate. But AI continues to get more intelligent and reliable in return, and security is becoming tighter. Different routes towards the actual use of that stuff in real clinics never look as hopeful as they are today. In conclusion, it can be stated that immersive environments, wearable AI, and the metaverse will change rehabilitation and neurotherapy forever. But, of course, nothing happens in a vacuum. Engineers, doctors, and policymakers need to ensure that prolonged cooperation eventually transitions such theoretical gems into our lives as real, practical, and equitable healthcare solutions for everyone.

References

[1] Riva, G., Wiederhold, B.K. and Mantovani, F. (2023). The metaverse in medicine: Clinical, technical, and ethical perspectives. *Journal of Medical Internet Research*, 25, e42119.

[2] Slater, M. and Sanchez-Vives, M.V. (2021). Enhancing presence in immersive virtual environments. *Frontiers in Robotics and AI*, 8, 622.

[3] Bortone, I., Leonardis, D., Solazzi, M., et al. (2020). Immersive virtual environments and wearable haptic devices in rehabilitation. *Journal of NeuroEngineering and Rehabilitation*, 17(1), 1–16.

[4] Li, X., Liu, H., Wang, Y. and Zhang, Y. (2023). Digital twins in healthcare: Foundations and applications. *IEEE Access*, 11, 115432–115447.

[5] Esteva, A., Robicquet, A. and Ramsundar, B., et al. (2019). A guide to deep learning in healthcare. *Nature Medicine*, 25(1), 24–29.

[6] Smith, A., Thomas, E. and Lee, J. (2024). Artificial intelligence-driven virtual rehabilitation systems. *npj Digital Medicine*, 7(1), 45.
[7] Kim, K., Yang, H., Lee, J. and Lee, W. G. (2023). Metaverse wearables for immersive digital healthcare: A review. *Advanced Science*, 10, 2303234.
[8] Jiao, D. (2025). AI-enhanced digital therapeutics for cognitive impairment: Integrating mobile applications, virtual reality, and wearable devices. *Discover Artificial Intelligence*, 5, 69.
[9] Sundaravadivazhagan, B., Balasubramaniam, B.S., Raj, P., et al. (eds) (2025). *Applying Metaverse Technologies to Human–Computer Interaction for Healthcare*. Auerbach Publications.
[10] González-Erena, P.V., Fernández-Guinea, S. and Kourtesis, P. (2025). Cognitive assessment and training in extended reality: Multimodal systems, clinical utility, and challenges. *arXiv preprint*, 14 January.
[11] Nairn, B., Tsakanikas, V., Gordon, B., et al. (2025). Smart wearable technologies for balance rehabilitation in older adults at risk of falls: Scoping review and comparative analysis. *JMIR Rehabilitation and Assistive Technologies*, 12, e69589.
[12] Yi-Lwern Yap, K. (2024). Navigating the healthcare metaverse: Immersive technologies and future perspectives. *Virtual Worlds*, 3(3), 368–383.
[13] Wang, Y., Zhu, M., Chen, X., et al. (2024). The application of metaverse in healthcare. *Frontiers in Public Health*, 12, 1420367.
[14] Garcia-Lizana, F., et al. (2022). Telerehabilitation using immersive virtual reality: A systematic review. *Journal of NeuroEngineering and Rehabilitation*, 19, 89.
[15] Maier, A., Rubio Ballester, A., Duff, E., et al. (2020). Effect of virtual reality-based rehabilitation on motor recovery after stroke. *Neurorehabilitation Neural Repair*, 33(2), 112–129.
[16] Patel, S., et al. (2020). Wearable sensors and rehabilitation systems: A review. *Journal of NeuroEngineering and Rehabilitation*, 17, 6515.
[17] Dias, R.D., Gupta, S. and Yule, M. (2022). Digital twins and the metaverse in healthcare: Emerging technologies. *IEEE Journal of Biomedical and Health Informatics*, 26(11), 5386–5398.
[18] Dhaliwal, A. and Singh, S.S. The role of metaverse technology in the healthcare supply chain: Identifying clustering patterns, application areas, and future directions, *Data Science and Informetrics*, vol. 6, Art. no. 100025, 2026.
[19] Mugisha, S., Job, M., Zoppi, M., Testa, M., and Molfino, R. Computer-mediated therapies for stroke rehabilitation: A systematic review and meta-analysis, *Journal of Stroke and Cerebrovascular Diseases*, vol. 31, no. 6, Art. no. 106454, 2022.

9 Wearable AI and Metaverse Initiatives for Management of Rheumatoid Arthritis: Past, Present, and Future Perspectives

M. Santhanamari[1], B. Aswini[2], B. Sreechandana[3], S. Sheik Asraf[4*], P. Nagaraj[5] and Raja Murugan[6]

Rheumatoid arthritis (RA) is a chronic autoimmune disorder. This chapter discusses in detail the convergence of artificial intelligence (AI), wearables, and the metaverse for managing RA. It focuses on fitness trackers, intelligent companions, and continuous health for the management of RA. The chapter also examines edge and cloud computing, remote patient monitoring, and AI-guided metaverse for management of RA. It highlights the issues of privacy, security, and data governance for the management of RA, besides discussing the regulatory challenges for AI-driven wearables for the management of RA. The chapter concludes by deliberating upon the future of personalized medicine and predictive health for the management of RA.

1. Rheumatoid Arthritis

Rheumatoid arthritis (RA) is a long-standing autoimmune disorder; it attacks a person's immune system and causes prolonged pain in the lining of the joints throughout the body. In the initial stage, the joint lining (synovial membrane) is affected. In severe cases, cartilage destruction, bone erosion, and disability might develop (Table 9.1). Pain starts with the joints of the feet and hands, which is followed by morning stiffness that lasts more than half an hour. This also affects the patients' organs, including the lungs, heart, blood vessels, skin, and eyes. RA is diagnosed by physical examination, blood tests, and X-ray scans [1].

The initial blood test for RA is the rheumatoid factor test, which confirms whether an autoantibody that wrongly targets healthy cells is present or not. But

[1-4] Department of Biotechnology, Kalasalingam Academy of Research and Education, Virudhunagar, Tamil Nadu, India.
[5] Department of Computer Science and Engineering, School of Computing, SRM Institute of Science and Technology, Tiruchirappalli, Tamil Nadu, India.
[6] School of Civil and Mechanical Engineering, Curtin University, Perth, Australia.
* Corresponding author: s.sheikasraf@klu.ac.in

DOI: 10.1201/9781003776291-9

doctors also recommend taking the anti-cyclic citrullinated peptide (anti-CCP) test [2]. Smoking is the major risk factor for RA [3].

Treatments with disease-modifying anti-rheumatic drugs (DMARDs) are effective in controlling inflammation and reducing bone destruction. But overall remission rates still stay at a low level. DMARDs are subdivided into three types:

i. Conventional synthetic DMARDs (csDMARDs)
ii. Targeted synthetic DMARDs (tsDMARDs)
iii. Biologic DMARDs

In clinical practice, csDMARDs (methotrexate, hydrochloroquine, and sulfadiazine) control inflammation. They are administered orally. Sometimes, methotrexate is used subcutaneously for better outcomes. It is the most widely prescribed medication, especially at the beginning of the disease, for long term. Doctors usually start the treatment with this drug because of its proven effectiveness and reasonable cost. The tsDMARDs (pan-JAK and JAK1/2 inhibitors) act on a specific pathway, like the JAK-STAT signalling pathway. The biological DMARDs (tumour necrosis factor (TNF)-α inhibitors, TNF receptor (R) inhibitors, IL-6 inhibitors, IL-6 receptor (R) inhibitors, B cell depleting antibodies, and inhibitors of co-stimulatory molecules) are produced by living cells, which are protein-based medicines. They play a major role in targeting the specific immune cells or inflammatory cytokines. Glucocorticoids and non-steroidal anti-inflammatory drugs (NSAIDs) are effective in controlling pain and inflammation, but treatment with these drugs is slow. A higher rate of adverse events led to treatment failure. That is why RA is typically a symmetric, erosive condition and is no longer considered curable [4].

In the initial stages, technological progressions in RA management data were stored in paper-based tools for assessing disease activity and patient-reported outcome measures. Tools like the Disease Activity Score (DAS), Health Assessment Questionnaire (HAQ), and visual analogue scales helped to measure disease severity and functional disability. The negative side of paper-based systems was that they required a lot of labour, were susceptible to transcription mistakes, and were frequently inadequate, mainly in hectic clinical environments. The disease recorded only particular moments and daily symptoms [5].

Electronic health records (EHRs) are better than paper-based records. They are useful to easily store data like clinical and laboratory results, X-Ray outcomes, and treatment. They aid in evidence-based decision-making. People who live in rural areas find this digital technology and tele-rheumatology more helpful [6].

The importance of usability, helpful relevance, and information integration has been emphasized by insights from the earliest digital initiatives in RA management. The foundation for today's wearable AI gadgets and fully immersive devices has been laid by previous technical developments, highlighting the need for patient-focused, continuous, and effective solutions in RA medical care [7].

Table 9.1 Overview of RA management: Past, present, future.

Stage	*Scientific Perspective on RA*	*Treatment Protocols*	*Advantages*	*Reference*
Past	Not clearly recognized as an autoimmune disease or age-related arthritis	Only pain, inflammation relief with aspirin, corticosteroids, NSAIDs	Short-term relief	[1]
Present	RA is established as a chronic autoimmune disease	DMARDs, physiotherapy and lifestyle modification	Aim to achieve low disease activity, prevent disability, and improve quality of life	[4]
Future	Expect evolved medicine	Preventive strategies, targeted therapies, and digital health monitoring	Transform RA care into proactive, individualized management	[6, 7]

2. Convergence of AI, Wearables, and the Metaverse for Management of RA

The application of AI is rapidly growing in the fields of medicine and healthcare. Machine learning and deep learning methods can provide high-quality care to patients with chronic diseases. They help to effectively analyse clinical data along with medical images, radiographs, patient histories, and molecular profiles. They also help to detect RA in the early stages and also provide better disease management. Machine learning helps doctors to understand which drug is suitable for the patient [8].

Rheumatoid arthritis leads to noticeable changes in several physical parameters of the patient. It affects body composition by causing muscle loss and changes in fat mass; reduces muscle function through weakness, stiffness, and fatigue; and compromises joint integrity, resulting in pain, swelling, stiffness, and, in some cases, deformities [2, 3]. These changes are mainly associated with chronic inflammation and reduced physical activity. Portable wearable devices, including smartwatches and biosensors, such as Apple Watch, Fitbit, and Oura ring, continuously monitor the user's data [9]. Wearable activity trackers are widely used and monitor physical parameters such as steps, inactivity time, activity intensity, sleep pattern, and energy expenditure, with data displayed as graphs and statistics on connected devices [10].

A variety of digital health tools that record physiological and functional characteristics are present in wearable technologies, which open up new possibilities for managing the symptoms of RA. Through objective data, these devices which are divided by design, sensing science and technology, and clinical application connect periodic evaluations with the unpredictable nature of the illness and help in proactive, specific treatment. While they lack joint-specific monitoring, smartwatches and health bands are the most common gadgets for tracking activity, rest, steps, and cardiac rate in an affordable and easy-to-use manner. While specific gloves and joint sensors focus on hand and fingers functionality, which is necessary for quality of life, yet often constrained by comfort, motion, and foot sensors applied on the wrist, ankle, or back offer insights regarding stiffness, stride, and action symmetry [9, 10].

Artificial intelligence (AI) supports automated tools. It is designed for analysing photographs of joints of individuals with RA. Manually diagnosis relies heavily on the experience and skill of every physician. However, the system can verify every image with ease. AI-assisted individuals also cut down on data review timing [7].

By enabling extensive data analysis, modelling of probabilities, and individualized therapy initiatives, AI has transformed the treatment of RA. AI changes administration from reactive consultations to proactive oversight by combining information from wearable devices, imaging, lab testing, and EHRs. While deep learning systems like recurrent and convolutional neural networks handle intricate time-series data from wearables, machine learning methods like support vector AI and random forests use data to classify disease activity. These concepts could introduce entirely new approaches to delivering patient care at low cost [11].

Creative approaches for controlling RA have emerged from metaverse-based applications, which provide psychosocial, educational, and therapeutic support outside of traditional healthcare settings. These apps reduce the need for in-person visitation while improving continuity of treatment, involvement of patients, and functional rehabilitation through the integration of immersive technology, real-time data, and interactive platforms. RA patients can engage in supervised exercises in stimulating conditions with individual feedback through virtual rehabilitation and therapy programmes, which may be especially helpful for people with limited availability of facilities. In addition to medical care, cognitive behavioural therapy (CBT) and immersive pain management offer coping mechanisms and methods for sleep and distraction to lessen mental discomfort and pain perception without the need for medication. By enhancing presence and conversation and incorporating wearable and medical data for improved illness monitoring (Figure 9.1) and collaborative decision-making, virtual clinics boost telemedicine [12].

Through interactive simulations, education for patients and training in self-management enable patients to learn about their disease, follow their treatment plan, and identify flare-ups early. In metaverse groups of people, social support increases quality of life, boosts psychological well-being, and fights feelings of isolation. Together, these mobile applications offer a thorough, individualized method of RA management that take into account social, psychological, and physical needs. However, there are certain limitations too (see Table 9.2) [12].

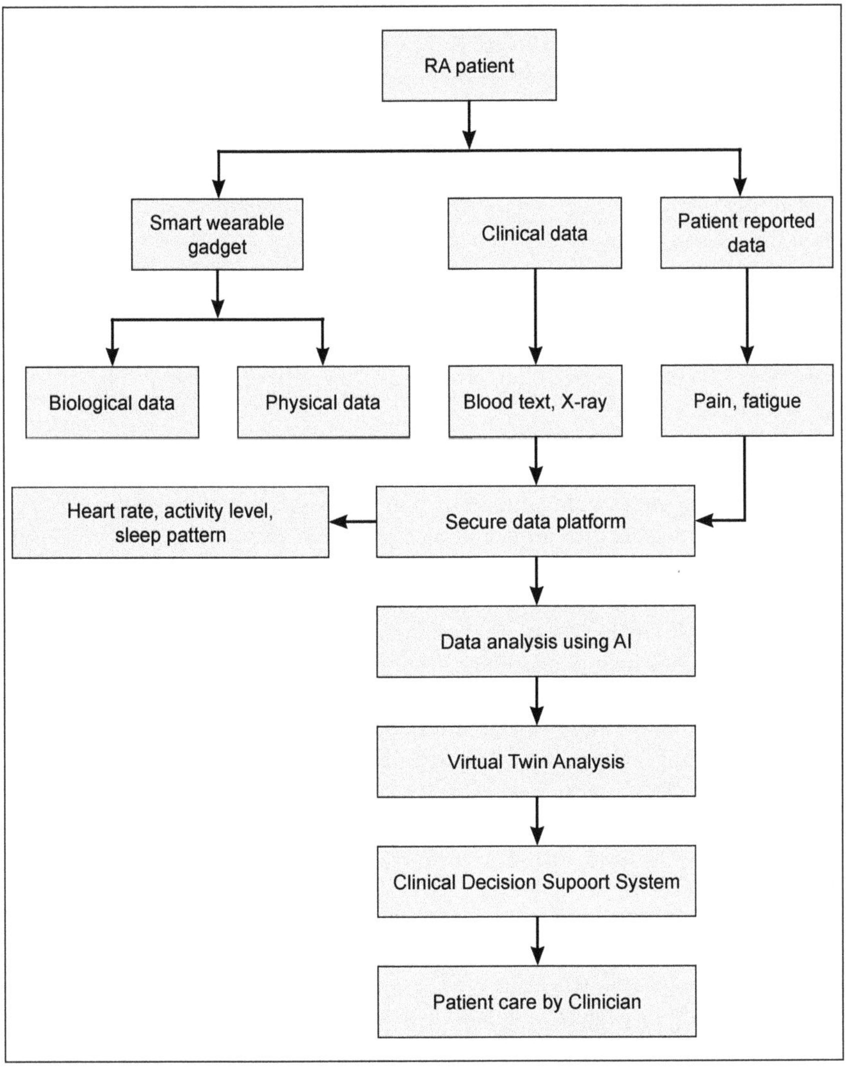

Fig. 9.1 Complete flow chart for patient data analyses.

3. Fitness Trackers, Intelligent Companions, and Continuous Health for the Supervision of RA

Fitness trackers put focus on people's physical activity, including their movement and overall stages of activity over the day. They collect data on the duration and quality of sleep, and also monitor the heart rate. These gadgets also track the duration of inactivity and calculate the calories burned. They gives users a detailed assessment of their daily physical health and exercise. Patients are becoming

Table 9.2 The primary limitations of wearable technology.

Factor	*Barrier*	*Sample*	*Impact*	*Reference*
Data Accuracy	Sensor errors, calibration issues	Misread joint movement or fatigue	Unable to monitor disease	[13]
User Compliance	Forgetting or misuse of devices	Patient forgot wearing tracker	Inconsistent data collection	[10]
Technical Issues	Battery, connectivity, malfunctions	Suddenly stop during use	Interrupted continuous tracking	[7]
Privacy Concerns	Risk of sensitive data exposure	Health data leaks or breaches	Loss of trust and engagement	[10, 13]

more aware of their physical activity levels, thanks to activity trackers. Wearable activity trackers gather data on their own in the background for self-monitoring, which helps in patient education and increases involvement in their care [7]. In rheumatology, wearable activity trackers are commonly used to monitor physical activity and track the health of patients with musculoskeletal and rheumatic conditions. Additionally, these technologies in quality clinical practice are still required since they help in checking activity levels and other health factors, and, when connected with AI, can support early diagnosis through sudden increase in symptoms. In most cases, the application of AI to RA can help doctors in the early detection of the condition. Machine learning may help rheumatologists in the future by improving disease estimation. Still, there are difficulties such as data accuracy, privacy problems, technical problems, and problems in finding the disease's course and key factors [9]. Wearable technology (Table 9.3) and cell phones can be used to track physical activity, which is important for reducing the intensity of RA.

Regular exercise increases joint function, reduces pain, and supports general health. According to the World Health Organization (WHO), to keep good health, adults should try to engage in balanced to strong physical activity, such as fast walking, for at least 150 minutes each week. Activity checks make patients more aware of their physical activity levels [7]. In case of self-monitoring, e.g., a wearable activity tracker checks data in the background, giving a push for patient education and involvement in their care [9]. Rheumatology Patient-Recorded results use of activity checkers to find clinical results. Public Health England published observations showing people in every regional government area were doing less than half an hour of physical activity per month. Usually, the application of AI in RA may help doctors to diagnose the disease earlier [7].

Machine learning could be a useful method to help rheumatologists by indicating worsening of the disease and by describing related diseases. While professionals appreciate physical activity trackers (PATs) for goal-setting and monitoring, they are worried about their long-term use and data quality. Patients find them motivating but also face problems including pain, tiredness, and lack of interest. Both the groups agree that the acceptance of PATs depends on their specific use [8]. Increasing exercises is the main non-pharmacological care for RA, which causes pain and disability. The best exercise dosage for RA is unknown, despite NICE's (National Institute of Health and Care Excellence) suggestion. The exercise regimens used in many clinical trials are not validated. Improved hand use and strength were associated with higher doses of hand-strengthening activities. The need for dosage improvement is shown by the fact that therapists change exercise level based on patient discomfort, and disease progression, and hand strength. The usefulness of strengthening activities for people with RA is greatly influenced by the types of exercises [12].

Twelve kids between the ages of 10 years and 18 years used a smartwatch and a smartphone app that reminded them to do daily physical activity and take medications. The study tested the system's usability and children's level of approval using a detailed method. Across the tools used in digital health research, wearable technologies help to collect health data. Osteoarthritis and inflammatory arthritis patients use activity checkers. Most studies had poor quality of reporting, which highlights the need for clearer reporting, else it becomes difficult to compare similar actions. The immune system commonly protects the body, but in autoimmune illnesses, it wrongly targets healthy tissues, resulting in inflammation. A wearable sensor-based smartphone app has the potential to help patients before inflammatory flare-ups by checking and controlling autoimmune illnesses [14].

Table 9.3 Wearables' application and clinical usage.

Domain in RA Management	*Specific Application*	*Data/Tool Used*	*Clinical Use in RA*	*Reference*
Self-management	Daily activity monitoring	Fitness trackers	Helps patients understand their daily activity, set personal goals, and notice how their symptoms change with different activities	[9]
Disease monitoring	Long-term activity trends	Wearable and digital platforms	Helps detect flare-ups, monitor movement problems, and track disease effects over time	[10]
Rehabilitation and exercise therapy	Strength and resistance exercise dosing	Exercise prescription frameworks	Helps design safe and personalized exercise plans for people with rheumatoid arthritis	[11]
Clinical decision support	Pattern recognition in activity data	Machine learning algorithm	Helps doctors easily understand large amounts of data collected from patients	[13]

Contd...

Table 9.3 *Contd...*

Domain in RA Management	*Specific Application*	*Data/Tool Used*	*Clinical Use in RA*	*Reference*
Patient–clinician communication	Sharing variable data during consultations	Digital dashboards	Enhances decision-making	[9]

4. Edge and Cloud Computing, Remote Patient Monitoring, and AI-guided Metaverse for Managing RA

Many existing systems used today are not very effective during emergencies and do not provide personalized care for patients with different health risks to overcome this issue. An edge and cloud computing–based smart healthcare system is proposed that can continuously monitor patient health by using intelligent technologies. This system regularly analyses patient health data and helps doctors to identify patients who need urgent care, while others can be normally monitored [15]. Healthcare technology is developing rapidly, and remote patient monitoring has become an important solution for managing health issues of the rising population with increasing medical problems. The early remote monitoring systems started as simple systems inside hospital rooms. But those have now advanced to allow patients to stay at home while still being continuously monitored. This monitoring system can be disease-based or situation-based depending on the patient's condition and healthcare needs. These technologies include body-worn sensors, environment-based sensors, and advanced contactless monitoring systems [16]. The metaverse is the next form of the internet, where people do not just watch a screen, but can also enter and interact inside a digital world. It uses technologies like AI, augmented reality (AR), virtual reality (VR), and fast internet connections, such as 5G, to connect the real world with the digital world. This close connection between real and virtual environments can help improve physical healthcare and mental healthcare services. This metaverse can change healthcare mainly by combining three main technologies: telepresence, digital twins, and blockchain [17].

To support the large-scale metaverse healthcare application, cloud services are used due to their scalability and flexibility. Amazon Web Services (AWS), Google Cloud, and Microsoft Azure are the major cloud platforms that use flexible, on-demand computer resources and storage solutions. The ability to scale the virtual resource is vital for managing periods of high demand and remote clinical consultation. Cloud platforms also provide secure, reliable, and easy-to-access storage for datasets (medical), records of patient data, and simulation files. It is economical because users pay only for the resources they consume.

Edge computing is necessary to improve the performance of VR and AR, and healthcare applications because it brings the resource closer to the data source. By reducing the latency, this setup confirms faster responsiveness for time-critical medical tasks and enables real-time experiences such as VR-based physical therapy. The main beneficial application is real-time processing and faster data transfer for the diagnostic tools.

Recently, governments, corporate companies, and some individuals are actively migrating their data to the cloud. So it creates a huge amount of data, which increases the possible threats, such as unauthorized access (Table 9.4), data breaches, sensitive information disclosure, and privacy disclosure [18].

Table 9.4 Digital tools for smart healthcare.

Applied Science	*Description*	*Role in Patient Management*	*Reference*
Edge computing	Works close to patient devices	Detect health problems quickly	[15]
Cloud-computing	Keeps health records on servers	Patient records are stored for long-term use	[18]
Remote patient monitoring	Monitors patient health at home	Fewer hospital visits	[16]
Metaverse healthcare	Provides medical care online	Gives medical support online	[17]
Contactless monitoring	Monitors health without contact	Makes patients more comfortable	[16]
Secure data systems	Keeps medical data safe	Ensures data safety	[17]

5. Privacy, Security, and Data Governance for the Supervision of RA

Data privacy refers to protecting the patients' clinical and personal information from any misuse. RA affects a person's data, such as disease activity scores and lab results. Informed consent is the voluntary agreement of the participants. They understand the purpose of a procedure, treatment, or study in research. They are also made aware of the potential benefits and risks and make an informed decision whether or not to be part of the research. It is also important to follow the regulations such as those of the Food and Drug Administration (FDA) in the US, the General Data Protection Regulation (GDPR) in the European Union, and the Indian Council of Medical Research (ICMR in India [19, 20].

The International Organization for Standardization (ISO), GDPR, and Health Insurance Portability and Accountability Act (HIPAA) (US) help to regulate data access, use, and sharing. The use of digital health tools such as electronic medical records, wearable health devices, mobile applications, and AI-driven clinical support systems generate more data [21].

Expanding HIPAA's scope (Table 9.5) could help, but its current framework does not fit the diverse non-clinical environments where health information is increasingly collected and exchanged [21].

6. Regulatory Challenges for AI-driven Wearables for the Management of RA

The progress of AI-driven wearable devices in the medical field has happened at a faster rate than the creation of rules and regulations meant to guarantee that they are safe and work well [8, 10]. Not having a clear idea about guidelines and standards could lead to using machines that are not checked well or do not work properly, which might put the health of patients at risk over the entire period of device malfunction [20]. The absence of regulatory frameworks and low trust and adoption rate of these technologies by doctors and patients are major challenges. The current Software as a Medical Device (SaMD) has FDA authorization. It is a structure, risk-based software used to ensure safety, effectiveness, and clinically reliability. Based on the medical condition, three types of classes (Class 1, Class 2, Class 3) are available [23, 24].

The clinical, regulatory, and approval processes for digital platforms in RA management are developing, with different frameworks in various countries (Figure 9.2) [25, 26, 27]. User safety, privacy, and scalability create new legal issues for medical products in the metaverse, notably those that involve full immersion and involvement by patients. To boost engagement and build trust among patients, it is still necessary to align with regulatory requirements and establish simple guidelines for digital health developments [24].

The WHO underlines the necessity of carefully examining the use of technology in healthcare from a variety of aspects. Evaluations must take into consideration the advantages, potential disadvantages, user approval, practical viability, and implementation resources. It is important to ensure that such efforts advance equity, i.e., the benefits and access are spread equitably across various populations. As a way to provide guidance for the creation and use of AI technology, the WHO has provided an in-depth review of the essential ethical concepts. WHO has provided in depth account of main principles of ethics to facilitate deeper examination. The various challenges at every stage of product lifecycle have been presented in Table 9.6 [23].

Human autonomy must be accepted, not supplanted, by medical autonomy protection. This suggests that effective information security systems must respect autonomy to protect confidentiality, privacy, and legitimate consent. Before being employed by everyone, AI tools must meet high standards for safety, accuracy, and efficacy to advance welfare, safety, and public interest. It must be ensured that everything is done in a clear, reasonable, and honest manner. Software developers, customers, and authorities must be able to understand AI systems. Transparency ensures patient safety, enhances system quality, and enables regulators and evaluators to effectively monitor the system. It has to be clear and adaptable to the people's thinking level.

Table 9.5 Fundamental principles of data governance with an explanation of importance and application.

Aspect	*Key Focus*	*Application in RA Supervision*	*Importance*	*Reference*
Patient Privacy	Confidential handling of personal health information	Protects clinical records, imaging data, genetic information, and patient-reported outcomes collected during RA monitoring	Maintains patient dignity and trust, long-term engagement in the disease	[18, 21]
Informed Consent	Transparency and patient control over data use	RA patients understand how their RA-related data from wearables, mobile apps, and hospital systems will be collected, stored, and shared	Empowers patients and supports ethical data collection practices	[20]
Data Security	Protection against unauthorized access and cyber threats	Implements encryption, secure servers, authentication mechanisms, and regular security audits for RA datasets	Prevents data breaches and preserves the integrity of clinical decision-making systems	[18]
Interoperability	Secure data exchange between systems	Enables safe sharing of RA data across electronic health records, wearable platforms, and clinical research databases	Supports coordinated care and improves continuity in RA management	[18]
Data Quality and Integrity	Accuracy and reliability of collected data	Ensures RA-related data from sensors, laboratory tests, and patient inputs are validated and free from errors	Enhances the reliability of disease monitoring and predictive analytics	[18, 21]
Regulatory Compliance	Alignment with legal and ethical frameworks	Ensures RA supervision systems comply with national and international data protection laws and ethical guidelines	Protects patients' rights and reduces legal and institutional risks	[22]
Ethical Use of Data	Data responsible and fair data utilization	Prevents misuse of RA patient data in research, AI-driven tools, and commercial applications	Promotes fairness, transparency, and socially responsible innovation in RA care	[23]
Data Governance	Policies for data management and accountability	Defines roles, responsibilities, and standards for storing, accessing, sharing, and deleting RA patient data	Ensures ethical data use and consistent data quality across healthcare and research settings	[21]

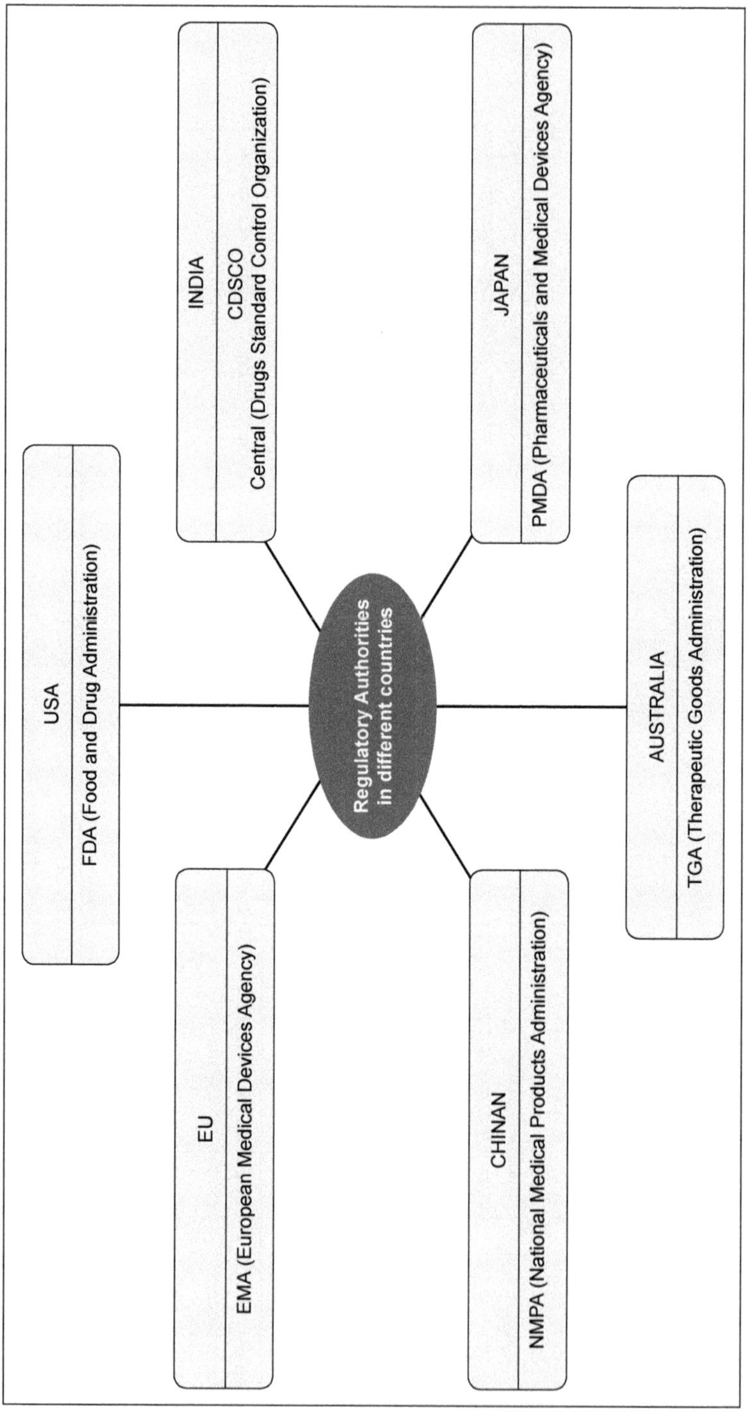

Fig. 9.2 Regulatory organizations in multiple countries.
Source: Reference 25, 26, and 27

Table 9.6 Certain stages and limitations faced by regulatory organizations.

Different Stages	*Challenges*
Product Design (SaMD/Wearable/AI Model)	• Device classification • Sensor accuracy and reliability • AI model explainability • Interoperability standards
Regulatory Strategy (Country-specific Planning)	• EMA, FDA, PMDA, NCA rules • Fragmented approval pathways • Varying risk classification • Pre-submission consultations
Data Privacy and Localization	• GDPR (EU) compliance • HIPAA (US) compliance • PIPL/CSL (China) • Cross-border data restrictions • Secure cloud storage and encryption
Clinical Evidence and Validation	• Demonstrating safety and efficacy • Limited real-world evidence • Device vs software updates • Validation for diverse populations
Regulatory Approval	• Long review timelines • Differences in documentation • Approval delays due to AI updates • Lack of harmonized global standards

Source: Reference 23

7. AI and Explainable AI Claims in Intelligent Systems and Healthcare

Artificial intelligence and explainable AI (XAI) have a foremost role in healthcare, conferring to current trainings. Fusion outlines like PVT-ResNet fusion improve malignancy forecast over combined image examination [28], while progressive deep learning models like enhanced NASNet are being employed for accurate lung adenocarcinoma cataloguing [29]. Furthermore, deep generative AI models are being examined for harmless biometric verification in the therapeutic arena [30]. Interdisciplinary submissions of AI skills include Internet of Things (IoT) systems for recognizing feelings and for detecting diseases [31, 32]. With schemes for diabetes forecast [33] and explainable Alzheimer's disease studies [34], XAI also helps in scientific policymaking, demonstrating AI's extensive variety of requests in healthcare.

8. Conclusion

Concerns about safety, security, and patient trust were raised by the quick development of AI-driven wearable technology in healthcare, as it has surpassed the creation of exact regulations. Global regulatory procedures for digital platforms in the field of treatment of RA are still inconsistent, despite the FDA's SaMD framework offering an organized, risk-based method to guarantee clinical efficacy across Class 1–3. Technology making diagnostic or therapeutic claims must provide evidence of effectiveness, security, and data protection, according to agencies like the FDA and European Medicines Agency (EMA). AI algorithms are also subject to further scrutiny with regard to bias and transparency. Emerging metaverse healthcare solutions increase complexity and necessitate user safety, interoperability, and safeguards for confidentiality. Harmonizing regulatory guidelines and creating simple rules will increase adoption rate and enhance trust between healthcare providers and patients.

Acknowledgement

We thank the management of Kalasalingam Academy of Research and Education for providing the necessary facilities.

References

[1] Smith, M.H. and Berman, J.R. (2022). What is rheumatoid arthritis? *JAMA*, 327(12), 1194.

[2] Rindfleisch, J.A. and Muller, D. (2005). Diagnosis and management of rheumatoid arthritis. *American Family Physician*, 72(6), 1037–1047.

[3] Gao, Y., Zhang, Y. and Liu, X. (2024). Rheumatoid arthritis: Pathogenesis and therapeutic advances. *MedComm*, 5(3), e509.

[4] Lin, Y-J., Anzaghe, M. and Schülke, S. (2020). Update on the pathomechanism, diagnosis, and treatment options for rheumatoid arthritis. *Cells*, 9(4), 880.

[5] Van der Kooi, E., Klarenbeek, N.B., Güler-Yüksel, M., et al. (2011). A decrease in disease activity score (DAS) level is associated with a decrease in health assessment questionnaire (HAQ) score, independent of follow-up duration, during 5 years of tightly controlled treatment: Results from the BeSt study. *Annals of the Rheumatic Diseases*, 70(1), 168–171.

[6] Carroll, R.J., Eyler, A.E. and Denny, J.C. (2015). Intelligent use and clinical benefits of electronic health records in rheumatoid arthritis. *Expert Review of Clinical Immunology*, 11(3), 329–337.

[7] Davergne, T., Kedra, J. and Gossec, L. (2021). Wearable activity trackers and artificial intelligence in the management of rheumatic diseases: Where are we in 2021? *Zeitschrift für Rheumatologie*, 80(10), 928–935.

[8] Momtazmanesh, S., Nowroozi, A. and Rezaei, N. (2022). Artificial intelligence in rheumatoid arthritis: Current status and future perspectives: A state-of-the-art review. *Rheumatology and Therapy*, 9(5), 1249–1304.

[9] Davergne, T., Rakotozafiarison, A., Servy, H. and Gossec, L. (2020). Wearable activity trackers in the management of rheumatic diseases: Where are we in 2020? *Sensors*, 20(17), 4797.

[10] Adepoju, V.A., Jamil, S., Biswas, M.S. and Chowdhury, A.A. (2025). Wearable technology in the management of chronic diseases: A growing concern. *Chronic Diseases and Translational Medicine*, 11(02), 117–121.

[11] Adil, M., Song, H., Khan, M.K., et al. (2025). Metaverse in health care: Security challenges and pathways for future research. *IEEE Systems, Man, and Cybernetics Magazine*, 11(1), 95–106.

[12] Wang, Y., Zhu, M., Chen, X., et al. (2024). The application of the metaverse in healthcare. *Frontiers in Public Health*, 12, 1420367.

[13] Tokatlıoğlu, T.Ş., Oflaz, F. and Semiz, B. (2025). Wearable technologies and psychiatry: Strengths, weaknesses, opportunities, and threats analysis. *Cyprus Journal of Medical Sciences*, 10(2), 111–115.

[14] Gupta, A. (2022). Using fitness tracker data to support self-management of arthritis. MSc Thesis, Simon Fraser University.

[15] Chen, M., Li, W., Hao, Y., et al. (2018). Edge cognitive computing-based smart healthcare system. *Future Generation Computer Systems*, 86, 403–411.

[16] Malasinghe, L.P., Ramzan, N. and Dahal, K. (2019). Remote patient monitoring: A comprehensive study. *Journal of Ambient Intelligence and Humanised Computing*, 10(1), 57–76.

[17] Wiederhold, B.K. and Riva, G. (2022). Metaverse creates new opportunities in healthcare. *Annual Review of Cybertherapy and Telemedicine*, 20, 3–7.

[18] Yang, P., Xiong, N. and Ren, J. (2020). Data security and privacy protection for cloud storage: A survey. *IEEE Access*, 8, 131723–131740.

[19] Neff, M.J. (2008). Informed consent: What is it? Who can give it? How do we improve it? *Respiratory Care*, 53(10), 1337–1341.

[20] Cohen, I.G. and Mello, M.M. (2018). HIPAA and protecting health information in the 21st century. *JAMA*, 320(3), 231–232.

[21] Ngesimani, N.L., Ruhode, E. and Harpur, P.A. (2022). Data governance in healthcare information systems: A systematic literature review. *South African Journal of Information Management*, 24(1), 1475.

[22] Babic, B., Gerke, S., Evgeniou, T. and Cohen, I.G. (2019). Algorithms on regulatory lockdown in medicine. *Science*, 366(6470), 1202–1204.

[23] Mennella, C., Maniscalco, U., De Pietro, G. and Esposito, M. (2024). Ethical and regulatory challenges of AI technologies in healthcare: A narrative review. *Heliyon*, 10(4), e26297.

[24] Food and Drug Administration. (2019). Proposed regulatory framework for modifications to artificial intelligence/machine learning (AI/ML)–based software as a medical device (SaMD). https://apo.org.au/node/228371?__cf_chl_f_tk=QIp_CFaHSq3U4RgN6bh84fDa58ZX788r3k1Tk6m4mXY-1782966533-1.0.1.1-HZ3MgKrOgqGI1I6fdpeTPxtZqreRZQegj4M_sh2Tt8Y. Accessed on 16.12.2025.

[25] Nagaraj, P. and Muneeswaran, V. (2023). A robust recession detective analysis system using IoT smart sensor devices. In *2023 2nd International Conference on Edge Computing and Applications (ICECAA)*, pp. 1260–1264. IEEE.

[26] Subash, M., Asraf, S.S. and Nagaraj, P. (2025). Diagnosis, prevention, and treatment approaches for rheumatoid arthritis using machine learning: AI-driven solutions for rheumatoid arthritis care. Ajibesin Adeyemi Abel, Naveen Sundar G, Senthil Kumar Thangavel (Eds). In *Synergizing Data Envelopment Analysis and Machine Learning for Performance Optimization in Healthcare* (), pp. 285–310. IGI Global Scientific Publishing.

[27] Palaniappan, K., Lin, E. Y.T. and Vogel, S. (2024). Global regulatory frameworks for the use of artificial intelligence (AI) in the healthcare services sector. *Healthcare*, 12(5), 562.

[28] Robert, R., Muneeswaran, V., Kumar, J.S. and Nagaraj, P. (2025). PVT-ResNet fusion: A hybrid DL framework for lung cancer prediction using image analysis and explainable AI. *Iranian Journal of Science and Technology, Transactions of Electrical Engineering*, 1–20.

[29] Lakshmi, G.G., Chinnasamy, P. and Nagaraj, P. (2026). Optimal NAS-MoE: Optimized NASNet and MoE model for lung adenocarcinoma classification with explainable AI. *Biomedical Signal Processing and Control*, 113, 109128.

[30] Vijay, M., Nagaraj, P., Sundareswaran, N. and Christopher, S.R.B. (2025). Deep generative AI-based multimodal biometric authentication system for enhanced security and accessibility in healthcare applications. Balasubramaniam S, Seifedine Kadry (Eds). In *Advances in Deep Generative Models for Healthcare and Medical Applications*, pp. 184–205. CRC Press.
[31] Nagaraj, P., Rajkumar, T.D., Rakesh, S., et al. (2023). AI-based leaf disease identification robot using IoT approach. In *2023 2nd International Conference on Edge Computing and Applications (ICECAA)*, pp. 1375–1379. IEEE.
[32] Pandiaraj, A., Nagaraj, P., Durga, B.V., et al. (2023). A comparative study on emotion AI using machine learning and deep learning models. In *2023 9th International Conference on Advanced Computing and Communication Systems (ICACCS)*, Vol. 1, pp. 900–904. IEEE.
[33] Nagaraj, P., Muneeswaran, V., Dharanidharan, A., et al. (2022). A prediction and recommendation system for diabetes mellitus using XAI-based lime explainer. In *2022 International Conference on Sustainable Computing and Data Communication Systems (ICSCDS)*, pp. 1472–1478. IEEE.
[34] Sudar, K.M., Nagaraj, P., Nithisaa, S., et al. (2022). Alzheimer's disease analysis using explainable artificial intelligence (XAI). In *2022 International Conference on Sustainable Computing and Data Communication Systems (ICSCDS)*, pp. 419–423. IEEE.

10 Privacy, Security, and Data Governance in Continuous Monitoring of Wearable AI and Metaverse

Mani Deepak Choudhry[1*], M. Sundarrajan[2], Karthic Sundaram[3], Arun Kumar R.[4] and Rama Abirami K.[5]

The rapid pace of change and evolution of hospitals into a more innovative ecosystem requires seamless integration, effective data sharing, and more intelligent decision-making. In this chapter, 6G communication technology, blockchain, and artificial intelligence (AI) are identified as trailblazers among the leading enablers of future innovations in the healthcare sector, as they can offer low latency, ensure reliability, and support a vast number of connected devices. The age-related privacy and trustworthiness issues have been addressed by introducing blockchain, which provides a decentralized, immutable system to ensure the secure exchange of patient data. These technologies would then be enhanced by AI, adding value through data analytics, automated diagnostics, and dynamic clinical decision-making. In this chapter, it has been identified that synergy among these three pioneer technologies, i.e., 6G communication, blockchain, and AI, will enable a high tide of enhancing clinical efficiency, patient outcomes optimization, and scalability of delivery in consideration of the future outcomes as the three are integrated collectively in a smarter hospital setting, given that this integration has been taken into account in terms of being part of the core challenges.

1. Introduction to Privacy, Security, and Data Governance in Wearable AI and Metaverse-enabled Healthcare

The proliferation of wearable artificial intelligence (AI) devices and metaverse-enabled healthcare environments has brought about significant changes in the

[1] Department of Computing Technologies, SRM Institute of Science and Technology, Chengalpattu, Tamil Nadu, India.
[2] Department of Networking and Communications, SRM Institute of Science and Technology, Chengalpattu, Tamil Nadu, India.
[3] Department of Computing Technologies, SRM Institute of Science and Technology, Chengalpattu, Tamil Nadu, India.
[4] Digital Forensics and Cybersecurity, University of South Wales, Treforest, United Kingdom.
[5] School of Engineering and Technology, PSB Academy, Singapore.
* Corresponding author: manideec@srmist.edu.in

DOI: 10.1201/9781003776291-10

way medical data is generated, transmitted, stored, and used. Modern wearable biosensors—EGGs (Electrogastrography), smartwatches, neural headsets, glucose monitors, motion tracking garments—are not standalone devices anymore, but they are the nodes of larger cyber-physical health ecosystems. These devices continuously monitor high-frequency physiological signals, behavioral patterns, geolocation data, and even emotional signals using multi-modal sensing.

While great strides have been made in remote diagnostics, preventive medicine, and personalized treatment strategies, the advancements also pose critical threats, such as privacy breaches, unauthorized surveillance, identity spoofing, biometric profiling, inference attacks, and cross-platform data exploitation. The risk surface is expanding not only because the volume of data is increasing, but also because velocity and variety of streaming data are increasing. The overall interaction among the wearable sensors, edge computing gateways, cloud repositories, and the virtual healthcare interfaces is depicted in Figure 10.1, which illustrates the multilayer data propagation as it creates more points of exposure and interception.

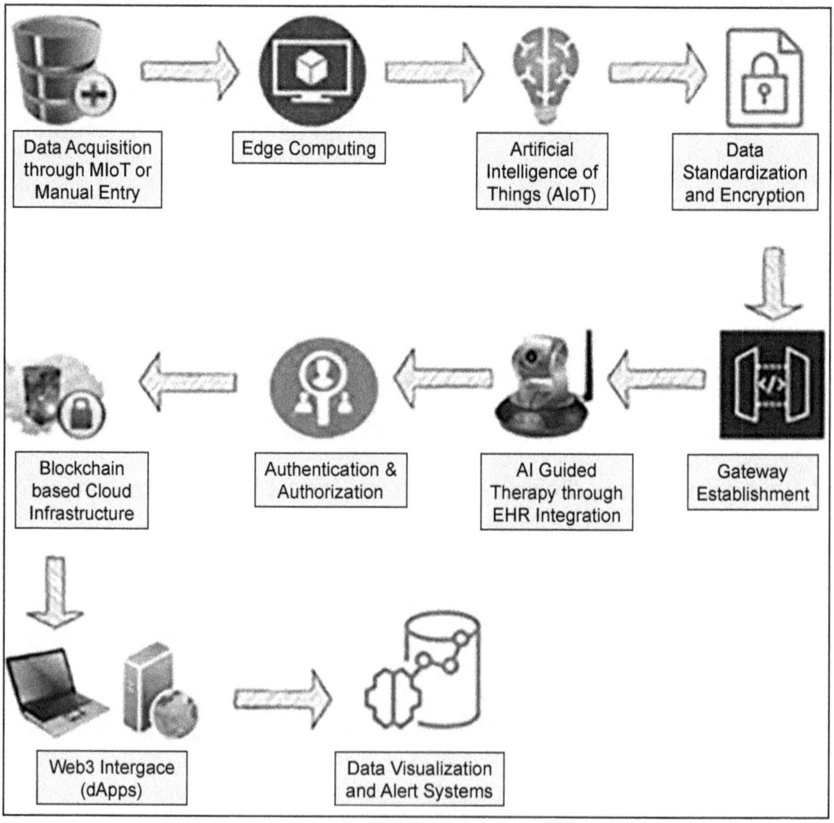

Fig. 10.1 Data flow framework of metaverse and wearable AI in healthcare.

Data governance, therefore, becomes a basic pillar of such ecosystems since healthcare information is very sensitive, long-term in its relevance, legally regulated, and multi-source. The data from wearable metaverse is different from traditional hospital records. The data from wearable metaverse usurps storage policies, retention timelines, and consent revocation procedures. In metaverse healthcare environments, we have digital twins, biometric avatars, holographic consultations, and simulations based on sensor-based information, which result in layered datasets that blur the lines of personal identity and medical information. This convergence forms complex issues in data ownership, compliance with local jurisdictions, legislation on data transfer across borders, accountability regarding algorithms as well as dynamic consent management.

The governance lifecycle presented in Figure 10.2 depicts how at each stage of the lifecycle—from first acquiring and preprocessing data to archival and secure deletion—privacy and compliance protections are built in. In addition, governance strategies increasingly use role-based access control, zero-trust architecture, and differential privacy techniques to reduce the risk of insider threats and external intrusions.

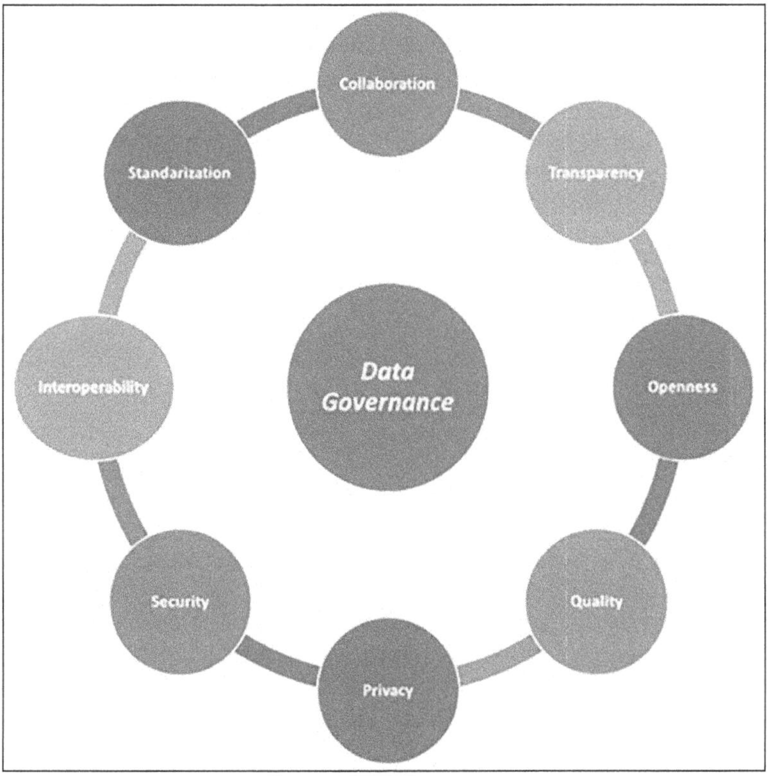

Fig. 10.2 Data governance lifecycle in smart healthcare.

A comprehensive framework for managing the entire lifecycle of data should be integrated into effective governance mechanisms, with standardized protocols for data interoperability, robust security measures, including encryption and anonymisation, federated identity and access management, transparent auditing mechanisms and well-defined ethical guidelines for the use of AI for decision making. This combination of components ensures that healthcare data is secure, with confidentiality, integrity, availability, and non-repudiation. Moreover, current studies show that the merging of explainable artificial intelligence (XAI) and blockchain technology with auditing trails can enhance transparency, traceability, accountability, and trust, leading to more robust reliability and governance in wearable healthcare systems [1, 2]. Explainability aims to make the clinical recommendations and identification of anomalies understandable for physicians and patients to limit their skepticism towards automated decisions. Blockchain, on the other hand, provides immutability in logging access requests, consent transactions, and data modifications, thus avoiding tampering and unauthorized changes to healthcare data. Complementary safeguards, including multi-factor authentication, decentralized storage architectures, homomorphic encryption, and secure key management, are identified as crucial in preventing breaches of centralized data use, misuse of data aggregation, and profiling of behavior [3, 4].

The growth of 6G connectivity is making governance even more demanding, as ultra-low-latency communication, massive device density, and terahertz-band data transmission enable even greater scale and speed. While 6G enables synchronization of digital twins in real time and immersive telepresence surgeries, it also increases the potential attack surface if encryption, intrusion detection, and adaptive access controls are not robustly implemented [5].

2. Secure Data Sharing and Governance Using 6G Communication and Blockchain Technologies

Secure data exchange in the next-generation healthcare ecosystem is inspired by the fusion of ultra-high-speed 6G communication infrastructure and blockchain-enabled decentralization mechanisms. Unlike previous wireless communication generations, 6G is expected to operate in the terahertz range of the frequency spectrum and therefore will offer extremely high bandwidth, microsecond latency, and near-instant device-to-device communication.

The concept of the multilayered interaction among wearable sensors, 6G base stations, an edge computing cluster, and distributed blockchain nodes is shown in Figure 10.3. This architecture makes the nodes in the blockchain act as checkpoints, verifying data packets before forwarding them to the hospital server or to metaverse healthcare platforms. In such a model, the network does not have a single central authority that implements it; instead, it distributes verification to several trusted nodes.

Blockchain technology possesses a number of transformational properties of particular relevance to healthcare governance such as immutability, decentralization,

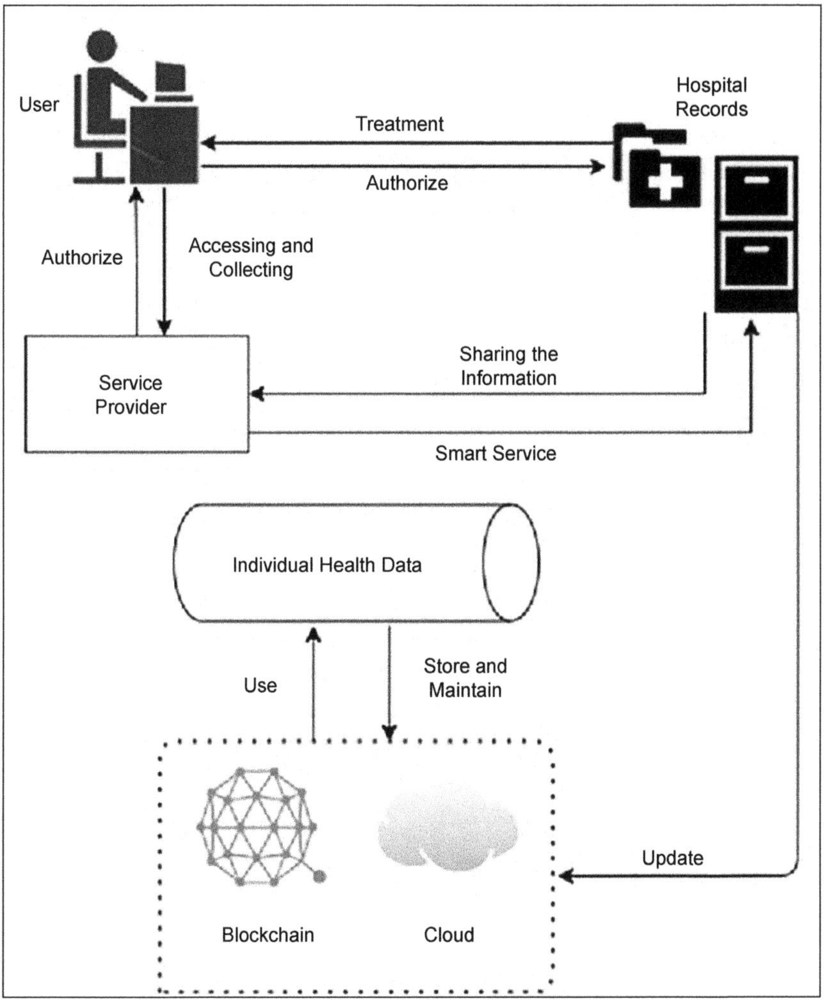

Fig. 10.3 Blockchain–6G integrated healthcare communication model.

transparency, traceability, and patient-centric ownership. Once medical data/access transactions are created and stored on the ledger, cryptographic hashing and a consensus algorithm make sure that they cannot be tampered with without consensus of the network. Smart contracts are also used to encourage governance via automating consent management, access expiration, conditional sharing policies, insurance verification, and compliance auditing. These programmable agreements remove the possibilities for manual administration, reduce the possibility of human error, and guarantee that all data interactions are time-stamped and verifiable. According to empirical research, Internet of Things (IoT) and Internet of Medical

Things (IoMT) frameworks based on blockchain are very helpful when used to enhance secure sharing and to lower the risk of unauthorized access of data by adding distributed cryptography identity verification and authentication layers [6, 7].

In addition, interoperability of electronic health records (EHRs) powered by the blockchain plays an important role in facilitating data exchange among hospitals, research labs, insurance agencies, and virtual healthcare platforms [3]. Blockchain is one solution to the challenge and this approach is likely to improve because it not only creates standardized and tamper-proof references to metadata but also allows for a more scalable approach to healthcare data by avoiding the duplication of the entire medical file, which in turn helps to comply with privacy laws such as the General Data Protection Regulation (GDPR).

The workflow of automatic consent and audit logging of patients can be represented as in Figure 10.4, which emphasizes the benefits of smart contract execution for governance.

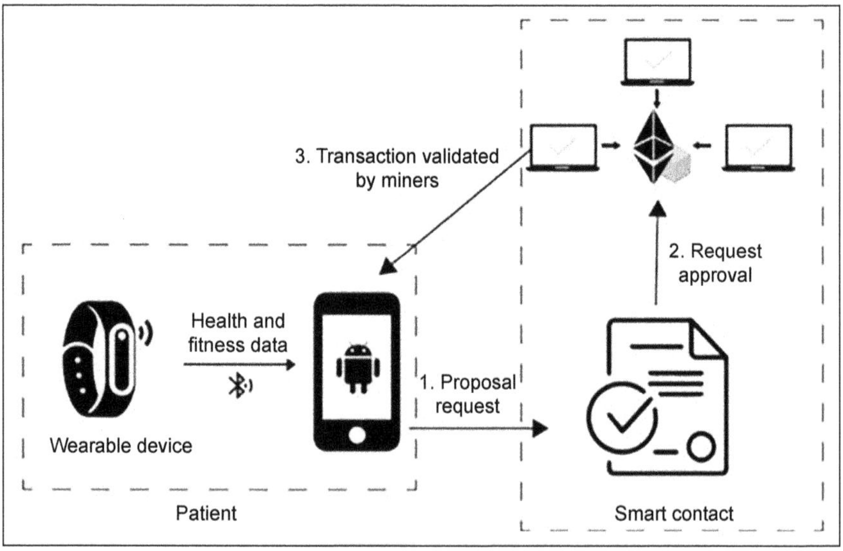

Fig. 10.4 Smart contract–based patient consent workflow.

When blockchain infrastructure is combined with 6G networks, it helps to offer way more scalability, reliability, and computational efficiency. Encrypted communication channels with blockchain verification will ensure that sensitive health information remains secret even with high-speed communications. Consensus algorithms, such as proof-of-authority or Byzantine fault tolerance, ensure trust by the institutions by validating transactions from well-known healthcare entities vs anonymity [8, 9].

Rather than sending unprocessed patient information to centralized databases, wearable sensors and hospital systems work to train machine learning models using their own devices, sending only secured models updates. The blockchain network captures and verifies these updates so that they cannot be tampered with and everybody can participate equally [4, 5, 10]. Through this approach, the chances of data exposure are reduced to a minimum, strict regulations for healthcare data protection are met, and sharing of intelligence across medical institutions that are geographically dispersed is made possible.

Overall, the synergy between 6G and blockchain helps to develop a secure, transparent, and patient-empowered data-sharing ecosystem that can serve the immense scale and sensitivity of wearable and metaverse healthcare environments. By adding cryptography-based verification, decentralized governance, automatic consent, and privacy-preserving analytics to the communication infrastructures, healthcare systems have the ability to shift from a reactive paradigm in security to a proactive, trust-centric paradigm that is resilient, scalable, and ethically consistent with future smart hospital systems.

3. Artificial Intelligence for Continuous Monitoring, Clinical Decision Support, and Trust Management

Artificial intelligence is the analytical and cognitive backbone of a wearable and metaverse-enabled healthcare ecosystem, helping transform raw multi-modal biosensor streams into predictive, prescriptive, and diagnostic intelligence. Modern wearable devices are used to produce heterogeneous data—ECG waveform, oxygen saturation, gait data, sleep cycle, emotional indicator, and environmental context—which are processed using machine learning, deep learning, convolutional neural network, recurrent architecture, and transformer-based model. These algorithms detect anomalies in real time, including arrhythmia prediction, glucose fluctuations, fall detection, deviations from neurological patterns, and stress-induced physiological changes. In immersive metaverse applications, these analytics power digital twin synchronization, virtual rehabilitation feedback, and avatar-assisted therapy personalization.

Clinical decision support systems (CDSS) take AI functionality beyond monitoring and provide healthcare professionals with context-aware, evidence-based, and explainable recommendations (Fig. 10.5). Rather than generating opaque probability scores, the latest AI-enabled CDSS platforms include XAI, interpretable feature attribution, causal inference mapping, and visual reasoning interfaces that help explain why a particular diagnostic suggestion or treatment pathway is recommended. This is a particularly important form of transparency in healthcare, made possible by the metaverse, where physicians communicate via virtual consultation rooms, AI-driven avatars, and holographic patient models. In such environments, trust and interpretability are not attributes of choice in clinical adoption, legal accountability, and patient confidence.

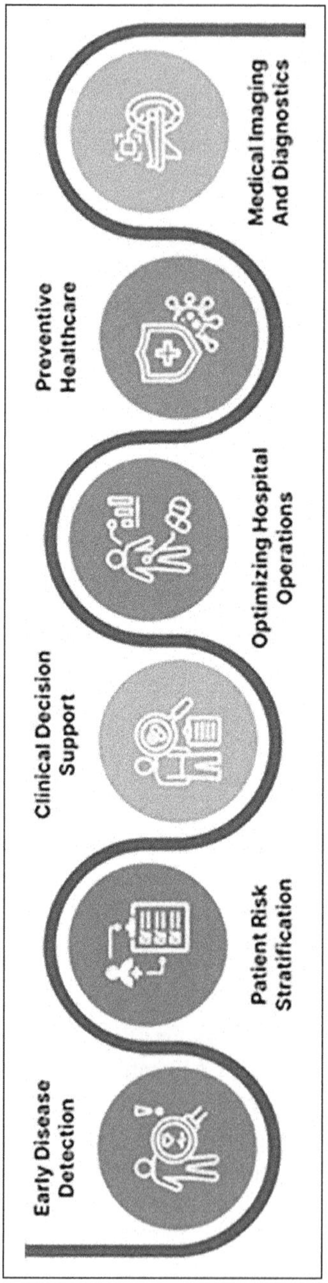

Fig. 10.5 AI-driven continuous health monitoring pipeline.

Trust management is therefore an important dimension of AI-augmented healthcare governance. Automated decision systems must be authentic, fair, bias-busting, accountable, and adversarial-attack-resistant. The AI-blockchain hybrid verification framework in Figure 10.6 is used to verify the outputs of AI system inference by cryptographic means and to ensure they are immutably registered in distributed ledgers before final clinical authorization. This two-layer validation mechanism ensures that diagnostic outcomes cannot be tampered with once generated and that any decision can be traced to the dataset, the version of the algorithm used, and the authority that granted access. Such tamper-resistant verification goes a long way towards minimizing the risks of data poisoning, model drift, insider tampering, and unauthorized access [1, 3].

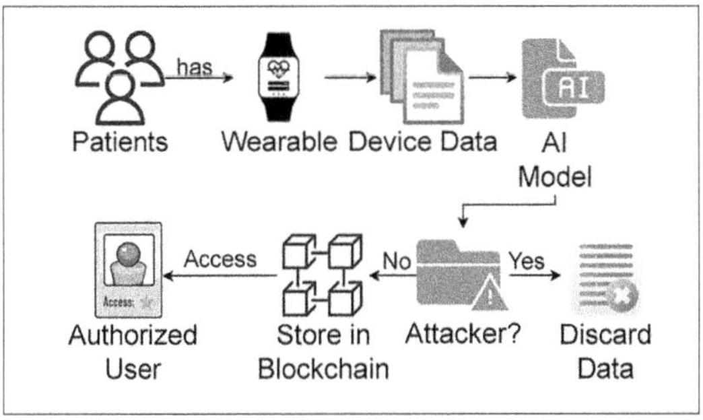

Fig. 10.6 Trust management framework with AI and blockchain.

Instead of having patient records at the centralized repositories, the local devices and institutional servers train the models independently and only pass the parameter updates in encrypted form. Blockchain governance then ensures the integrity of contributions. It prevents the injection of malicious models, thereby enabling secure multi-institutional analytics, personalized medicine, and cross-border medical research without breaching confidentiality [11-13].

4. Conclusion and Future Directions for Smart Hospital Ecosystems

This chapter focuses on the fact that the smart hospital ecosystem is a holistic convergence of wearable AI, metaverse-enabled healthcare platforms, 6G communication network, blockchain-based security model, and intelligent data governance frameworks. Such integration is a definite step away from the traditional and institution-centred approach to healthcare, towards decentralized, patient-centred, and always-connected medical environments. This chapter reflects the importance of the following: future healthcare infrastructure must be more focused on explainable diagnostics, interoperable digital twins, autonomous monitoring capabilities, and ultra-safe communication layers that enable seamless integration of the physical and virtual clinical spaces [7, 8, 14].

References

[1] Ali, S., Abdullah, A., Tagne Poupi, T.A., et al. (2023). Metaverse in healthcare integrated with explainable AI and blockchain: Enabling immersiveness, ensuring trust, and providing patient data security, *Sensors*, 23(2), 565.

[2] Letafati, M. and Otoum, S. (2023). On the privacy and security for e-health services in the metaverse: An overview. *Ad Hoc Networks*, 150, 103262.

[3] Othman, S.B. and Getahun, M. (2025). Leveraging blockchain and IoMT for secure and interoperable electronic health records. *Scientific Reports*, 15, 12358.

[4] Ghadi, Y.Y., Shah, S.F.A., Waheed, W., et al. (2025). Integration of wearable technology and artificial intelligence in digital health for remote patient care. *Journal of Cloud Computing*, 14, 39.

[5] Taleb, H., Andrieux, G., Khalife, D., et al. (2025). Exploring healthcare in the 6G and AI era: Opportunities and challenges. *Internet of Things*, 34, 101744.

[6] Yang, W., Hou, C., Zhang, Z., et al. (2024). Secure and efficient data sharing for IoT based on blockchain and reputation mechanism. *IEEE Internet of Things Journal*, 11(11), 20631–20647.

[7] Azzi, R., Chamoun, R.K., Serhrouchni, A. and Sokhn, M. (2025). Unlocking the potential of data: Toward a secure and privacy-preserving blockchain-based health data governance framework. *Blockchain: Research and Applications*, 7(1), 100318.

[8] Ghadi, Y.Y., Mazhar, T., Shahzad, T., et al. (2024). The role of blockchain to secure internet of medical things. *Scientific Reports*, 14, 18422.

[9] Taherdoost, H. (2023). Privacy and Security of Blockchain in Healthcare: Applications, Challenges, and Future Perspectives. *Sci*, 5(4), 41. https://doi.org/10.3390/sci5040041.

[10] Bhasker, B., Rao, P.M., Saraswathi, P., Patro, S.G.K., Bhutto, J.K., Islam, S., Kareemullah, M., and Emma, A.F. (2025). Blockchain framework with IoT device using federated learning for sustainable healthcare systems. *Scientific Reports*, 15(1), 26736. https://doi.org/10.1038/s41598-025-06539-z.

[11] Olyanasab, A., Hosseini, S., Khosravi, A., Nahavandi, S. and Buckley, J. (2024). Leveraging machine learning for personalized wearable health monitoring: A review. *Sensors*, 24(4), 1258. https://doi.org/10.3390/s24041258.

[12] Zhao, H., Yang, J., Zhang, H., Li, X. and Wang, Y. (2025). Privacy-preserving federated learning framework for multi-source electronic health records prognosis prediction. *Sensors*, 25(8), 2374. https://doi.org/10.3390/s25082374.

[13] Kumar, A., Alharbi, A., Alsubhi, K., Alharthi, S., Hossain, M.S. and Ghoneim, A. (2025). Integrating 6G technology in smart hospitals: Challenges, enabling technologies, and future directions. Frontiers in Medicine, 12, 1534551. https://doi.org/10.3389/fmed.2025.1534551.

[14] Sheejakumari, V., Sundravadivelu, K., Pushparani, S., et al. (2025). Diabetic retinopathy detection based on mobile maxout network and weber local descriptor feature selection using retinal fundus image. *Scientific Reports*, 15(1), 13858.

11 Digital Identity and the Self: Psychological Implications of Health in Virtual Worlds

Vijay Priya V.[1], Uma M.[2], Geetha A.[3*],
Nebojsa Bacanin[4] and Yuvaraja Teekaraman[5]

A major cause of road accidents is drowsiness, which is usually associated with a state of less alertness and slow thinking. This chapter suggests a driver-monitoring wearable gadget that comprises of behavioural and physiological sensing strategies to provide an early warning of fatigue. Including physiological techniques, behavioural techniques such changing head posture different techniques can be utilized to determine whether a driver is sleeping, including behavioural techniques such changing head posture, observing eye movement, and yawning. Vehicle techniques including steering wheel control, lane position, and vehicle speed control can determine the driver's vehicle speed; hybrid techniques can be used for the purpose of identifying driver intoxication, and any two or three approaches may be combined. The performance measure is used in the proposed model using Weka machine learning software. SMOTE is included in the suggested method for the class imbalance to enhance accuracy. Each performance in the suggested models was assessed using 10-fold cross-validation and compared with various accuracy metrics. Support vector machines (SVMs), Random Forest, J48 Decision Tree, K-Star, and K-Nearest Neighbours have accuracy rates of 71.67%, 96.60%, 93.31%, 95.65%, and 93.89%, respectively. Random Forest, utilizing a straightforward colour histogram feature, outperformed all classifiers in terms of performance and accuracy.

1. Introduction

Road transport is the backbone of modern society, powering growth, opportunities, and social connections. Human error is the cause of most crashes, along with

[1] Department of Computer Science and Engineering, SRM Valliammai Engineering College, Chengalpattu, Tamil Nadu, India.
[2] Department of Computational Intelligence, School of Computing, SRM Institute of Science and Technology, Chengalpattu, Tamil Nadu, India.
[3] Department of Electrical and Electronics Engineering, College of Engineering and Technology, SRM Institute of Science and Technology, Chengalpattu, Tamil Nadu, India.
[4] Faculty of Informatics and Computing, Singidunum University, Belgrade, Serbia.
[5] Department of Electrical Engineering, Chair-Research and Ethics Committee, School of Engineering and Computing, American International University, Kuwait.
* Corresponding author: geethaa2@srmist.edu.in

DOI: 10.1201/9781003776291-11

driver fatigue and drowsiness, which are significant and under-recognized factors. Drowsiness is the sense of being tired during the day. Drowsiness and fatigue are important contributing factors in car accidents. Driving while fatigued increases the risk of collisions and injuries to other road users. The National Highway Administration reports that traffic crashes caused by drowsy driving resulted in 800 fatalities, 50,000 injuries, and 100,000 police-reported incidents over the course of the year 2019 [1]. According to annual research on traffic safety done by the AAA (American Automobile Association) Foundation, there were over 3,28,000 crashes involving fatigued drivers, over 109,000 injuries, and over 6,400 fatalities. The National Safety Council (NSC) records show that each year, over 100,000 crashes involving drowsy drivers result in 71,000 injuries and 1,550 fatalities [2]. Driver drowsiness is a multifaceted and psychophysiological situation that occurs when a person has been awake for a long time, has had insufficient sleep, has irregularity in sleep period, and deals with continuous mental workload. It is associated with the human circadian rhythm which controls the regular sleep–wake cycle. Human cognitive performance is at its lowest when drivers operate vehicles during biologically low-alertness periods like late at night or in the early morning hours. Attention span, perception, and reaction times are the factors considered in the importance of driving safely. Microsleep is extremely dangerous and it turns off the sections of the brain that process external stimuli, leading to the driver not being aware of the road surroundings. Thus, a two-second microsleep at highway speeds can allow a vehicle to move uncontrolled dozens of metres, dramatically increasing the probability of the vehicle crashing. Drowsiness affects executive functions, including decision-making, situational awareness, and working memory. Fatigued drivers are slower to receive and process visual information, recognize traffic signs, and react to an unexpected hazard. Fatigue behaviourally appears as signals from the face and body. Brief non-blinking, slow blinking, yawning, eyelid droop, and head tilt are known signs of decreasing vigilance. These symptoms represent the brain trying to respond to sleep deprivation by decreasing sensory input and conserving energy. Consequently, eyes and mouth play the most important role for detecting fatigue. Such behavioural changes can be observed in a non-invasive manner, thereby making them an effective foundation for automated driver monitoring. While physiological sensors are contact based, vision-based systems can detect subtle facial expressions via cameras mounted inside the vehicle. Using these cues along with machine learning models, we can assess the mental state of the driver in real time and provide early warnings before fatal levels of fatigue are attained.

The major signs of tiredness include closing the eyes, yawning frequently, leaning forward, and continual blinking [3]. Four major techniques are commonly employed to detect driver drowsiness: the hybrid method, the vehicle-based method, the physiological method, and the behavioural method. Each of these approaches monitors different indicators of fatigue, ranging from driver biological signals and physical behaviour to vehicle dynamics and combined multi-source data, thereby enabling more reliable and accurate detection of drowsy driving conditions. The behavioural technique relies on various facial actions, including head position changes, eye closure, eye gazing, blinking, and yawning, that can be recorded using a front camera or smartphone [4]. The last decade has seen rapid urbanization, longer work hours, long commuter distances, and night-shift jobs, all of which have drastically heightened the risk of drivers driving vehicles when they are physically and mentally fatigued. Newer vehicles are designed with sensors, cameras, and embedded computing systems to capture real-time data on vehicle behaviour and the driver state. The physiological approach relies on a variety of body-worn sensors that the driver must wear. In real life, drivers are not distracted by physiological techniques. Photoplethysmogram (PPG), electroencephalogram (EEG), electrooculogram (EOG), and electrocardiogram (ECG) are the physiological techniques used in the current procedures. The vehicle's technique is based on a number of mechanical components, including lane location, steering wheel control, and speed control. The hybrid technique accurately detects driver drowsiness by combining any two or three methods.

Dasgupta et al. (2018) created a smartphone-based front camera for detecting drowsiness. In the three-stage process, the first stage employed PERCLOS to detect the driver's eye open and closed states, the second stage used the voiced-to-unvoiced ratio to determine the drivers alertness, and the third stage evaluated the drivers touch response using the smartphone. This multi-stage approach improved the detection accuracy to 93.33% [5]. Deng and Wu (2019) proposed a driver monitoring framework called Dricare to detect multiple driver fatigue states, including yawning, prolonged eye closure, and abnormal blinking patterns [6]. The system examined the Yawdd Dataset to analyse yawning behaviour and the CelebA dataset to evaluate eye closure duration and blinking frequency. To accurately track facial landmarks and key points in real time, they employed the Multitask Convolutional Neural Network–Kernelized Correlation Filters (MC-KCF) algorithm, whose primary function is robust facial feature tracking. The proposed approach achieved an overall detection accuracy of 93.6%, demonstrating its effectiveness in fatigue recognition. Similarly, Dua et al. (2021) investigated multiple deep learning architectures for driver drowsiness detection, including AlexNet, VGG-FaceNet, Flow ImageNet, and ResNet [3]. Their comparative analysis showed that deep convolutional neural networks are highly effective in extracting discriminative facial features and improving the accuracy and reliability of driver fatigue and drowsiness detection systems. The final output is predicted using an ensemble algorithm. Hashemi et al. (2020) used deep learning algorithms and a fully designed neural network (FD-NN) to predict drowsiness using eye open and eye closed states in the ZJU (Zhejiang University) dataset [7]. When compared to three models, FD-NN produced 98.15% accuracy. Savaş and Becerikli (2020) used two datasets, Yawdd and NthuDDD, for detecting driver eye and mouth conditions using multitask CNN (Convolutional Neural Network) models with three classes: very tired, less tired, and not tired [8]. Perclos and frequency of mouth are used from two video datasets to analyse eye and mouth regions for detecting drowsiness states.

Jamshidi et al. (2021) proposed a detection of drowsiness network for driver behavioural features like face, eye, and mouth state. Various scenarios such as daytime driving with glasses, were analysed using Resnet 18 and VGG-16 for drowsiness state detection, and for temporal information, long short-term memory (LSTM) is used to classify drowsy and non-drowsy people [9]. Hossain et al. (2022) proposed a list of driver distraction behaviours, including unsafe driving, texting with both hands, talking on cellphone with both hands, radio operation, and drinking [10]. Driver distraction is classified using different architectures like VGG-16, CNN, Resnet 50, and Mobilenetv2. Compared to all models, Mobilenetv2 produced 98.12% accuracy. Saurav et al. (2020) used two datasets, Yawdd and NthuDDD, for detecting yawning features using a video stream [11]. A facial recognition system is implemented to collect data from the mouth region. Park et al. (2016) carried out three deep detection methodologies: Alexnet for tuning the learned features, flowImageNet for training behavioural features like facial and head movements, and VGG-FaceNet for facial features like gender and ethnicity [12]. Drowsiness is detected using the NthuDDD dataset with 73.06% accuracy. Zhang et al. (2016) used three datasets: the FDDB dataset, the WIDER face dataset for face detection, and the AFLW dataset for face alignment, and the model was designed using a cascaded CNN-based framework for analysing joint face detection and alignment [13]. Kholerdi et al. (2016) proposed a decision-making algorithm and a sharpening module using three features: head-dropping, yawning, and closed eyes for estimating the level of consciousness for detecting driver drowsiness [14]. Gupta et al. (2018) used a non-intrusive behavioural method for detecting driver sleepiness and yawning features [15]. An RGB camera is implemented in the car to collect driver images. Images of driver's face are found using support vector machines (SVMs). Gu et al. (2018) proposed a multitask-based CNN for driver fatigue detection that simultaneously learns multiple facial cues [16]. Their approach extracts critical behavioural features such as the percentage of eye closure (PERCLOS) and mouth opening frequency, which are strong indicators of drowsiness. The proposed MSP-Net model was trained and validated using three benchmark datasets, namely the ZJU dataset, EMD dataset, and CEW dataset. Experimental results demonstrated that MSP-Net performs effectively and robustly across different driving conditions, making it suitable for accurate real-time fatigue state detection. Testing is done in a real-time driving scenario using the NVIDIA Jetson TX2 development board on an embedded platform. Yan et al. (2016) used four driving postures like normal driving, using a cell phone while driving, eating, and smoking while driving as considered driver distraction states [17]. Convolutional neural networks are used to test driving postures on the Southeast University dataset and the driver poster dataset. Fatima et al. (2020) state that the driver fatigue detection system is based upon microsleep patterns, and an alert is used to warn the driver [18]. Whether the driver's eyes are open or closed is classified using two classification methods named SVM and Adaboost.

Different types of systems are either multi-modal or hybrid systems: multi-modal systems utilize diverse sources of data including behavioural, physiological, and vehicle-based data to improve robustness. While these systems enable higher reliability, they are more complex, increase the cost, and make the user feel uncomfortable since they require multiple sensors and also demand data fusion mechanisms. Moreover, sensor calibration and synchronization are still among the biggest challenges to drive better. Classical machine learning methods like SVM, KNN, and decision tree–based methods have faster training, reduced computational cost, and higher interpretability. But conventional methods are not always transferable to different datasets and illumination conditions. Additionally, class imbalance is not appropriately addressed in conventional methods, which means that the predictions usually are not quite good. The proposed framework combines a data-balancing technique based on Synthetic Minority Oversampling Technique (SMOTE) with a very simple feature extraction by colour histogram and a Random Forest for classification. The proposed framework fills the gap between performance and utility, resulting in a scalable solution for real-time driver drowsiness detection.

Despite the advancements in this research area as enabled with deep learning and multi-modal sensing systems, a few practical challenges still remain unaddressed. Despite the high accuracy of systems such as CNNs, large-scale datasets, hand-related datasets, or high-performance hardware platform like GPUs or embedded platform, they are typically computationally expensive, slow to train, and unsuitable for real-time deployment in resource-constrained environments. Additionally, conventional research study is often limited to small, curated datasets that may not be representative of real-world driving. Some challenges like class imbalance, dataset bias, and overfitting still affect the reliability of the models. Moreover, the physiological indicator-based system and the hybrid system usually need wearable sensors or special hardware, which may decrease user comfort and acceptance. Most of the conventional systems suffer from performance and accuracy issues and also rely on complex architectures, utilizing high computation power, or specialized hardware components, which hinders implementation in real-world vehicles. The high memory, computation time, and constant high-performance resource demand of such models are unsustainable for low-cost or embedded platforms. So, they are also difficult to maintain and cannot adapt to other driving environments. This drives the demand for simple, effective, and robust machine learning frameworks that can achieve high detection accuracy. To address these challenges, this work presents a behavioural-based drowsiness detection framework employing classical machine learning algorithms. The proposed method aims to provide an accurate identification with low complexity by using SMOTE to handle class imbalance, a simple colour histogram filter to extract the feature, Random Forest as the main classifier, and proves effective for driver drowsiness detection methods. The organisation of the chapter is as follows: Section 2 discusses the proposed methodology. Section 3 explains the different machine learning classifiers and comparative analysis. Section 4 presents the experimental results for the proposed methodology. Section 5 concludes.

2. Proposed Methodology

The aim of the proposed framework is to build an efficient and reliable driver drowsiness detection system with minimum computational complexity and high predictive accuracy. This approach is drastically different from modern deep learning models that rely on special hardware to train on massive datasets, employing classical machine learning techniques paired with low-weight image feature descriptors for practical real-time deployment into real-world driving scenarios. This work utilizes a behavioural-based detection approach using facial expression and eye–mouth active region for detecting driver fatigue. From various observable symptoms of drowsiness, long duration eye closure and frequent yawn are chosen to be the key indicators as they explicitly suggest assumptions in decreased alertness and tendency of microsleep. Facial images are taken from the D3S dataset, a rich dataset representing different driving behaviours under real-time settings. The dataset used is from real-time situations that reflect the drowsiness patterns rather than artificially simulated, ensuring that the evaluation is conducted under realistic driving conditions. Since there is an inherent imbalance of classes in the dataset between drowsy and non-drowsy samples, SMOTE is employed during the preprocessing step. The pseudo-gradient-balancing does not let classifier suffer from majority class bias and therefore can enhance the learning capability which helps to improve generalization performance. Unlike other conventional approaches which depend on elaborate facial landmark detection or deep convolutional layers, this method uses an effective and yet simple colour histogram descriptor to transform face images into useful numerical features.

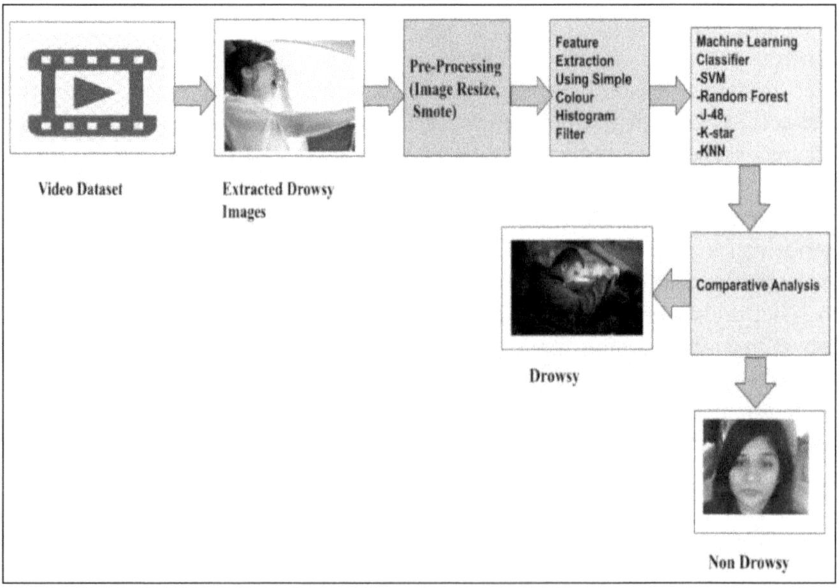

Fig. 11.1 Proposed methodology for detecting driver drowsiness [15].

The systematic comparative evaluation of classifiers points out Random Forest as the best performing classifier due to the valid generalization and ensemble-based discrete decision structure of the Random Forest architecture. The proposed method makes a significant contribution by conducting a driver drowsiness detection experiment in Waikato Environment for Knowledge Analysis (Weka) machine learning software. To accurately predict drowsiness symptoms, two important features are used: percentage of eye closure and yawning. The publicly available D3S dataset is used, and the dataset is manually labelled with two classifiers: Drowsy and Non-drowsy. To balance the dataset, SMOTE class imbalance is used. Different accuracy and performance measures are compared using five machine learning algorithms: K-Nearest Neighbour, SVM, K-Star, J48 Decision Tree, and Random Forest. Compared to all machine learning algorithms, Random Forest predicts with good accuracy using a simple colour histogram feature. The proposed method to detect driver drowsiness is described in Figure 11.1.

The proposed method uses six different steps to detect drowsiness.

Input: Videos from the D3S dataset are converted to images and uploaded to the Weka machine learning software.

Output:

1. Loads D3S dataset images into Weka machine learning software.
2. In the preprocessing stage, D3S dataset images are resized and classified into two classes: drowsy and non-drowsy.
3. The two class images in the D3S dataset are balanced using SMOTE-based preprocessing methods.
4. In the D3S image dataset, different features are extracted using a simple colour histogram filter.
5. After feature extraction methods, the D3S dataset is evaluated using a 10-fold cross-validation for evaluating drowsy and non-drowsy methods.
6. Different performance measures are compared with the D3S dataset and analyzed with five different machine learning classifiers.

2.1 D3S Dataset (Driver Drowsiness Dataset)

Videos of four participants engaging in various driving behaviours, such as eye closure, eye opening, yawning, and talking while driving, can be found in the D3S Dataset. Happy and neutral emotional measures are included in the D3S dataset. An RGB camera is continuously positioned in front of the driver's face and placed before the front windows to record the D3S video dataset. Three male subjects and one female subject performed various sleepiness symptoms throughout the 3 hours and 14 minutes of the D3S video, which is in MP4 format [15]. In Figure 11.2, a few sample images from the D3S dataset are shown.

2.2 Preprocessing

Data preprocessing is a crucial step in a generic machine learning–based image analysis system as the accuracy and precision of the final predictions are largely affected by the quality of the input data. Driver drowsiness detection commonly deals with raw video frames, which may not contain well-controlled variations in lighting, facial orientation, resolution, and background noise that allow feature extraction and classification. This indicates the necessity of an organized and standardized preprocessing pipeline to maintain uniformity in the input samples. Initially, facial images are extracted from the D3S video dataset and made uniform for machine learning analysis in the suggested framework. All images are resized to fixed dimension to reduce computational load and to avoid the difference between samples. With this process of normalization, all of the images can have the same contributed feature extraction process as inputs without taking the original eye settings or recordings. Resize also reduces superfluous spatial information that does not contribute to fatigue detection, thereby forcing the model to attend on the most discriminative visual features. As per the normalization, the dataset is labelled manually into two classes, drowsy and non-drowsy, based on the presence of visual behaviour indicators such as prolonged eye closure and yawning. As depicted in Figure 11.3, there is a substantial class imbalance for these two types. This imbalance may cause a biased learning process such that the model may be biased towards the majority class to assign the correct label to the samples of the minority class. The proposed methodology operates on a dataset of 4,671 facial images of drivers which are extracted from a video dataset of driver behaviour (D3S) collected at 1920 × 1080 in JPG format. To minimize computational cost and standardize input, all images were pre-processed and rescaled to 640 × 480 pixels. The images were resized, pre-processed, and imported into the Weka machine learning environment for analysis using both Explorer and Knowledge Flow modules. These tools were used for feature extraction, classification, and performance evaluation to train the proposed driver drowsiness detection framework and improve testing efficiency. The D3S dataset is classified into two classes: Drowsy with 1,754 instances and Non-drowsy with 2,918 instances.

2.2.1 SMOTE

Class imbalance is a common concern in the real-world classification problem, especially in safety-critical applications like driver drowsiness detection. Machine learning models become biased towards the majority class, and class imbalance is thus significant. The number of non-drowsy samples is naturally greater than drowsy samples in the context of this study, which may significantly hinder the learning ability of the classifiers. In response to this problem, the abnormal data balancing strategy SMOTE is included in the preprocessing stage of the proposed framework. Instead of simply copying instances from the minority class, SMOTE synthesizes new minority class instances in the feature extraction between the examples of the minority class and their nearest neighbours. It also enables the

Fig. 11.2 Sample images from Driver Drowsiness Dataset.

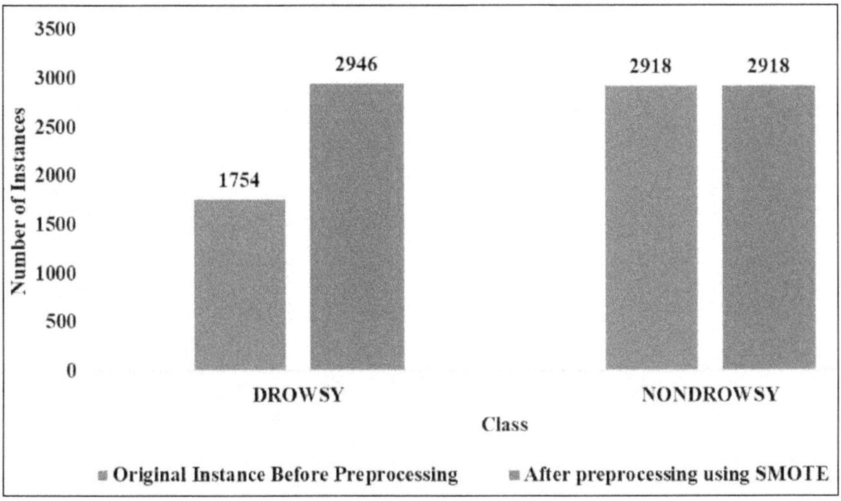

Fig. 11.3 D3S class data distribution during Preprocessing.

model to learn a more general decision boundary and not simply copying the samples of minority classes which can lead to an overfitting behaviour. The D3S dataset has the effect of SMOTE applied, shown in Figure 11.4 and Figure 11.5. In Figure 11.4, the original distribution is illustrated, where the drowsy class is highly imbalanced. Simultaneously, Figure 11.5 shows a more balanced and synthetic class structure that comes after applying SMOTE where minimum class increased to get a similar distribution to the maximum sample class. Further, each of the classifiers has equal chance of learning about both of the classes, resulting in higher sensitivity towards drowsy instances. If the dataset before training is balanced, it can obtain performance metrics that cannot be misleading or too favourable to any of the classes. Additionally, it improves the consistency and strength of the prediction models across different folds of validation. SMOTE is used to handle multiclass imbalance problems [19]. In machine learning algorithm, imbalanced data is an important problem for classification-based methods. By using SMOTE in training data, it reduces the overfitting problems during training process. SMOTE contains two classes: Majority class and Minority class. To balance the dataset, Minority class should be increased with the training and testing ratio. In the proposed method, the D3S datasets are imbalanced with two classes: Drowsy and Non-drowsy. The proposed method used Synthetic Minority oversampling technique from WEKA tool to balance the D3S dataset classifier named Drowsy.

The entire D3S dataset is composed of 1,754 drowsy instances and 2,918 non-drowsy instances, which reflects a class imbalance before preprocessing. To mitigate the problem and ensure an equitable training of the model, the dataset is initially separated into 70% for training and 30% for testing the model. SMOTE implements the synthetic sample generation method in order to balance the training set by creating synthetic samples for the minority class. This strategy of maintaining a balance enhances the robustness and generalization ability of the proposed system.

Table 11.1 Data distribution during preprocessing.

Class	*Original Instance before Preprocessing*	*After Preprocessing using SMOTE*
Drowsy	1,754	2,806
Non-drowsy	2,918	2,918

Source: Reference [15]

Table 11.1 shows the class distribution of the D3S dataset before and after applying the SMOTE technique. The dataset was originally composed of 1,754 drowsy instances and 2,918 non-drowsy instances, which is relatively imbalanced. The drowsy class was synthetically increased to 2,806 using SMOTE-based resampling. This updated distribution mitigates bias towards the majority class during training through more equal contribution of both classes,

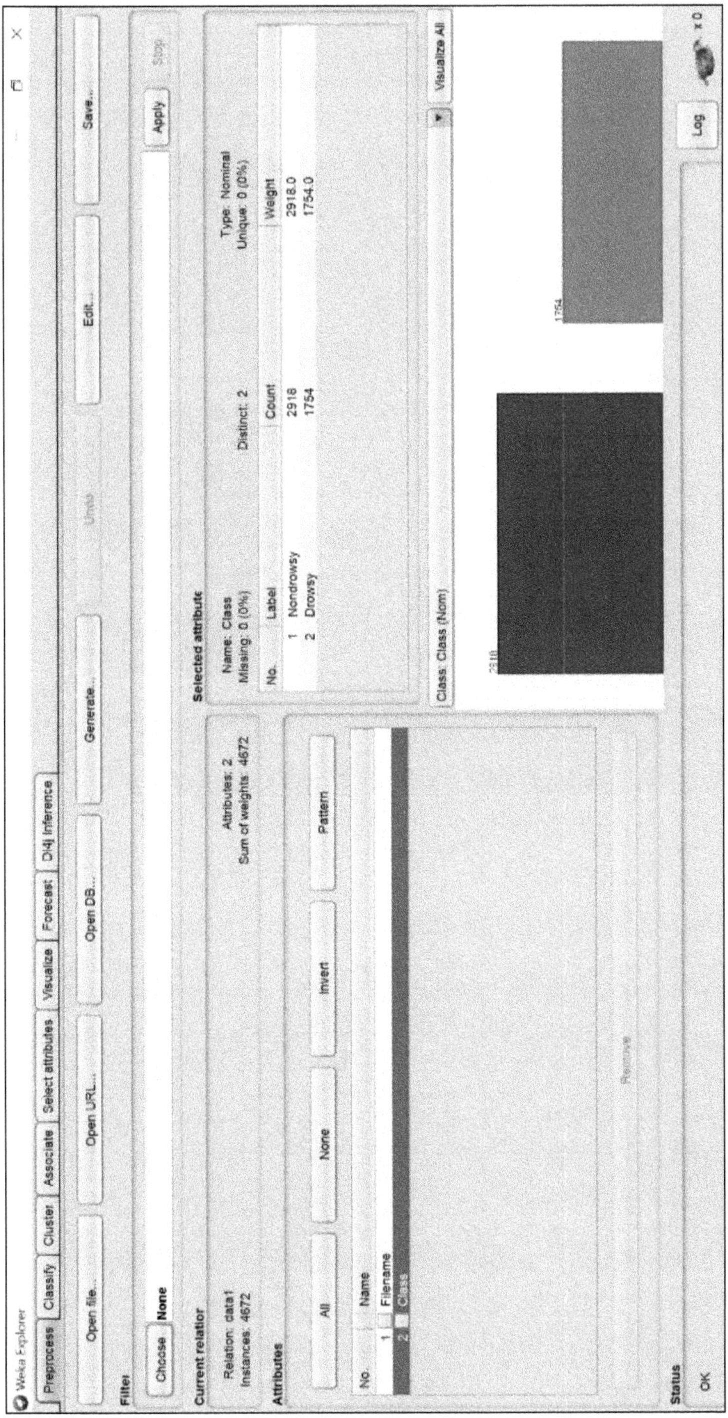

Fig. 11.4 Original instance before preprocessing D3S dataset.

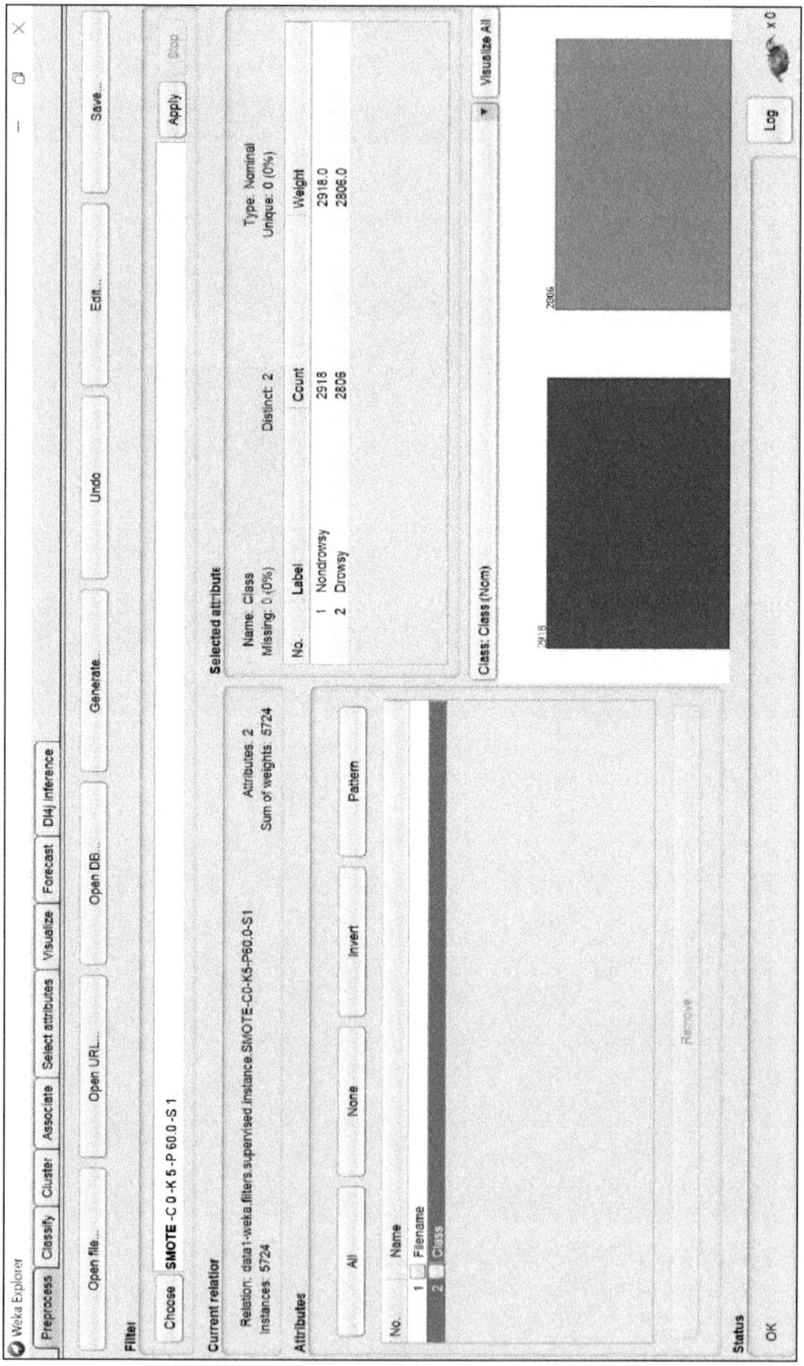

Fig. 11.5 After preprocessing D3S dataset using SMOTE.

which enhances the reliability and generalization capability of the developed classification models.

2.3 Feature Extraction

The transformation of visual patterns related to fatigue in facial images into informative features is the key step in characterizing the driver state from driver facial images. The proposed method targeted visual patterns through the tracking of facial appearance induced by fatigue rather than complex landmark tracking or supervised deep neural networks by focusing on global features. By eliminating the need for these interfaces, system complexity is reduced and the model can run efficiently on high-level computing platforms. The facial region colour distribution summary for detecting subtle changes in skin tone and shadow patterns associated with eye closure, yawning, and head movement behaviour is a strong cue for a decrease in alertness. The colour-based descriptor has some benefits in real time. It is computationally efficient, tolerant to small spatial variations, and insensitive to exact face alignment. In contrast to the multidimensional high-level deep features, histogram-based representations result in compact feature vectors that capture salient visual information but need comparatively little storage and processing resources. Subsequently, they are suitable for lightweight driver assistance systems that require speed and efficient use of resources. Feature extraction stage creates the link between the visual facial image input and the machine learning classification by converting each facial image into feature vector according to structured numerical features. It allows analysis across thousands of samples in a consistent and scalable manner and provides the basis for accurate model training and evaluation during the task classification step. The feature is extracted using the filters image package, which consists of various image processing filters and is based upon a Java library for image retrieval and Lucene Image Retrieval [20]. D3S dataset experiences using simple colour histogram image filters process. Simple colour histogram filters are applied to the D3S dataset to extract feature descriptors from images.

2.3.1 Simple Colour Histogram Filter

Colour distribution forms a compact representation of visual content and is useful for image-based pattern recognition tasks. In the context of driver drowsiness detection, slight modifications in facial appearance such as shadow around eyes, patterns near mouth for yawning, and skin colour variations due to lighting can be well captured by colour-based statistical-based representations. This chapter observes that existing models often use an elaborate facial landmark tracking with temporally complex deep convolutional features to extract pixel intensity, while using only simple colour histograms to summarize the pixel intensity across red, green, and blue channels. This method transforms each picture into a stable vector that expresses the overall colour profile of the area containing the face.

The simple colour histogram filter offers the speed of the computation, necessary time, and memory for processing extraction.

The simple colour histogram filter maps visual information into a compact feature vector to strike a balance between performance and speed. This allows the machine learning classifiers to differentiate between drowsy and non-drowsy states by utilizing light but descriptive features, which assists with the main objective of creating an efficient and scalable driver monitoring system. Simple colour histogram filter is used to transform each image into pixels to numerical features [21]. Simple colour histogram filter is used for extracting colour histogram feature from images. The colour histogram features have three colours: red, green, and blue with 32 bins in each histogram.

In the proposed method, simple colour histogram features are extracted from the D3S dataset by using the simple colour histogram filter from the Weka tool, where the D3S dataset was divided into 66 features, as depicted in Figure 11.6. For each feature it contains name, type, missing value, distinct, and unique, and statistical values like maximum, minimum, mean, and standard deviation were calculated using the Weka tool.

2.4 WEKA Tool

The WEKA is open-source software that originated from the University of Waikato, New Zealand, and is used for machine learning and data mining. WEKA provides a GUI that enables modelling to be performed quickly, and tested and evaluated without the need for large amounts of programming. WEKA provides a large collection of tools for performing tasks such as classification, clustering, data visualization, data preprocessing, feature selection, and regression analysis. The software contains five main applications classified into Explorer, Knowledge Flow, Experimenter, Simple CLI, and Workbench [22], where each application specializes in building, evaluating, and managing data flows for machine learning workflows.

3. Performance Measure

3.1 Correctly and Incorrectly Classified Instances

In the proposed method, several machine learning classifiers such as K-Star, Random Forest, SVM, K-Nearest Neighbour, and the J48 Decision Tree are employed to evaluate the performance of the drowsiness detection model. The effectiveness of each classifier is assessed by analysing both correctly and incorrectly predicted instances. In particular, the total count of correctly predicted samples is obtained from adding up true positive (TP) and true negative (TN) values while the number of misclassified samples is computed from the sum of false positive (FP) and false negative (FN) values [23]. The strategy provides a quantitative measure of the prediction accuracy and reliability of the different models.

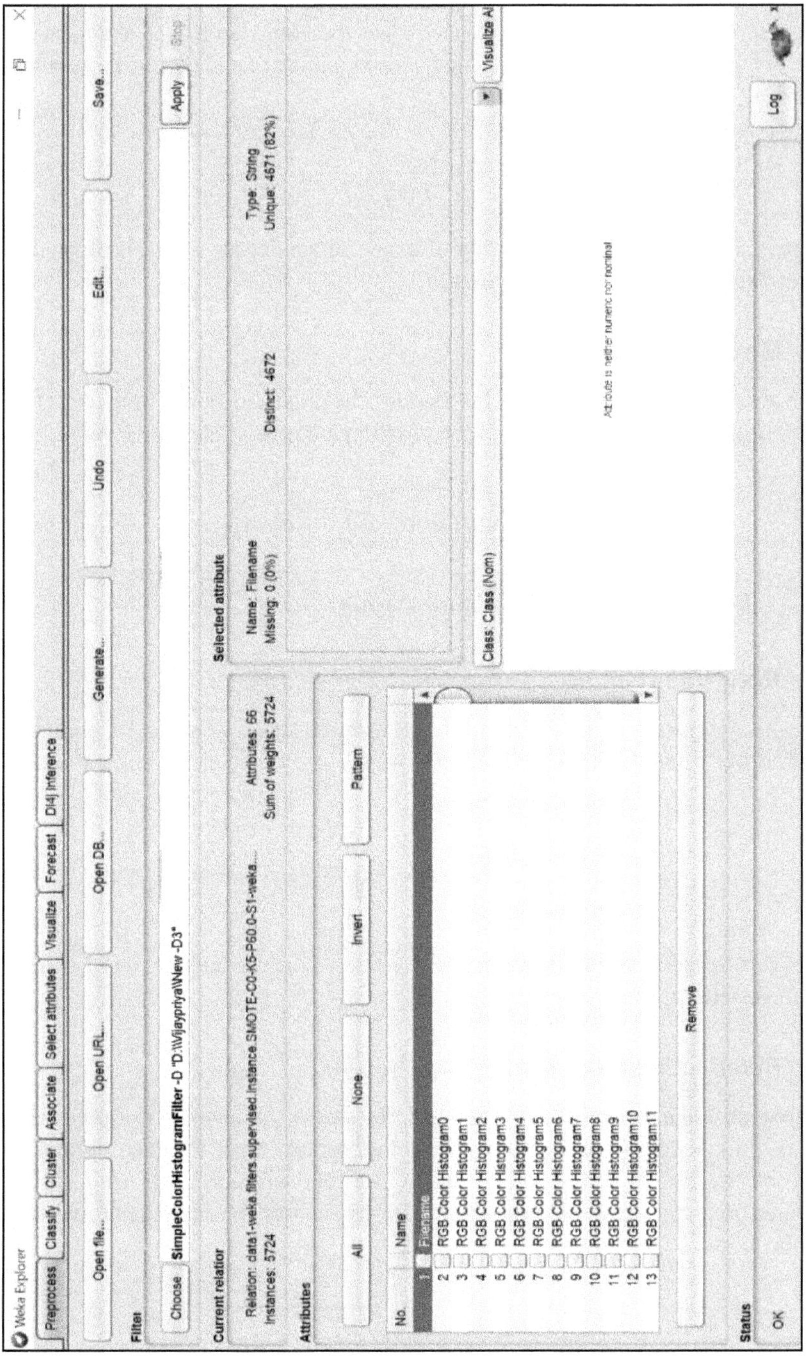

Fig. 11.6 Extracted features using simple colour histogram filter for D3S dataset.

3.2 Kappa Statistics

To assess the multiclass and imbalanced class methods, the Kappa statistics are used. Kappa statistics are used to evaluate the significance and performance of the classifier. The kappa statistic is defined as

$$k = \frac{a_o - a_e}{1 - a_e} \quad ...(11.1)$$

where a_e is defined as the probability of expected agreement and a_o is defined as the probability of observed agreement.

3.3 Mean Absolute Error

Mean absolute error (MAE) is used to measure the predicted values from the actual values. It shows the average size of the errors in the prediction model.

$$\text{Mean Absolute Error} = \frac{1}{n}\sum_{i=1}^{n}|x_i - x_p| \quad ...(11.2)$$

where x_i is the prediction and x_p is the true value.

3.4 Root Mean Squared Error

Root mean squared error (RMSE) is used to measure how much the predicted values differ from the actual values. It shows the size of the errors in the model.

$$\text{Root Mean Squared Error} = \sqrt{\frac{\sum_{i=1}^{n}(p_i - p_p)^2}{n}} \quad ...(11.3)$$

where p_i is defined as the actual value, n is considered as the number of observations, and p_p is stated as the predicted value.

3.5 Relative Absolute Error

Relative absolute error (RAE) is a metric to assess the quality of a prediction model. This is computed by taking the total absolute error for each prediction made by the model and dividing that by the total absolute error of a simple baseline predictor. This illustrates the performance of the model relative to a simple reference method.

$$\text{Relative Absolute Error} = \sqrt{\frac{\sum_{i=1}^{n}|p_i - p_p|}{\sum_{i=1}^{n}|p_p - x|}} \quad ...(11.4)$$

where p_i is defined as the realized value, x is considered the relative absolute error, and p_p is stated as the absolute value.

3.6 Root Relative Squared Error

Root relative squared error (RRSE) is used to evaluate the performance of a prediction model, especially in regression tasks. It is calculated as the square root of the total squared error of the prediction model divided by the total squared error of a simple baseline model.

$$\text{Root Relative Squared Error} = \sqrt{\frac{\sum_{i=1}^{n}(p_i - p_p)^2}{\sum_{i=1}^{n}(p_p - x)^2}} \quad ...(11.5)$$

where n is considered as the number of observations, p_i defined as realized value, x is considered as the average of the realized values, and p_p is stated as predicted value.

4. Experimental Result

In the proposed model, different machine learning algorithms such as K-Star, SVM, K-Nearest Neighbour, J48 Decision Tree, and Random Forest are implemented using the WEKA Explorer module. In WEKA, Sequential Minimal Optimization (SMO) is used as the training algorithm for the SVM classifier. SMO is an efficient method for solving SVM optimization problems. SVM can be utilized for various binary and multiclass classification tasks. It also assists in converting nominal (textual) values into numeric formats, and machine learning model can process the corresponding data. SVM is an efficient methodology that can perform classified tasks by constructing hyperplanes. Random Forest is termed as both classification and regression learning algorithm model. The Random Tree classifier considers the input vector of every tree in the forest and the majority of output votes received during classification. K-Star is defined as an instance-based classifier on the class of training the sum of similarity function. J48 was developed by Ross Quinlan. Hence, C4.5 algorithm is implemented for building decision trees and also developed in Weka as a classifier named as J48. J48 is defined as the machine learning decision tree classification algorithm based upon Iterative Dichotomiser3 in the Weka tool. The J48 Decision Tree algorithm builds decision trees based on a set of D3S training datasets. A J48 Decision Tree is used for categorical and continuous data. A decision tree is used for both classification and regression. A decision tree generates a tree structure to classify various data, starting from the root node and moving downward through the branches until a prediction is made or concluded.

To perform training and testing, the D3S dataset is first divided into 70% for training and 30% for testing. To further improve the reliability and accuracy of the proposed model, cross-validation is applied. After the initial data split, the model

Table 11.2 Different performance measures compared with different machine learning algorithms.

Algorithm	*Support Vector Machine*	*Random Forest*	*J48*	*K-Star*	*K-Nearest Neighbour*
Mean Absolute Error	0.3092	0.3092	0.0948	0.0889	0.061
Correctly Classified Instances	69.07%	96.06%	92.64%	95.42%	93.89%
Root Mean Squared Error	0.5561	0.1874	0.2576	0.1948	0.244
Incorrectly Classified Instances	30.92%	3.93%	7.35%	4.57%	6.10%
Kappa Statistics	0.3787	0.9213	0.8528	0.9084	0.870
Root Relative Squared Error	111.23%	37.48%	51.53%	38.97%	50.39%
Relative Absolute Error	61.86%	18.95%	18.97%	17.78%	13.05%

is evaluated using the 10-fold cross-validation technique in WEKA (version 3.9.2) under the classification environment. For this technique, the whole D3S dataset is split into 10 equal parts (folds). In each iteration, one fold is treated as validation data and the remaining nine folds function as training data. We provide the average performance from all these 10 runs to be the final result in order to have more reliable and unbiased predictions. All the experiments are performed on a batch size 100. The D3S dataset is used to conduct several experiments in WEKA Explorer classifier tab. As reported in the classifier output section, Table 11.2 provides the detailed performance results of each classifier.

Compared to other machine learning algorithms, Random Forest produced good accuracy using 10-fold cross-validation testing samples. Using SMOTE as preprocessing method, the D3S dataset is balanced and a simple colour histogram filter is used for extracting the drowsiness features from the D3S dataset. The different performance measures are compared with different machine learning algorithms, as depicted in Figure 11.7.

In the proposed model, different accuracy measures like precision–recall curve (PRC) area, MCC, F-measure, recall, receiver operating characteristics (ROC) area, and precision are compared with the performance of each machine learning algorithm, as depicted in Figure 11.8. In the proposed method, the frequently used graphical display of classifier for accuracy contains ROC and PRC curves. PRCs show the precision values for corresponding sensitivity values and recall values are used to compare multiple classifiers on class imbalanced datasets [24]. ROC curves show the evaluated graphical method to represent the trade-off which occurs in between true positive and false positive rates. Compared to other algorithms, Random Forest produced higher accuracy, as depicted in Table 11.3.

In classification methods, correct or incorrect classifications are used to specify the cost or benefit. In the proposed method Random is defined as the cost of a random classifier and Gain is evaluated as the difference of classifier than the random classifier. Cost–benefit analysis has two plots: threshold curve and ROC curve. Threshold curve is similar to the ROC curve. In ROC curve, Y axis contains true positive rate and X axis contains false positive rate, depicted in Figure 11.9. In cost–benefit analysis using Random Forest, threshold curve contains X axis with sample selected instances and Y axis with true positive rate. Cost–benefit curve contains X as sample selected size and Y axis as cost/benefit, depicted in Figure 11.10. Different confusion matrix for the D3S dataset–based machine learning algorithm are compared with actual drowsiness and non-drowsiness along with predicted drowsiness and non-predicted drowsiness. As a comparison statement in Table 11.4, the output result of the confusion matrix for SVM using the D3S dataset shows the actual drowsy according to predicted drowsy value output is 1718 and the actual drowsy according to predicted non-drowsy value output is 433. Using the confusion matrix for Random Forest predicts using the D3S dataset shows the actual drowsy according to predicted drowsy value output is 2820 and the actual drowsy according to predicted non-drowsy value output is 73 (Table 11.5). Similarly, in Table 11.6, by using the confusion matrix for J48 using the

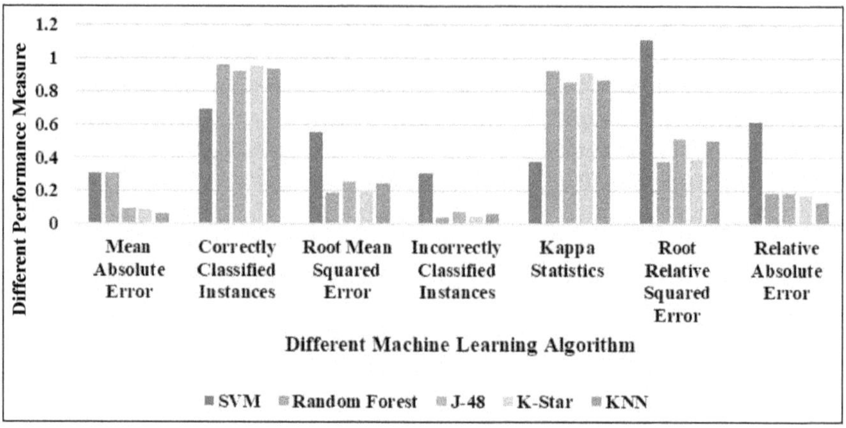

Fig. 11.7 Performance measure results based on different machine learning algorithms.

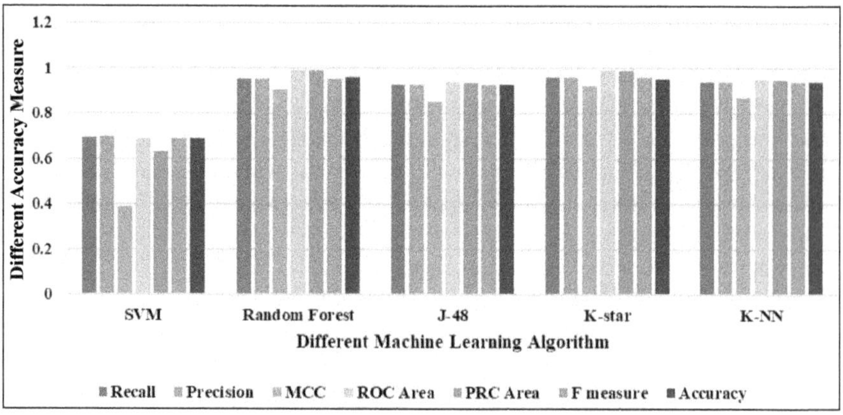

Fig. 11.8 Accuracy measure results based on different machine learning algorithms.

Table 11.3 Different accuracy measures compared with different machine learning algorithms.

Algorithm	*Recall*	*Precision*	*MCC*	*ROC Area*	*PRC Area*	*F-measure*	*Accuracy*
SVM	0.691	0.699	0.388	0.689	0.632	0.687	69.07%
Random Forest	0.954	0.954	0.909	0.989	0.988	0.954	96.06%
J48	0.926	0.927	0.853	0.940	0.934	0.926	92.64%
K-Star	0.961	0.961	0.922	0.989	0.988	0.961	95.42%
K-NN	0.939	0.939	0.870	0.954	0.949	0.939	93.89%

D3S dataset, the actual drowsy according to predicted drowsy value output is 2,707 and the actual drowsy according to predicted non-drowsy value output is 153. Accordingly, in Table 11.7, by using the confusion matrix for K-Star using the D3S dataset, the actual drowsy according to predicted drowsy value output is 2791 and the non-drowsy value output is 100.

As a similar comparative result, actual non-drowsiness was compared with predicted drowsiness and non-predicted drowsiness. As an evaluation statement, the output result of the confusion matrix for SVM using the D3S dataset shows the actual non-drowsy according to predicted drowsy value output is 1228 and the actual non-drowsy according to predicted non-drowsy value output is 2485. Similarly, by using the confusion matrix for J48 using the D3S dataset, the actual non-drowsy according to predicted drowsy value output is 239 and the actual non-drowsy according to predicted non-drowsy value output is 2,765. Accordingly, by using the confusion matrix for K-Star using the D3S dataset, the actual non-drowsy according to predicted drowsy value output is 155 and the actual non-drowsy according to predicted non-drowsy value output is 2818. Using the confusion matrix for Random Forest predicts using the D3S dataset shows the actual non-drowsy according to predicted drowsy value output is 126 and the actual non-drowsy according to predicted non-drowsy value output is 2845.

Compared to the above results, the Random Forest classifier performed better on the D3S dataset. Significantly, It correctly predicted 2820 drowsiness cases, while 73 drowsiness cases were incorrectly predicted as non-drowsiness. Similarly, having a value output of 126 under the actual non-drowsiness along with predicted drowsiness and a value output of 2845 under the actual non-drowsiness along with non-drowsiness is predicted.

Table 11.4 Confusion matrix for SVM – D3S dataset–based machine learning algorithm.

Confusion Matrix for SVM	*Predicted Drowsy*	*Predicted Non-drowsy*
Actual Drowsy	1718	433
Actual Non-drowsy	1228	2485

Table 11.5 Confusion matrix for Random Forest – D3S dataset–based machine learning algorithm.

Confusion Matrix for Random Forest	*Predicted Drowsy*	*Predicted Non-drowsy*
Actual Drowsy	2820	73
Actual Non-drowsy	126	2845

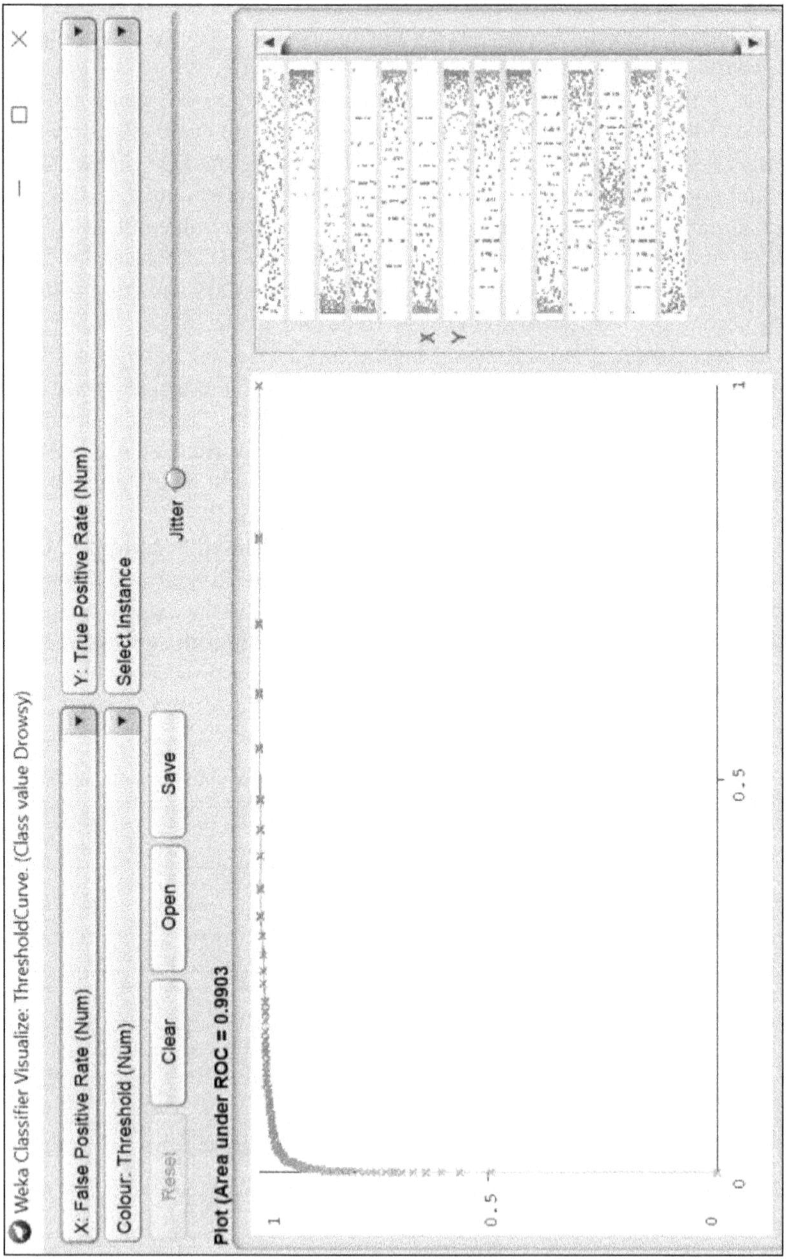

Fig. 11.9 Proposed model ROC curve with class drowsy.

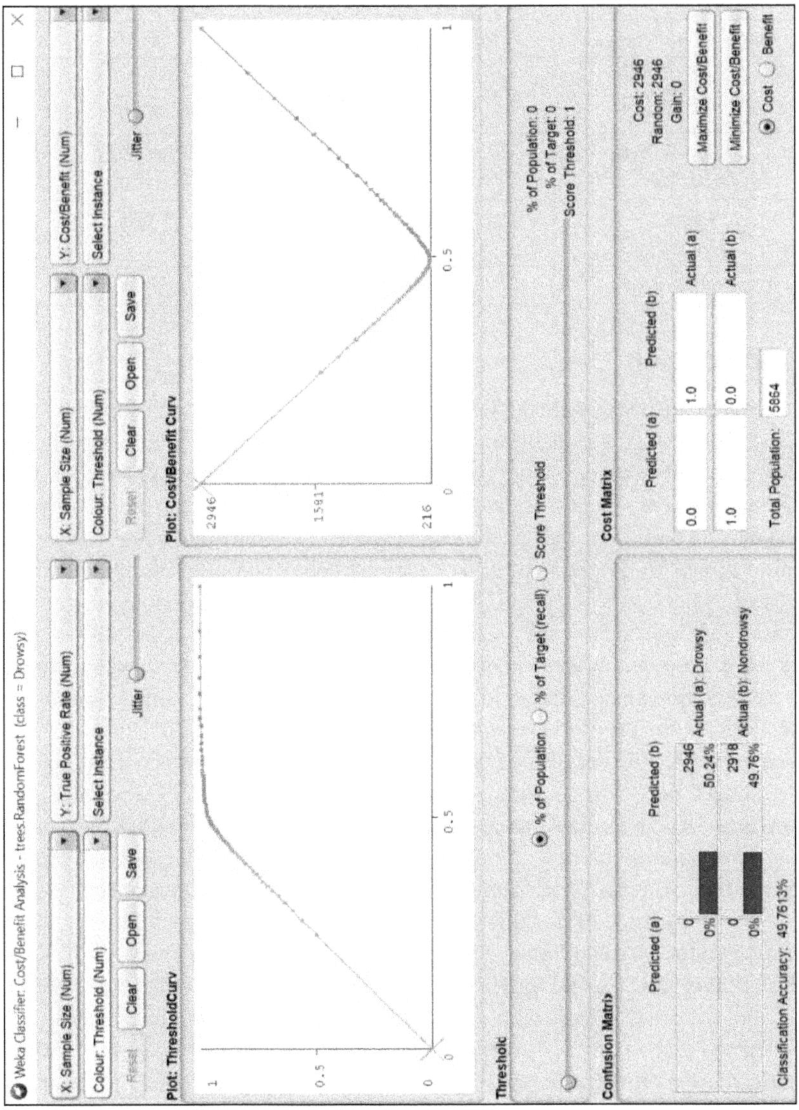

Fig. 11.10 Cost or benefit analysis for Random Forest classifier.

Table 11.6 Confusion matrix for J48 – D3S dataset–based machine learning algorithm.

Confusion Matrix for J48	*Predicted Drowsy*	*Predicted Non-drowsy*
Actual Drowsy	2707	153
Actual Non-drowsy	239	2765

Table 11.7 Confusion matrix for K-Star – D3S dataset–based machine learning algorithm.

Confusion Matrix for K-Star	*Predicted Drowsy*	*Predicted Non-drowsy*
Actual Drowsy	2791	100
Actual Non-drowsy	155	2818

5. Conclusion

The recommended wearable device aims to prevent fatigue-related accidents and driver drowsiness. A reasonable analysis was conducted for calculating significant model performance based on two classifiers: drowsy and non-drowsy. To accurately predict drowsiness symptoms, two important features were used: the percentage of eye closure and yawning. The proposed work was carried out using a machine learning model by implementing five various controlled algorithms, including K-Nearest Neighbours, K-Star, SVM, J48 Decision Tree, and Random Forest. The proposed method made a substantial impact by conducting a driver drowsiness detection experiment in Weka machine learning software. Weka machine learning software is implemented and used for evaluating significant model performance. Henceforth, in the proposed research methodology, the class imbalance SMOTE is used to balance the dataset and enhance the accuracy performance. Each output was evaluated for various accuracy measures like Recall, MCC, FP, Precision, TP, F-measure, PRC area, ROC area, correctly and incorrectly classified instances, root mean squared error, root relative squared error using 10-fold cross-validation, Kappa statistics, relative absolute error, and mean absolute error. Hence, the accuracy performance of classifiers is evaluated in percentages such as for SVM it is 71.67%, for Random Forest it is 96.60%, for J48 Decision Tree it is 93.31%, for K-Star it is 95.65%, and for K-Nearest Neighbours it is 93.89%, as calculated. Compared with all the above outputs of classifiers, Random Forest produced higher performance and accuracy levels by using a simple colour histogram feature. Overall, the experimental results validate that the proposed driver drowsiness detection framework delivers an efficient solution for distinguishing between drowsy and non-drowsy driving conditions. The integration of SMOTE for class balancing, simple colour histogram-based feature extraction, and Random Forest classification significantly improved the overall detection performance with low computational complexity. These findings determine the effectiveness of the proposed methodology for real-time driver drowsiness detection and highlight its potential to improve road safety through reliable drowsiness monitoring.

References

[1] National Safety Council. (n.d.). Drivers are falling asleep behind the wheel. Available at https://www.nsc.org/road-safety/safety-topics/fatigued-driving (accessed on 1 October 2022).

[2] Bank Rate. (n.d.). Driver drowsiness statistical data. Available at https://www.bankrate.com/insurance/car/drowsy-driving-statistics (accessed on 1 September 2022).

[3] Dua, M., Shakshi, Singla, R., et al. (2021). Deep CNN models-based ensemble approach to driver drowsiness detection. *Neural Computing and Applications*, 33, 3155–3168.

[4] Priya, V.V. and Uma, M. (2021). Comparison of multimodal features for detecting driver drowsiness using different dataset. In *2021 5th International Conference on Trends in Electronics and Informatics (ICOEI)*, pp. 1429–1437. IEEE.

[5] Dasgupta, A., Rahman, D. and Routray, A. (2018). A smartphone-based drowsiness detection and warning system for automotive drivers. *IEEE Transactions on Intelligent Transportation Systems*, 20(11), 4045–4054.

[6] Deng, W. and Wu, R. (2019). Real-time driver-drowsiness detection system using facial features. *IEEE Access*, 7, 118727–118738.

[7] Hashemi, M., Mirrashid, A. and Beheshti Shirazi, A. (2020). Driver safety development: Real-time driver drowsiness detection system based on convolutional neural network. *SN Computer Science*, 1, 1–10.

[8] Savaş, B.K. and Becerikli, Y. (2020). Real time driver fatigue detection system based on multi-task ConNN. *IEEE Access*, 8, 12491–12498.

[9] Jamshidi, S., Azmi, R., Sharghi, M. and Soryani, M. (2021). Hierarchical deep neural networks to detect driver drowsiness. *Multimedia Tools and Applications*, 80, 16045–16058.

[10] Hossain, M. U., Rahman, M. A., Islam, M. M., et al. (2022). Automatic driver distraction detection using deep convolutional neural networks. *Intelligent Systems with Applications*, 14, 200075.

[11] Saurav, S., Mathur, S., Sang, I., et al. (2020). Yawn detection for driver's drowsiness prediction using bi-directional LSTM with CNN features. In *Intelligent Human Computer Interaction: 11th International Conference, IHCI 2019, Allahabad, India, December 12–14, 2019, Proceedings 11*, pp. 189–200. Springer International Publishing.

[12] Park, S., Pan, F., Kang, S. and Yoo, C. D. (2016). Driver drowsiness detection system based on feature representation learning using various deep networks. In *Asian Conference on Computer Vision*, volume 10118, pp. 154–164. Cham: Springer International Publishing.

[13] Zhang, K., Zhang, Z., Li, Z. and Qiao, Y. (2016). Joint face detection and alignment using multitask cascaded convolutional networks. *IEEE Signal Processing Letters*, 23(10), 1499–1503.

[14] Kholerdi, H. A., TaheriNejad, N., Ghaderi, R. and Baleghi, Y. (2016). Driver's drowsiness detection using an enhanced image processing technique inspired by the human visual system. *Connection Science*, 28(1), 27–46.

[15] Gupta, I., Garg, N., Aggarwal, A., et al. (2018). Real-time driver's drowsiness monitoring based on dynamically varying threshold. In *2018 Eleventh International Conference on Contemporary Computing (IC3)*, pp. 1–6. IEEE.

[16] Gu, W. H., Zhu, Y., Chen, X. D., et al. (2018). Hierarchical CNN-based real-time fatigue detection system by visual-based technologies using MSP model. *IET Image Processing*, 12(12), 2319–2329.

[17] Yan, C., Coenen, F. and Zhang, B. (2016). Driving posture recognition by convolutional neural networks. *IET Computer Vision*, 10(2), 103–114.

[18] Fatima, B., Shahid, A. R., Ziauddin, S., et al. (2020). Driver fatigue detection using Viola Jones and principal component analysis. *Applied Artificial Intelligence*, 34(6), 456–483.

[19] Santoso, N., Wibowo, W. and Himawati, H. (2019). Integration of synthetic minority oversampling technique for imbalanced class. *Indonesian Journal of Electrical Engineering and Computer Science*, 13(1), 102–108.

[20] Janković, R. (2019). Machine learning models for cultural heritage image classification: Comparison based on attribute selection. *Information*, 11(1), 12.

[21] Vijayan, T., Sangeetha, M., Kumaravel, A. and Karthik, B. (2020). Feature selection for simple color histogram filter based on retinal fundus images for diabetic retinopathy recognition. *IETE Journal of Research*, 69(2), 987–994.

[22] Weka 3-data mining with open-source machine learning software in Java. Available at https://www.cs.waikato.ac.nz/ml/weka (accessed on 18 May 2026).

[23] Villavicencio, C.N., Macrohon, J.J.E., Inbaraj, X.A., et al. (2021). Covid-19 prediction applying supervised machine learning algorithms with comparative analysis using weka. *Algorithms*, 14(7), 201.

[24] Rao, R.R. and Makkithaya, K. (2017). Learning from a class imbalanced public health dataset: A cost-based comparison of classifier performance. *International Journal of Electrical and Computer Engineering*, 7(4), 2215.

12 Vision 2035: The Next Frontier of Wearable AI and Immersive Healthcare

Ashwini A.[1*], G. Santhiya[2], Lavanya M.[3] and Balasubramaniam S.[4]

Passive data collection devices act as an active, intelligent assistants that completely pervade the healthcare ecosystem. The next generation of this kind of wearable is built on the most recent sensor miniaturization, neural-interface systems, and ultra-low-power edge artificial intelligence (AI) controllers to continuously record physiological, behavioural, and environmental measures with clinical precision. Immersive healthcare extends the future of the healthcare industry with the help of augmented reality, virtual reality, and mixed reality. As part of AI, wearable-based and immersive interfaces by 2035 will give doctors, nurses, and patients the opportunity to interact with health data in spatial workflows, allowing them to be more accurate when it comes to diagnoses, treatment adherence, and recovery performance. The vision of the digital future proposed in Vision 2035 is where preventive digital therapeutics, emotion-sensitive biosensing, AI-assisted mental health assistants, and decentralized care at home will become the new norms. Such a change will also transform the number of individuals to manage the clinical load, as it makes human-centred, adaptive, and immersive healthcare the force behind the future of medical innovation.

1. Introduction to Vision 2035

Immersive vision introduces the next new frontier in the sphere of healthcare development with wearable artificial intelligence (AI) and immersive technologies that radiate as ancillary objects [1]. By 2035, healthcare will not be an episodic, clinical-based experience but a continuous, anticipatory, and intensely personal

1 Department of Electronics and Communication Engineering, Vel Tech Rangarajan Dr. Sagunthala R&D Institute of Science and Technology, Chennai, Tamil Nadu, India.
2 Department of Information Technology, SRM Valliammai Engineering College, Kattangulathur, Tamil Nadu, India.
3 Department of Artificial Intelligence and Data Science (AI&DS), Adhiparasakthi College of Engineering, Ranipet, Tamil Nadu, India.
4 School of Computer Science and Engineering, Kerala University of Digital Sciences, Innovation and Technology (Formerly IIITM-K), Digital University Kerala, Thiruvananthapuram, Kerala, India.
* Corresponding author: a.ashwinivel@gmail.com

DOI: 10.1201/9781003776291-12

experience. Wearable technology in the future will be replete with miniaturization of sensors and bio-integrated electronics along with edge AI so that wearable systems can be used as intelligent companions continuously tracking physiological, cognitive, and emotional states [2]. Such systems will be able to bridge the gap between patients and the healthcare providers because they will be able to provide real-time health intelligence, anticipate risks in advance, and take proactive measures, as well as refocus on prevention and prediction of care rather than providing reactive care.

The convergence of wearable AI and immersive technologies (augmented reality [AR], virtual reality [VR], and mixed reality [MR]) is one of the points in Vision 2035. These virtual worlds will modify the perception and reaction to medical data. To enhance the quality of diagnosis and clinical decision-making, clinicians will communicate with patient data using 3D spatial interfaces, digital twins, and holographic dashboards. At the same time, patients will benefit by getting the opportunity to receive immersive rehabilitation, virtual therapy rooms, and interactive health education, which increase the level of engagement, adherence, and recovery rates [3]. This corporeal, informatization, and virtual healthcare will enable one to comfortably offer care in hospital, at home, and everywhere. The labour force disparities will be bridged and the underserved and rural areas will gain access to on-demand healthcare with the assistance of smart avatars and virtual physicians. Wearable computing, immersive intelligence, and generative AI will converge to result in the provision of healthcare that is always personalized, constant, and predictive.

Equity, scalability, and sustainability in the global health systems are also areas that Vision 2035 has focused on. The issue of workforce shortage will be resolved through AI-based virtual clinicians, smart avatars, and smart care coordination with smart wearables and virtual telemedicine environments. The digital services will be decentralized on-demand to provide quality healthcare to rural and underserved populations [4]. Responsible use and trustful building of ethical AI models, privacy-enabling cloud-edge systems, and ethical data management will be crucial in the development of trust. Finally, there is a scenario of Vision 2035 where healthcare is responsive, welcoming, and enabling to people in front of a smart, immersive, and shifting healthcare model, as depicted in Figure 12.1.

2. Smart Biosensors and Nanowearables

Vision 2035 relies on a technological platform of smart biosensors and nanowearables that make non-invasive monitoring of health, at unprecedented scales, continuously and extremely accurate. These devices of the new generation are nanoscale sensing materials, flexible electronics, and biocompatible substrates that can record the full spectrum of physiological signals, including biochemical signals, neural signals, cardiovascular signals, and metabolic signals, as illustrated in Figure 12.2. Compared to the more traditional wearables, nanowearables are

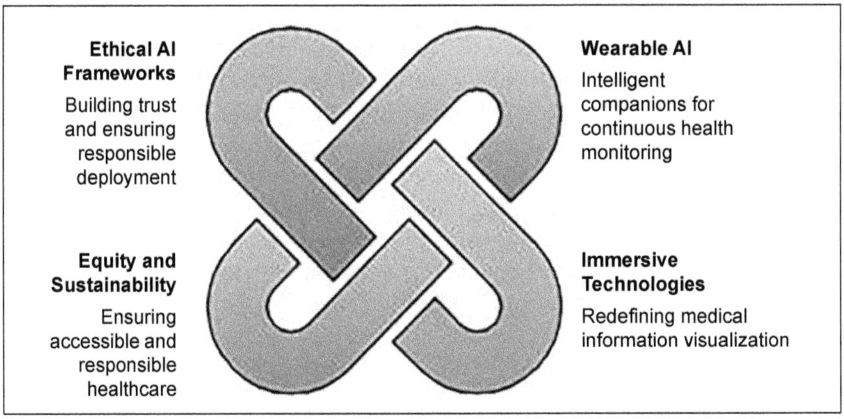

Fig. 12.1 Vision 2035—The Future of Healthcare.

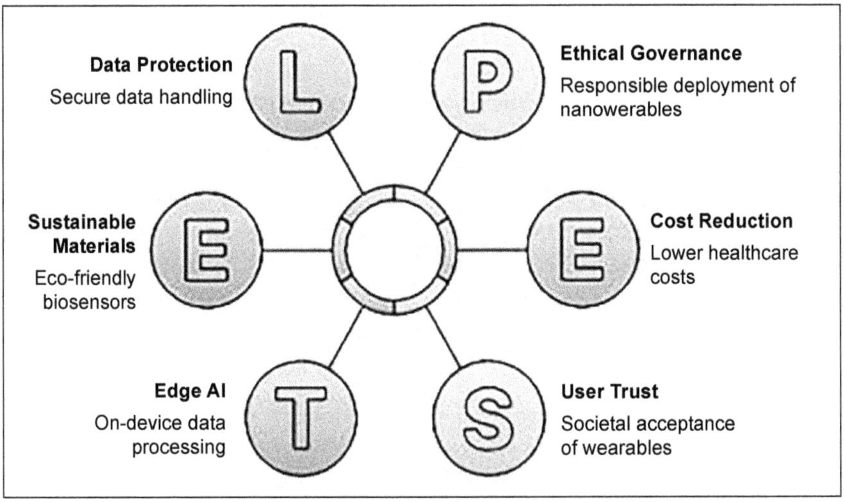

Fig. 12.2 Smart Biosensors and Nanowearables.

able to identify slight shifts in health states and early signs of a disease at the clinical level of accuracy due to their ability to take periodic measurements [5].

2.1 Evolution of Smart Biosensing Technologies

The emergence of smart biosensing technologies has been defined by how extensive and discrete measurement instruments can be transformed into smart and continuous monitoring systems which are miniature. First-generation biosensors are only able to measure a single parameter and have to be manually operated or with laboratory analysis. The development of microelectronics, nanofabrication, and biomedical engineering has enabled modern biosensors to detect a number of physiological and biochemical signals in real time, and they can significantly improve diagnostic accuracy and responsiveness. Smart biosensors will be independent health trackers that will be incorporated into normal lives by 2035. These systems will introduce the ability to combine sensing, computation, and communication into a single system that can modify itself to the health profile of a particular individual. The shift to predictive biosensing, replacing reactive sensing, will allow early detection of diseases, real-time assessment of threats, and proactive health measures, reforming the role of diagnostics in future healthcare systems.

2.2 Nanoscale Materials for Advanced Biosensing

Graphene, carbon nanotubes, quantum dots, and nanowires are nanoscale materials that have transformed biosensors in terms of sensing and selectivity. They possess a high surface-to-volume ratio and distinctive electrical, optical, and mechanical properties, thus enabling the detection of biomarkers at trace levels that cannot be detected using conventional materials. These nanomaterials are easy to transduce and bio-recognize rapidly, and thus are suitable for wearable and implantable sensing devices. Under Vision 2035, smart nanomaterials will be integrated with biosensors for real-time molecular-based health monitoring. Functionalized nanostructures are selective towards biomarkers of metabolic disorders, cardiovascular diseases, infections, and neurological disorders [6]. This molecular accuracy will enable early-stage diagnosis, custom therapeutics, and constant monitoring of disease progression at the clinical grade.

2.3 Flexible, Stretchable, and Implantable Nanowearables

The design of flexible and stretchable nanowearables is highly significant for human-centric healthcare. Constructed using soft materials such as elastomers, hydrogels, and biocompatible polymers, the devices are shaped in a natural form that fits the skin or internal tissues and can thus be monitored over a long period without any inconvenience. In contrast to stiff devices, flexible wearables do not lose sensor accuracy due to motion and can therefore be used for continuous self-measurement of physiological data. Nano wearables that can be implanted will also go beyond the surface-level measurements of healthcare monitoring. Virtual assistants will contribute to lowering workforce shortages and increasing efficiency, accuracy, and consistency in healthcare provision by automating routine activities and providing a better clinical understanding.

2.4 Biochemical and Physiological Signal Monitoring

Smart biosensors have been developed to measure both physiological and biochemical signals, which provide a complete picture of human health. The biochemical sensing system encompasses glucose, cortisol, lactate, electrolytes, and inflammatory proteins, whereas physiological sensing encompasses heart rate, respiration, muscle activity, and oxygen saturation in the blood. These signals can be combined to profile holistic health, together with the conventional vital signs. The possibilities of multi-modal sensing in the future are AI-based biochemical changes and physiological correlation of trends. Such an integrated data system will enhance precision in the forecast of disease prediction, allow adaptive care settings, and assist in the detection of acute health scenarios in a timely manner. They will transform clinical decision-making processes into longitudinal health through episodic evaluations based on constant tracking.

2.5 Energy-Efficient and Self-Powered Biosensor Systems

Continuous biosensing implementations are a major problem as far as energy conservation is concerned. Conventional batteries shorten the lifestyles of devices and make them very cumbersome to use as they have to be charged or changed so often. To eliminate this, the next generation of nanowearables will have ultralow-power electronics and smart power management solutions, which will guarantee maximum service life. By 2035, nanogenerators and bio-energy harvesting methods will enable self-powered biosensor systems to use body heat, movement, biochemicals, or ambient light to generate power. Such inventions will allow work without any maintenance, making constant health monitoring feasible and viable. Wearables that are energy autonomous will be particularly useful in implantable healthcare devices and remote medical care.

2.6 Edge AI Integration for Intelligent Health Monitoring

Edge AI incorporated into biosensors allows the processing of data at the device level and lowers latency and the need to rely on cloud infrastructure. Edge AI enables biosensors to remove noise, realize higher-order features, and conduct real-time health-related activities. The method increases the responsiveness and at the same time maintains the privacy of data and minimizes the communication bandwidth. Vision 2035 intelligent nanowearables will be based on adaptive learning models, which will be applied to customize health monitoring according to individual baselines. Such systems will improve as the user improves, and they will continue to improve predictions and interventions. Edge AI–powered biosensors will also serve as real-time decision-support agents, which will raise alerts, offer suggestions, or provide immersive therapeutic feedback in case anomalies are identified.

2.7 Emotion-Aware and Neuro-Biosensing Wearables

Emotion-sensitive biosensors can also be used to monitor health, in addition to physical factors, such as mental and emotional conditions. These wearables can predict stress, anxiety, fatigue, and cognitive workload by examining physiological measures, including heart rate variability, electrodermal activity, brain activity, and hormonal indicators. This is required for mental health and neurorehabilitation evaluations. As 2035 approaches, the monitoring of brain–body interaction will be performed continuously through neuro-biosensing nanowearables. Combined with immersive healthcare ecosystems, these systems will facilitate adaptive mental health therapy, cognitive training, and neurofeedback therapies. Individualized mental health will include emotion-responsive biosensing and will enhance the quality of life and well-being.

2.8 Data Security, Privacy, and Ethical Considerations

The deliberate collection of sensitive health information is an issue of enormous concern as far as the security, privacy, and ethical conduct of the operation are concerned. The control of unauthorized access and misuse of smart biosensors should be limited by use of strong encryption, secure authentication, decentralized data structures, and secure encryption. Privacy-preserving measures, which will become the key elements of biosensing ecosystems, are federated learning and anonymized analytics. The responsible use of nanowearables will be regulated in Vision 2035 through the use of ethical governance systems [7]. The transparent data ownership models, informed consent mechanisms, and regulatory compliance will ensure that users have trust and acceptance in society. By overcoming these challenges, it will be possible to realize the full potential of smart biosensors in the healthcare systems at a later stage.

2.9 Role in Preventive, Predictive, and Personalized Healthcare

The transformation to preventive and predictive approaches to healthcare will target smart biosensors and nanowearables. Regular monitoring aids in detecting deviations in health at an early stage and in a timely manner before the symptoms turn into a serious disease. This is a preventive approach that reduces hospitalization, medical spending, and the load of patients. Individual healthcare plans will be customized to lifestyles, genetic composition, and the environment through the application of biosensing information over the long term. The nanowearables of the future in Vision 2035 will give the population a chance to manage their health and give clinicians a chance to act [8]. Such a paradigm revolution will streamline healthcare and make it more effective, equitable, and patient-centred.

By 2035, nanotechnology and material science will facilitate easy integration of biosensors in clothes, skin patches, implants, contact lenses, and in ingestible platforms. These non-invasive devices will also continuously detect biomarkers, such as glucose, cortisol, lactate, oxygen levels, hydration level, and indicators of inflammation, without disrupting daily lifestyle [9]. Energy-efficient designs can be made in such a way that frequent recharging is done away with by the use of energy collection in the form of body heat, motion, or ambient light. In combination with ultra-low-power edge AI, smart biosensors will process data on the device, identify anomalies, and send immediate warnings, enabling faster interventions and maintaining data privacy.

3. Intelligent Virtual Assistants and Avatars

In addition to personal health monitoring, smart biosensors and nanowearables are important in the management of population health and precision medicine. Anonymous and aggregated sensor data will facilitate mass epidemiology, individualized drug therapy, and digital therapeutic adaptation. Emotion-sensitive biosensors will be used in the fields of mental health and neurology to measure stress, fatigue, and cognitive load to implement interventions in response to them, using immersive or AI-assisted environments, as shown in Figure 12.3. Altogether, these technologies will transform healthcare into a proactive, personalized, and preventive healthcare model to provide individuals and clinicians with continuous actionable health intelligence within the ecosystem of Vision 2035.

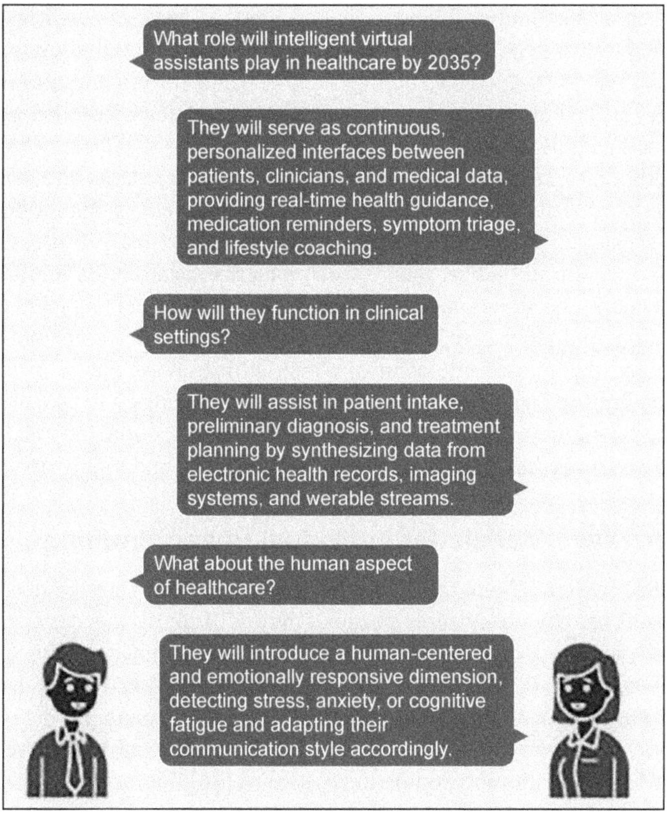

Fig. 12.3 Intelligent Virtual Assistants in Healthcare 2035.

Smart virtual assistants and AI-based avatars will have a transformational role in the healthcare ecosystem of the future in 2035 as continuous and personalized interfaces between the patient and inter-professional and medical data [10]. These virtual agents, which aim to assist people in both cognition and emotional states, will evolve beyond rule-based chatbots to become empathetic, adaptable companions able to comprehend user intent, emotional conditions, and health backgrounds through both cognitive and emotional understanding and empathy [11]. Together with wearable AI and biosensor connections, virtual assistants will provide real-time health information, medication notifications, symptom management, and lifestyle counselling that will enable proactive and preventive care in the everyday environment. The clinical settings will have intelligent avatars that play the role of virtual clinicians and decision support agents to complement the efforts of healthcare professionals. Using the synthesis of multi-modal data based on electronic health records, imaging systems, and continuous wearable streams, they will assist with patient admission, initial diagnosis, and planning of treatment. These avatars show patient-specific 3D data, simulate disease progression, and enable remote consultations and tele-surgeries with the help of the immersive AR/VR/MR platform [12]. The virtual assistants will also help to decrease the workforce shortages and enhance the efficacy, accuracy, and consistency of healthcare delivery through the automation of routine operations and enhancing clinical acumen.

In addition to functional assistance, smart virtual assistants and avatars will bring a human-related factor of emotional responsiveness to digital healthcare. Emotion-sensitive AI cognitive models allow avatars to analyse stress, anxiety, or cognitive strain and adjust their speech patterns accordingly, allowing users to trust avatars and maintain a relationship over time [13]. In mental health, rehabilitation, and elder care, customized avatars will offer companionship and cognitive and therapeutic interactions, which will decrease social isolation and enhance compliance with care plans. These intelligent beings will take the place of trusted digital partners in Vision 2035, which will grant people the independence they need and make healthcare approachable, inclusive, and highly personal.

4. Generative Models for Individual Health Profiling

Vision 2035 will use generative models as the central intelligence layer in personalized healthcare systems because they will allow the development of dynamically engaged, data-based individual health profiles. Generative AI models are also used to learn the underlying distributions of multi-modal health data, which comprise physiological measurements, clinical imaging, genomic data, lifestyle behaviours, and environmental conditions, unlike traditional predictive models, which use fixed features and population dynamics [14]. Variational autoencoders, diffusion models, and generative adversarial networks will be used to synthesize heterogeneous data streams into coherent changing representations of the health state of an individual to better understand normal baselines and subtle changes over time.

One such innovation made possible by generative models is the creation of digital health twins—personalized virtual representations of people that continually evolve as new information is provided by wearables, biosensors, and clinical records. Digital twins will model disease progression, response to treatment, and lifestyle interventions before being implemented in the real world [15]. With the help of generative models, clinicians will be able to choose the most appropriate treatments, modify prescriptions, and anticipate adverse outcomes more accurately by creating counterfactual health conditions for patients. Such a change from population-based medicine to individual-based modelling will be a tremendous boost in clinical outcomes and lessen the use of trial-and-error in planning treatment.

In addition to clinical decision support, generative models will enable individuals to work with personal health paths [16]. Intelligent virtual assistants and smart visualization applications generate personal health, risk, and wellness educational content in a contextual and easy-to-understand format. Generative techniques that are privacy-conscious, like federated and synthetic data generation, make sure that the model is not trained in any way and no personal information that might be considered sensitive is revealed. Through the assistance of generative models, healthcare will be predictive, adaptive, and more personalized in the upcoming Vision 2035, transforming the process of individual health profiling into a participatory, ongoing, and intelligent process.

5. Real-Time Anomaly Detection

The Vision 2035 healthcare ecosystem will require real-time anomaly detection as an important feature that will allow continuous monitoring of physiological, behavioural, and environmental measurements to determine the initial indicators of worsening health [17]. In contrast to traditional threshold-based surveillance systems, next-generation anomaly tracking models will use AI-based models to find personalized baselines using wearable and biosensor data over time. Such models will identify slight, context-dependent changes in essential parameters of heart rate, oxygen saturation, neural activity, motion modes, and biochemical indicators, enabling the timely prevention of the onset of acute clinical events, as shown in Table 12.1.

Table 12.1 Real-Time Anomaly Detection in Vision 2035 Healthcare Ecosystem.

Aspect	*Description*
Purpose	Continuous monitoring of physiological, behavioural, and environmental signals to detect early signs of health deterioration in real time

Contd...

Table 12.1 *Contd...*

Aspect	*Description*
Data Sources	Wearables, biosensors, nanowearables capturing heart rate, oxygen saturation, neural signals, motion patterns, and biochemical markers
Baseline Modelling	AI-driven personalized baseline learning using long-term individual sensor data instead of static threshold-based rules
Detection Approach	Identification of subtle, context-aware deviations from normal patterns rather than abrupt threshold violations
AI Techniques Used	Self-supervised learning, probabilistic modelling, and generative reconstruction-based anomaly detection models
Computational Paradigm	Edge AI and streaming analytics enabling ultra-low latency, on-device anomaly detection
Latency and Connectivity	Minimal latency with reduced dependence on cloud connectivity, suitable for remote and resource-constrained environments
Privacy and Security	On-device data processing ensures enhanced data privacy and trustworthiness
Response Mechanisms	Clinician alerts, adaptive digital therapeutics, and immersive support systems providing immediate care guidance
Context Awareness	Integration of personal health history, lifestyle, and environmental context to reduce false positives
Advanced Capabilities	Use of customized health profiles and digital twins for intelligent, decision-aware anomaly interpretation
Clinical Applications	Chronic disease management, mental health monitoring, elderly care, and post-operative recovery
Healthcare Impact	Reduction in emergency cases, optimized healthcare resources, and shift towards proactive and preventive care
Vision 2035 Outcome	Enables continuous, personalized, and patient-centred healthcare monitoring with high clinical relevance

The development of edge AI and streaming analytics will also ensure that anomaly detection can run with ultra-low latency on wearable and nanowearable devices. Self-supervised learning, probabilistic modelling, and generative reconstruction-based detection are some of the techniques that provide systems with the capability to differentiate between benign variations and clinically significant abnormalities. These systems minimize reliance on cloud connectivity, maximize the trustworthiness of using remote locations, and maintain data privacy by conducting on-device analyses [18]. The identified anomalies will cause adaptive changes, such as the provision of a clinician alert, digital therapeutics modification, or the use of an immersive support environment to provide immediate care instructions.

Vision 2035 will go beyond issuing alerts and move to real-time anomaly detection, which will be an intelligent and decision-aware process, as well as customized health profiles and digital twins. The detected anomalies will be placed in context with respect to personal history, lifestyle, and the environment to maximize the reduction of false positives and increase clinical significance. This will be more helpful in the treatment of chronic diseases, checking mental health, taking care of the aged, and post-operative recovery. Real-time anomaly detection will remove the issue of emergency cases, enhance healthcare resources, and add to a preventive and patient-centred healthcare paradigm in a significant way by enabling proactive, continuous, and personalized healthcare monitoring [19].

6. Interoperability, Data Governance, and Security

The healthcare ecosystem in Vision 2035 will be based on the idea of interoperability, according to which data will be carried among wearable devices, biosensors, clinical systems, immersive platforms, and AI services in a fluid manner [20]. The diversity of data sources—such as nanowearables or home monitoring devices—and tools—such as electronic health records or digital twins—requires the application of common data formats, data communication protocols, and semantic models. Through the development of open interoperability frameworks and healthcare standards, heterogeneous systems will be in a position to relay and interpret data reliably, ensuring continuity of care across institutions, geographies, and care environments without the occurrence of data silos. There is a need for strong data governance systems that will control the lifecycle of sensitive health data in this well-interconnected environment.

By 2035, governance models will focus on patient-based data ownership, disclosure consent, and access to patient data based on purpose [21]. Methods such as federated learning, data minimization, and synthetic data generation enable the training of AI models in a distributed manner without access to raw personal data. Fairness, accountability, and explainability of AI-driven healthcare decisions will be ensured by ethical governance policies to inspire trust among patients, clinicians, and regulatory bodies. Security will become a priority because ongoing data sharing will expand the attack area of digital healthcare systems. Data will be secured using advanced encryption, secure identity management, and zero-trust architectures throughout their transmission, storage, and processing [22]. Wearable devices will be secured against tampering and unauthorized access using edge-based security schemes, and data integrity and traceability will be ensured by blockchain-inspired audit trails. This interoperability, strong data governance, and strong security convergence will create a trusted digital health infrastructure that achieves innovation in Vision 2035—infrastructure that brings privacy, safety, and ethical responsibility [23].

7. Applications across Medical Domains

The integration of wearable AI, smart biosensors, generative models, and immersive technologies in Vision 2035 will enable the use of applications across a wide range in different areas of medicine. In cardiology, continuous observation of heart rhythm, blood pressure, and biochemical parameters is important for the early identification of arrhythmias, ischemia, and exacerbation of heart failure. Within the endocrinology profession, smart wearables will enable the real-time monitoring of glucose, hormone, and metabolic levels, enabling the use of adaptive insulin and tailored lifestyle treatment for diabetes and metabolic diseases [24]. Such apps will be used to ensure that chronic disease management is less episodic and more comprehensive in the form of data-based supervision.

Immersive intelligence and advanced biosensing will be particularly helpful in neurology and mental health. Neuro-wearables monitoring brain activity, stress, and sleep patterns will be used for the early diagnosis of neurological indicators in epilepsy, Parkinson's disease, and Alzheimer's disease. In the context of mental healthcare, emotion-sensitive wearables with the help of AI-powered virtual assistants will allow for assessment of anxiety, depression, and cognitive overload on a constant basis [25]. VR-based therapies include immersion that offers customized rehabilitation, exposure therapy, and neurofeedback that enhances compliance with treatment and long-term outcomes.

Vision 2035 technologies will improve accuracy, accessibility, and interpersonal interactions in areas such as oncology, orthopaedics, paediatrics, and geriatrics. Wearable biosensors can be used to measure the side-effects of treatment and progress of recovery in patients with cancer, thus allowing timely measures. Motion-sensing wearables and digital twins will direct custom physical therapy in orthopaedics and rehabilitation. The non-invasive and unobtrusive monitoring systems will help in care of the paediatric patients and in elderly care, where safety is ensured and independence is enhanced. Together with these cross-domain applications, the immersive technologies will make healthcare delivery personalized, preventive, and inclusive, bringing high-quality medical care to populations and clinical specialties.

8. Challenges and Research Opportunities for 2035

Although wearable AI and immersive healthcare technologies have the potential to transform the healthcare field and contribute to the Vision 2035 paradigm, a range of critical issues must be resolved to support the implementation of the proposed changes. The technical issues are to provide long-term reliability of biosensors, control noise and drift of the continuous data streams, and provide clinical-grade accuracy in varying populations and environments. Scalability and interoperability problems also exist because of discontinuous standards and device ecosystems. Moreover, issues of data privacy, AI bias, AI decision explainability, and user trust are all prior ethical issues regarding adoption at scale. Next-generation wearables will have a complicated design issue of balancing continuous monitoring with user comfort, energy efficiency, and affordability.

From a regulatory and societal perspective, adopting wearable AI in the mainstream healthcare context casts doubt on accountability, consent, and fair access. Laws are usually slow to keep up with rapid technological change; therefore, the process of clinical validation and certification of AI-based wearables is complex and time-consuming. The other problem is workforce adaptation: clinicians will be required to undergo training to receive the insights generated by AI, to communicate with immersive systems, etc. Furthermore, with regard to connectivity, literacy, and infrastructure, the vulnerable groups will be neglected by digital divides unless there is a shift to embrace and use inclusive design and deployment models.

These problems give a broad research scope in the field of interdisciplinary innovation. Further studies will revolve around explainable and reliable AI models, adaptive multi-modal learning, and privacy protection intelligence, like federated and edge learning. The latest developments in bio-compatible materials, self-powered nanowearables, and emotion-related sensing will determine the future of incessant health-checking. Ethical AI governance, human–AI interaction, and immersive clinical processes are other key areas of research. Tackling these concerns wholesomely, Vision 2035 offers unparalleled opportunities to redefine healthcare as smart, immersive, preventive, and with a highly human-centred approach.

9. Clinical Validation and User Acceptance

By 2035, translating wearable AI and immersive healthcare technologies from experimental innovations into trusted medical solutions will be a decisive factor for clinical validation. Strict validation systems are needed to prove the safety, accuracy, reliability, and clinical effectiveness of these models in different populations and under different real-life conditions. Unlike conventional medical devices, wearable AI systems are continuous and evolve over time, which requires longitudinal clinical trials, the generation of real-world evidence, and post-market surveillance. Multi-modal data evaluation, AI performance measures, and comparison with gold-standard clinical diagnostics will also be included in the validation protocols to achieve consistent and reproducible results.

Next-generation healthcare technologies will also rely on user acceptance as a key to success. For patients, comfort, ease of use, transparency, and value in everyday life are the key attributes for long-term adoption. Smart clothes and interactive interfaces should be non-obtrusive, user-friendly, and culturally friendly, and indicate in an easy-to-understand manner how health data are used and safeguarded. The dependency on AI-grounded recommendations will grow with understandable insights, feedback, and better health outcomes. Immersive healthcare environments need a thoughtful human design to prevent cognitive overload and positive user experiences.

Wearable AI systems have to be incorporated without any hindrance into the existing workflow and clinical decision-making processes. The administrative overhead or excessive alarms which are added by technologies are likely to be resisted and underutilized. The systems will be developed via co-design approaches by 2035 to include clinicians, patients, and policymakers, hence ensuring that the system is pertinent and helpful. Education, training, and clear instructions to regulations will also help in adoption. Wearable AI and immersive healthcare technology are highly trusted by users, strongly clinically verified, and engaged, and this will render them sustainable and fruitful when used at a colossal scale of adoption and transform the healthcare delivery system into a new era.

10. Conclusion: A Future of Intelligent, Immersive Health

As per the paradigm of Vision 2035, the development and delivery of healthcare and its experience have evolved significantly. Wearable AI, smart biosensors, generative models, and immersive technologies put together are an indication of the shift from episodic-reactive care to continuous, predictive, and highly personalized health ecosystems. Real-time intelligent systems that sense, reason, and modify themselves will offer clinicians and individuals real-time actionable intelligence to intervene and transform health outcomes throughout various medical fields. The immersive healthcare settings made by smart virtual assistants and digital twins will be redesigned using the human technology–based approach to medicine. Such systems will provide more clinical reasoning, patient interaction, and treatment outcomes because the complicated health data will be converted to consumer-friendly, spatial, and interactive applications. The home-based and decentralized model of care will make high-quality healthcare accessible to underserved and remote communities to solve workforce shortages and establish equity. Innovation will be built in a responsible and inclusive way because of creative AI applications, efficient data management, and interoperability frameworks. Finally, the smart interactive prospective of health puts the patient at the central point of treatment with the assistance of adaptive technologies that protect human values, self-direction, and confidence. Vision 2035 is not a technological approach but a human-focused change in the healthcare sector, in which prevention turns out to be the main focus, insight replaces uncertainty, and digital intelligence complements compassion. The vision will result in a more interwoven and empowered world as far as health is concerned since research, policy, and clinical practice are equal.

References

[1] Corbeil, J.R. (2025). The future of learning: AI-driven education in 2040. In Corbeil, J. R. and Corbeil, M.E. (eds), *Teaching and Learning in the Age of Generative AI*, 362–390. Routledge.

[2] Aloqaily, M., Bouachir, O. and Karray, F. (2023). Digital twin for healthcare immersive services: Fundamentals, architectures, and open issues. In El Saddik, A. (ed.), *Digital Twin for Healthcare*, 39–71. Academic Press.

[3] Damar, M., Aydin, O. and Erenay, F.S. (2025). Blockchain technology in digital health and medical technologies. *Blockchain in Healthcare Today*, 8(3). https://doi.org/10.30953/bhty.v8.409

[4] Latif, S., Qadir, J., Farooq, S. and Imran, M.A. (2017). How 5G wireless (and concomitant technologies) will revolutionize healthcare? *Future Internet*, 9(4), 93.

[5] Kim, K., Yang, H., Lee, J. and Lee, W.G. (2023). Metaverse wearables for immersive digital healthcare: A review. *Advanced Science*, 10(31), 2303234.

[6] Huang, G., Chen, X. and Liao, C. (2025). AI-driven wearable bioelectronics in digital healthcare. *Biosensors*, 15(7), 410.

[7] Abhinav, V., Basu, P., Verma, S.S., et al. (2025). Advancements in wearable and implantable BioMEMS devices: Transforming healthcare through technology. *Micromachines*, 16(5), 522.

[8] Konstantinou, G.N., Anderson, W.C., Bagkis, E., et al. (2025). Artificial intelligence–driven wearable and connected technology for allergy: Real-time monitoring and predictive management for personalized care. *The Journal of Allergy and Clinical Immunology: In Practice*, 13(11), 2903–2913.

[9] Murala, D.K., Panda, S.K. and Dash, S.P. (2023). MedMetaverse: Medical care of chronic disease patients and managing data using artificial intelligence, blockchain, and wearable devices state-of-the-art methodology. *IEEE Access*, 11, 138954–138985.

[10] Hancock, K. (2022). Virtual healthcare visits, wearable devices and ambient sensors, and biomedical big data in the metaverse environment. *American Journal of Medical Research*, 9(2), 73–88.

[11] Lăzăroiu, G., Gedeon, T., Halicka, K. and Szpilko, D. (2025). Generative artificial intelligence–driven medical digital twin technologies in blockchain Internet of Things wearable sensor and computer vision–based extended reality healthcare metaverse. *Engineering Management in Production and Services*, 17(3), 27–50.

[12] Maqbool, K.Z., Ali, A., Asghar, S., et al. (2025). Challenges and opportunities in integrating generative AI with wearable devices. In Pandey, B., Pandey, D., Khamparia, A., et al. (eds), *Artificial Intelligence in Microbial Research: Bridging the Gap*, 385–398. Springer Nature.

[13] Diwakar, D. and Raj, D. (2025). Generative AI in wearables: Exploring the impact of GANs, VAEs, and transformers. In Khamparia, A. and Gupta, D. (eds), *Generative Artificial Intelligence for Biomedical and Smart Health Informatics*, 1–34. Wiley.

[14] Veeravalli, B., Deepu, C.J. and Ngo, D. (2017). Real-time, personalized anomaly detection in streaming data for wearable healthcare devices. In Khan, S.U., Zomaya, A.Y. and Abbas, A. (eds), *Handbook of Large-scale Distributed Computing in Smart Healthcare*, 403–426. Cham: Springer International Publishing.

[15] Yang, X., Qi, X. and Zhou, X. (2023). Deep learning technologies for time series anomaly detection in healthcare: A review. *IEEE Access*, 11, 117788–117799.

[16] Diaconu, I.D. (2024). Wearable patient monitoring and metaverse-enabled healthcare systems, immersive medical simulation and remote care technologies, and deep learning disease prediction and diagnosis algorithms for artificial intelligence–powered individualized treatments in virtual clinical settings. *American Journal of Medical Research*, 11(1), 39–54.

[17] Bindu, N., Kumar, R.A., Radhakrishnan, T., et al. (2025). Virtual realities: The influence of the metaverse on healthcare e-governance. In Sundaravadivazhagan, B., Balasubramaniam, S., Raj, P. and Kumari, K.S. (eds), *Applying Metaverse Technologies to Human–Computer Interaction for Healthcare*, 254–277. Auerbach Publications.

[18] Awotunde, J.B., Adeniyi, A.E., Randle, O., et al. (2025). Definition of metaverse in the framework of smart healthcare system. In Barsocchi, P., Awotunde, J. B., Brahma, B. and Bhoi, A. K. (eds), *HealthTech Horizons: AI-Infused Metaverse Solutions for Smart Healthcare Systems*, 173–208. Cham: Springer Nature Switzerland.

[19] Lakshmi, D., Kondurkar, I., Kumar, R. and Banerjee, R. (2024). Intelligent healthcare systems in the metaverse: Architecture, applications, challenges, and opportunities. In Chowdhary, C. L. (ed.), *The Metaverse for the Healthcare Industry*, 17–32. Springer Nature.

[20] Awotunde, J.B. (2025). Data privacy in virtual healthcare environments and ethical guidelines for metaverse health applications. In Barsocchi, P., Awotunde, J. B., Brahma, B. and Bhoi, A.

K. (eds), *HealthTech Horizons: AI-Infused Metaverse Solutions for Smart Healthcare Systems*, 543–576. Cham: Springer Nature Switzerland.

[21] Qu, Z., Lau, C. W., Simoff, S.J., et al. (2022). Review of innovative immersive technologies for healthcare applications. *Innovations in Digital Health, Diagnostics, and Biomarkers*, 2(2022), 27–39.

[22] Samuel, S. (2022). Immersive technologies in the healthcare space. In Mishra, S., Tripathy, H. K., Mallick, P. and Shaalan, K. (eds), *Augmented Intelligence in Healthcare: A Pragmatic and Integrated Analysis*, 433–451. Singapore: Springer Nature Singapore.

[23] Yang, E. (2023). Implications of immersive technologies in healthcare sector and its built environment. *Frontiers in Medical Technology*, 5, 1184925.

[24] Sharma, A. and Rani, S. (2025). Transforming healthcare in the metaverse with impact of wearable technology. In Rani, S. (ed.), *Healthcare Frontiers in the Metaverse: Innovations and Impacts*, 335–349. Academic Press.

[25] Fawkes, A. and Burden, D. (2025). Digital human twins and the military metaverse: Opportunities and challenges. *AI & SOCIETY*, 41(3), 2529–2541.

Index

About the Editors

Dr. Balasubramaniam S is an Assistant Professor at the School of Computer Science and Engineering, Kerala University of Digital Sciences, Innovation and Technology, Digital University Kerala (DUK), Thiruvananthapuram, Kerala, India. Prior to joining DUK, he was with the school of computer science and engineering, Vellore Institute of Technology (VIT), Chennai where he worked as a senior associate professor. He has over 15 years of experience in teaching, applied research, and industry. He was a postdoctoral researcher in the Department of Applied Data Science at Noroff University College, Kristiansand, Norway. He has a PhD in Computer Science and Engineering from Anna University, Chennai, India (2015). He has published more than 30 research papers in reputed SCI/WoS/Scopus indexed journals. He has been granted one Australian patent and two Indian patents and has also published two additional Indian patents. He has presented papers at conferences, received a best paper award, contributed 40 chapters in edited books, and has been an editor in 15 books published by international publishers. His research and publication interests include machine learning, deep learning, federated learning-based healthcare and security applications, cloud computing security, generative AI and agentic AI.

Prof. Seifedine Kadry has a bachelor's in 1999 from Lebanese University, MS degree in 2002 from Reims University (France) and EPFL (Lausanne), PhD in 2007 from Blaise Pascal University (France), HDR degree in 2017 from Rouen University (France). At present his research focuses on Data Science, education using technology, system prognostics, stochastic systems, and applied mathematics. He is an IET and AAIA fellow and he is a full professor of data science at the Department of Computer Science and Mathematics, Lebanese American University, Beirut, Lebanon.

For Product Safety Concerns and Information please contact our EU representative GPSR@taylorandfrancis.com
Taylor & Francis Verlag GmbH, Kaufingerstraße 24, 80331 München, Germany

www.ingramcontent.com/pod-product-compliance
Ingram Content Group UK Ltd.
Pitfield, Milton Keynes, MK11 3LW, UK
UKHW022026061126
477531UK00002B/60
* 9 7 8 1 0 4 1 3 0 8 1 4 0 *